Spiritual Exercises

SPIRITUAL EXERCISES

Karl Rahner

Translated by Kenneth Baker, S.J.

ST. AUGUSTINE'S PRESS
South Bend, Indiana

Manufactured in the United States of America

1 2 3 4 5 6   20 19 18 17 16 15 14

Library of Congress Cataloging in Publication Data
Rahner, Karl, 1904–1984.
[Betrachtungen zum ignatianischen Exerzitienbuch. English]
Spiritual exercises / Karl Rahner; translated by Kenneth
Baker, S.J. – Reprint of 2nd edition.
pages cm
ISBN 978-1-58731-850-4 (paperbound: alk. paper)
1. Ignatius, of Loyola, Saint, 1491–1556. *Exercitia
spiritualia*. 2. Spiritual exercises. 3. Spiritual retreats.
I. Title.
BX2179.L8R33 2014
248.3 – dc23   2014009449

∞ The paper used in this publication meets the minimum requirements of the American National Standard for Information Sciences
– Permanence of Paper for Printed Materials, ANSI Z39.481984.

ST. AUGUSTINE'S PRESS
www.staugustine.net

Contents

Foreword

The author owes the reader some explanation about the origin, meaning, and purpose of this book. He has often given eight-day retreats, based on the Spiritual Exercises of St. Ignatius, to young candidates for the priesthood—especially in the Berchmannskolleg in Pullach near Munich, and also in the Germanicum in Rome. In the last two instances, some eager retreatants took down the talks verbatim. From the side of the author, there never was a written text. Also, the notes taken down by the seminarians were neither controlled nor edited by the author.

Some of my former students in Innsbruck, among whom Dr. Ernst Niermann and Dr. Miran Vodopivec deserve special mention, gathered all these notes together, and edited and published them in mimeograph. This mimeographed manuscript was well received, and even found favor beyond the circle of my former students. This explains the frequently repeated request that this collection of meditations on the Spiritual Exercises be published in book form. My fellow Jesuit, Hans Wulf, S.J., and Dr. Paul Neuenzeit of Kösel publishing house took up this project and set about giving these notes a form that would permit their publication. At this stage also, I had nothing to do with the redaction of the text. I trust in the judgment of these colleagues that these printed meditations will help those interested in them. I am strengthened in this trust by the English and Spanish translations which have been undertaken.

In giving these meditations, my desire was to explain the Spiritual Exercises of St. Ignatius; I was not attempting to present pious meditations and theological considerations, no matter how useful they might be. I attempted to give these meditations on the Spiritual Exercises the kind of theological foundation that my listeners had the right to expect, without falling into the kind of theological investigations that really have nothing directly to contribute to the purpose of spiritual exercises. The reader himself must judge whether or not I have been successful in this.

There is one further point I would like to make very clear: These printed considerations—even including those that quote directly from Ignatius' book of the Spiritual Exercises—are not in themselves *exercises,* and, as they are presented here, they are not meant to be an adequate commentary on the Spiritual Exercises of St. Ignatius. For, leaving all other considerations aside, a real commentary should not restrict itself to the presentation of the meditation-themes as they are given by St. Ignatius—and this completely independent of the fact that here, as in all eight-day retreats, only a part of the whole Exercises of St. Ignatius can be dealt with. A commentary must give a detailed analysis of the directions given by St. Ignatius for the methods to be employed in making a retreat.

Moreover, it should never be forgotten that true spiritual exercises, as they are envisioned by St. Ignatius, are not a series of pious meditations that a person with good will can make anywhere and anytime, or that he can present to a larger group of people all gathered together for this purpose. Rather, real spiritual exercises are the serious attempt, following a certain plan, to make a definite decision or choice at a decisive point in one's life. This is the kind of decision that cannot be deduced from the general principles of the faith or from common human wisdom alone; a decision such as this is received from God and from His grace alone in a kind of logic of existential knowledge gained in prayer. Therefore, spiritual exercises in this sense, which is their true meaning, cannot be made where many people

8

go through the Exercises together; much less can they be imparted through printed meditations of a general theological content.

Therefore, it is my hope that this book will not be the occasion for the common error that, when a person has read through some theological considerations based on the themes of the Spiritual Exercises of St. Ignatius, he then knows what the Spiritual Exercises are, or, even worse, thinks he has already made the Spiritual Exercises. With regard to the formal structure of the logic of existential knowledge and decision as it is found in the Exercises of St. Ignatius, I refer the reader to my express treatment of this subject in *The Dynamic Element in the Church* (New York, Herder and Herder, 1964), pp. 84–170. That consideration attempts to bring out the great difference between real "exercises" and theological meditations, even when these latter are explicitly based on the Spiritual Exercises of St. Ignatius. Nevertheless, it is my hope that these present meditations will be of some help to those who give or make retreats.

In conclusion, I would like once again to thank Father Hans Wulf and Dr. Paul Neuenzeit for their dedicated work on this book. Without their help, it never would have been published.

KARL RAHNER, S.J.

Introduction

I. *The Situation of the Exercises*

From an historical point of view, our age, the twentieth century, is more difficult to live in than were ages past. But this is our age; it is an age of momentous change, and therefore also a time of new orientation for Christian living. This is our great opportunity. Certainly, we do not want to over-dramatize our life, but at the same time we should not let monotonous everyday life blind us to the great risks involved. Nor should we act as if everything in our life is perfectly self-evident. We should be conscious of the fact that we can only master our life with constantly renewed effort—that life of ours that is so dependent on our good will; but still, we are always a bit afraid of that good will of ours, since we do not know for sure how long it will last.

If we consider the above seriously, then we should like to experience the actuality of the Spiritual Exercises for our own individual situation—and it is only from that situation that one can make the Spiritual Exercises.

II. *The Essence of the Spiritual Exercises*

The Spiritual Exercises are not a theological system. From a theological point of view, the Spiritual Exercises are nothing but an election or choice: the choice of the means and the concrete way in which Christianity can become a living reality in us. St.

11

Ignatius is only interested in this: that a man place himself before the Lord of the "Kingdom of Christ" and the "Two Standards" and ask: What should I do? What do You want from me according to the sovereignty of Your divine will?

This brings us to the problem of the present retreat. Certainly, one can set aside some time in which to reflect on oneself, to be silent, to try to be more recollected and more fervent, to learn how to pray again and make one's prayer more intense— spiritual exercises of this kind are praiseworthy and helpful, but this is not what St. Ignatius had in mind. It seems that an election cannot be imposed on one from the outside, nor, especially, be repeated sincerely once a year. For the historical character of our human existence strives for finality and irrevocability, which, in turn, seem to exclude a constantly renewed election. It might flow from all this that, for us, in this retreat, there is no real question of a basic decision for or against God, or of the choice of a vocation. But are we so sure that our past decision was truly honest and not just apparently so? Occasionally, certainly not always, it can be advisable to enter once again into one's own election-situation in order to examine its genuineness.

But this is even more important: Our finite freedom can never embrace the totality of our life in one act. Thus, every decision that we make leaves room for further decisions, which, to be sure, are conditioned and determined by those that have gone before, but are not simply a linear extension of them. Hence, in our yearly retreat we find ourselves in an election-situation. And we can see it, if we will only move aside the debris of everyday life.

In our annual retreat, therefore, instead of choosing a way of life, we will ask ourselves with regard to some concrete point: What does God want from me now? Is He pleased by the way I make my meditation, choose my reading material, and so forth? What about my determination to make progress in the spiritual life? We only really begin to make a retreat when we have found such an Archimedean point in our lives. In this regard, no retreat master can tell me precisely what God is asking of me. St. Ignatius presupposes that God says to each and every one in a very personal way where his or her election should begin. That is a shocking presupposition! It says that God Himself manifests to the retreatant—going beyond whatever is presented by the retreat master—what only He can manifest. Ignatius knows well that each man cannot properly build up his own life from the publicly revealed propositions. Certainly, these propositions are very important. But St. Ignatius believes that God says to each and every man—beyond his own personal reflections on the matter: I want that and that particular thing from you! If I have the courage and the vitality to believe (something that I can never accomplish with my own powers) that God will say something to me during this retreat that I will never be able to disregard in the future, then my retreat could really be Ignatian. That will only come to pass, however, if God is ready. But even the self-preparation and the waiting to see if God will act are worth the trouble.

III. *The Right Way to Make a Retreat*

The retreat should be made earnestly and with recollection, but still calmly and peacefully. We must be patient and try to make an election with constantly renewed effort. It is important that we do not pass anything up. We have a tendency to change gears too quickly. Then there is a danger that we jump ahead of our own reality. Then it can happen that a person prays, makes resolutions, sighs for the everlasting hills, and in the whole process falls into the illusion that the "old man" is no longer present and thinks that he will not return for some time. If everything is the same after the retreat as it was before, frequently the reason for this is that the "old man" was not invited to come along and make the retreat. It should not surprise us if the various exercises annoy us at first, and we should let the less pious side of our nature have its say. It does not matter if the battle gets a bit hot—the important thing is that there be some positive results.

Each one of us should try to discover what question he should put to God in his own regard—even if his question seems ever so small and unimportant. And it is important that we muster the courage so to go out of ourselves that we can figure that God must answer us! For even though a retreat is a very subjective activity (making resolutions, etc.), it contains hidden within it a quasi-sacramental happening. Granted that God has given us no assurance that He will speak clearly and definitely in each retreat, still it is and remains true that we Christians have a real (though perhaps a permanently anonymous) entrance to the grace of God: through the pierced heart of Jesus Christ.

Hence, by means of a true retreat a person is able to get out of his own desperate situation and into the infinite breadth of God. If we do what we can, then God will bless us with His grace during these days, even though we may not be able to perceive it, and perhaps we will then be able to say with Jacob: "I have seen God!"

1. God and Man
(23)*

A personal election is the most important thing in an Ignatian retreat. This can be made in many different ways. But in each case, it must proceed from what St. Ignatius calls the "Foundation." St. Ignatius added the Foundation to the Spiritual Exercises at a rather late date. It is, as it were, the framework of the Exercises placed at the beginning, containing the key ideas that are to run through all the meditations.

The Christian concept of God that interests us here is essentially "practical." It demands a decision either for or against God, and is itself only attainable in decision. It is a turning to the living God (1 Th 1,9; Lk 1,16). The demands of this "turning" apply to us believers also, at least insofar as we have to suffer through the godlessness of the world. The affliction of all Christian confession of God is especially tangible at that point where we are supposed to find God in the dark bitterness of the world and in the obscurity of the future, while addressing Him as "Father" with a feeling of security against all insecurity.

I. *The Infinite God*

According to the First Vatican Council, God is "infinitely beyond everything that can be said of Him." Let us run through the theological statements about God's attributes (His life, His truth,

* The number refers to the number in the *Spiritual Exercises* of St. Ignatius.

15

His justice, His eternity, His knowledge, His power, His love),
in order to understand that we do not grasp Him with these
statements no matter how legitimate they are, and that we must
take everything away from God that has been thought about Him
so that we can give ourselves to Him, to His inexhaustible life
and to His mysteriousness. "*Deus semper maior.*"

II. *The Living God*

God is the One Who constitutes me in mysterious freedom, deals
with me, and disposes over me in such a way that through the
divine absoluteness my autonomy and self-direction are not
diminished, but rather firmly established.

III. *The Father of Our Lord Jesus Christ*

He is also our Father! We only know this by faith and revelation,
and it is truly something astonishing when we consider what
God is and what we are. Modern man is not so much an atheist
as he is one for whom the transcendence of God means something;
to him it is very improper for man to act as if God can be grasped
by human perception. But for us Christians, God is not the
absolutely other, beyond all experience, but rather the Lord Who
has come near to us in Jesus Christ.

IV. *The Trinitarian God*

The Spirit, in Whom we cry: "Abba, Father" (Rom 8,15), has
been sent to us from the Son. Thus, we must familiarize ourselves
with the way to the Father from the Son in His Spirit. This
Trinitarian way was essential to the attitude of life of St. Ignatius;
it was the basis of his piety, and we meet it at every turn in his
Spiritual Exercises.

V. *God is Love*

We should try to appreciate the grandeur and the weight of this sentence, and at the same time look at the brutality, the darkness, the division, the poverty and sinfulness of the world and our own hearts, and then say: He is still infinite love! And that not in a vague, indefinable sense, but in such a way that He in His glory wants to be our inheritance and life. His love is absolutely unowed, and it is given to me precisely as such. It is this that constitutes the dangerous incomprehensibility of our life; that is, that I, as a creature, can decide for myself in the face of this love. God's love is the basic foundation of the human existence of each one of us. This is not an ordinary gift; it is rather the self-gift of God of Himself to each and every one of us in our own unique situation. We can not only say "we," but each one must also say: "I" am here . . .

VI. *The Still Distant God*

We have been created by God, placed before Him, destined for Him, called to the immediate participation in His glory. But now we are still in the world—we are not yet there where we will be for all eternity. This demands humility of us (recognition of the fact that we are still "on the way") and courage (striving for the future community with God). These various aspects of our human situation give us an idea of what St. Ignatius means by *praise, reverence,* and *service.*

2. Man and the Other Things
(23)

Note

"The other things on the face of the earth are created for man to help him in attaining the end for which he is created. Hence, man is to make use of them inasfar as they help him in the attainment of his end, and he must rid himself of them inasfar as they prove a hindrance to him."

Let us try to experience interiorly the supreme clarity of these statements. They make it easy for us to say: Yes, that's just the way it is! But we must not confuse clarity of statement with existential appropriation. If, according to St. John, a man only has the truth to the extent that he acts in truth, then true understanding consists in performing and appropriating to oneself the reality that lies behind these statements. This kind of understanding, as far as we are concerned, is necessarily in a state of becoming, for the complete integration of all things into the service of God occurs only in a state of perfection. This holds also for the saints who have not yet attained the end.

For us, the union of God and creature is still a mystery, yes, even a scandal. The danger is always present that we will either make our way in life in opposition to God, or not take creatures seriously within the horizon of the Absolute. That is, if we have ever even become aware of this dilemma! For in our familiarity with the things of our experience, most probably we have not

18

once noticed that they have not yet been integrated into the service of God.

We should not let ourselves be deceived by the polished clarity of the Foundation. We must still meditate on it very often until we have understood what it means.

I. *The Other Things*

By the "other things" St. Ignatius understands everything between my ego and God. They embrace many natural gifts with which I am perhaps "actually identified," and with which I naïvely try to identify myself. In this retreat, I should try to separate myself from them, and I should try to understand that I am different from them. I should realize interiorly that nothing can take the place of my pure ego, that I cannot run away from it, that I cannot relinquish my self-responsibility to the world around me. This type of separation from self is one of the main tasks of the Christian—and it takes a whole life to complete it. It is a necessary part of the road to Christian sanctity.

Let us ask ourselves very concretely what these "other things" are from which we must separate ourselves. They are not only material possessions, time, friends, but also my activity, my abilities, even my nature that has been formed by my own free decisions, health and sickness, honor and dishonor, thoughts and desires, and so forth. This process of freeing the self from the self includes everything that can be said about the ego—these all belong to the "other things." That which remains is the "peak of the soul," that is, the free, self-surrendering person posited by God. This person has mastery over all other things, takes them or leaves them, orders them or forms them, and in this dealing with things finds God and itself and comes to an understanding of the relationship between God and self. Therefore, the "other things" are not an obstacle between God and me. I cannot desire simply to eliminate them. We may not strive stoically to remove

19

ourselves from them in such a way that we are no longer affected by them. The question here is how to use them properly and how to direct all of them to God.

II. *Using and Leaving the "Other Things"*

St. Ignatius says that the "other things" that have an objective relationship to me and to God should be used or not used to the extent that they help me attain the end for which I was created. Surely, in the last analysis there is nothing that cannot be integrated into the service of God in some way, and one can say without hesitation: God grows in men to the degree that their relationship to things is a more positive one, and vice versa. This point must be emphasized because man is always tempted to consider earthly things meaningless and of little value. For our relationship to God, the "other things" are absolutely necessary—they are the place of our service and worship.

On the other hand, there is the fact of sin, which consists precisely in the disturbance of the objective order of things. The Christian cannot maintain a naïve, trusting relationship to things which, in their objective relation to God and man, have become really disordered by sin. Therefore, for the Christian there is also a true leaving of things. But this leaving is not, as it were, a simple "jumping over." Even a man who lives according to the evangelical counsels, who gives up many things and must give up many things, can only have a positive relationship to things, and must experience them in their finiteness as good and desirable. And it is only after this positive experience of them that he can properly give them up without resentment. It would be a type of un-Christian idealism if we desired to come down to things from God. We are placed in the midst of these things that make up our world, and nobody asked our permission for this beforehand. They are the unrelinquishable position for man as far as his attaining God is concerned. Moreover, "leaving" things is a type of intensive relationship to them: That which has never been the object of a decision because we have never really "encountered" it, also cannot be given up by us in a free decision. By leaving or giving up things in the Christian way, we bring them into the relationship with ourselves that God desires, and which must, therefore, be a valid relationship. The things that we give up are not simply lost. They do not leave behind a dull, spirit-killing emptiness, but, because they are left for Christ, they come back to us in a glorious manner. The one who can give things up in the right way becomes not poorer, but richer.

Therefore, we must make a choice and we must decide. That is easy to say, but difficult to carry out in concrete circumstances. We give up many things, or at least imagine that we do, because they seem to be bad or because they impede the attainment of something else that we desire more. But when it comes to giving up something that is really important, then we return to the real order and realize how difficult it is, for the sake of the God who seems to have abandoned us, to bear the dark night of the soul and watch the world disappear from under our feet.

Consider the Christological structure of what has just been said! In the Incarnation, all things have been basically integrated into God by the Logos. In Christ, everything has been taken over, but also called to the cross and to death, and only by passing through both of these destined for glory. This shows that "using" and "leaving" are not two different things placed next to one another, but two aspects of the same thing: Death is the radical, differentiating separation between the person and everything else that is not the person. In death, the sinful identification of myself with the "other things" is completely dissolved, but also through death the proper, positive relationship to them becomes possible, so that they are able to attain their "glorification."

III. *A Self-Examination*

Each one of us should ask himself now whether God's will is really his goal, whether he affirms it not only theoretically, but also in such a way that it has a true influence on his use of things. We should ask ourselves whether we are truly determined

21

to belong to God with our whole will, to serve Him and to be dedicated to Him; whether we realize that ultimately we will have to render an account of our stewardship to Him alone, and that a person becomes a slave of passion, the world, and the devil if he does not serve God with his whole freedom. We should ask ourselves whether we live according to the "*Suscipe*"; whether we can profess to be "slaves of Christ" with the same pride with which St. Paul said this of himself. Do I have the courage to ask God unconditionally what He wants me to do? What are the "natural" reservations that I make in such an offer?

Our meditation should reveal our life to us in such a way that it becomes of itself a prayer for the "more," so that we are able to mold our human existence in such a way that it is always striving for the greater glory of God.

3. Indifference and the "More"

Note

The conclusion of the Foundation manifests a double aspect: the necessity of indifference, and of the choice of those things that are "more conducive to the end."

I. *Indifference*

Indifference is a kind of removal or distance away from things that makes true vision possible and is required for a proper decision. As pilgrims and strangers on this earth, we must choose and decide—we who have here no lasting city and who see things as only temporary and in certain respects as not so important. Certainly, our free decisions never take place in a state of absolute reflection or under the influence of a comprehensive knowledge that would perfectly illumine this particular decision. Often we have already chosen before we begin to decide. We cannot indicate the point up to which we were undecided and at which we reached our decision. The unencompassable and the unreflective always exercise a certain influence on our decisions. From this arises the possibility of prejudices or pre-decisions, which, of course, can themselves be the result of former decisions.

This brings us to the real subject. The very possibility of the influence of previously held views (for example, "That would be stupid!" or, "That cannot possibly be for me!") points up the fact that by our very nature we are not indifferent when it comes to making a free decision. Indifferent is what we must become. But this does not come about through good will alone, or by saying that I am indifferent; for indifference is something that must enter into the nerves and the very marrow of the bones. Nor is indifference the mere resolution not to let oneself be carried along by the crowd; it demands, rather, the existential distance from things that is self-appropriated in such a way that it even frees the will to reject its own previous prejudices. Even the attitude of accepting everything that happens in silence—which in itself is very difficult—is less than what is demanded here. The Spiritual Exercises propose an *active indifference* in virtue of which we are to act in such a way that both the using and leaving of things can and must be our own responsibility.

This active indifference is surrounded and protected by man's humble handing over of himself to God's good pleasure. God levels out in the only proper way the differences in the reality of our human existence, even those that we ourselves may not level out. And, finally, we lose everything in death. In death, despite our great freedom, we do not have control of ourselves, but can only endure, and say: "Into your hands I commend my spirit." In death, we must let the incomprehensible dispose of us in such a way that we believe that this disposition is the work of an infinite love, and is preserving our spiritual human existence from meaninglessness.

This distance from things is a goal that must always be re-won again and again. We are never at a perfect distance from the world—a distance so perfect that it cannot be questioned. We love things, we have confidence in them because of the immediate relationship to our own corporality, we have tasted them in sweetness and in sorrow, we have absorbed them in love or in fear. Therefore, we need the courage to undertake ever new beginnings, and we need the power to break loose from that which holds us.

The number of things about which we must make ourselves indifferent is very great, and their natures very diverse, but I cannot remove myself from God, nor may I write off the personal value of my fellow men. Even though my relationship to things must be determined in accordance with sound morality, still I cannot make my absolute decision on the basis of morality alone. Above and beyond universally valid morality, this decision must form my own irreducible history by also proceeding from God's will for me.

If we consider all this, then it seems that we can never attain this kind of indifference by ourselves and permanently. If we could truly attain this indifference to all created things over which our freedom has some control, then we should know for sure that we love God, that we have His grace, and that we can leave "fear and trembling" behind us once and for all. On the other hand, we may not let ourselves become obdurate in a complete doubt: that would also be, but in a negative direction, the self-presumption of the creature. Therefore, the only thing that remains is to place our choice completely in the hands of God. In any event, we are called on to free ourselves from our own prejudices and pre-decisions in accordance with the grace given us, so that we can quietly and peacefully say to ourselves: According to God's will, I have desired and striven for what is right.

II. The "More"

The true essence of indifference is its "elevation" into the decision to do "more." Indifference is distance from things with the goal of willing them or leaving them: Therefore, it must change itself into non-indifference. For example, when I have chosen a way of life, I may no longer be hesitant about it. Indifference does not exist for its own sake, but for the choice of "what is more conducive to the end." It is freedom for decision, which is really no longer mine, but God's: I am seeking His will in the election.

From this point of view, indifference appears as the distance from things that must be determined from God and not from man; it appears as man's freedom—that freedom that man does not want to keep selfishly for himself, but wants to leave to God so that He can decide.

In this way, then, the *"Tantum-quantum"* of indifference must be surpassed by the "what is more conducive to the end" of the decision that I leave to God to demand. We must not let ourselves be deceived in this regard by an excessively heroic attitude. Essentially, what I am saying is that we have here no lasting city, that God is the always-greater One, that He will respond to us if we remain supple and do not direct ourselves in one way and one way only. We should protect ourselves from that inner hardening that can be observed sometimes in the so-called "patent ascetics." We should remain elastic—always ready for that call of God that will lead us to higher things. The more we love God, the more we will experience His ever greater distance from us, and the more we will want to be in awe at the holy unconditionedness of His demands. What we have to do in this meditation in the depths of our souls is to utter a clear "Yes" to that which is, not to that which is made by us, that is, to God and His immeasurable love.

Hence, it should be clear that indifference is the exact opposite of all attitudes of unconcern. The difference that God has put into things is all around us, and it must be affirmed by us. Man moves in the midst of this difference, and suffers through it. A person may not and cannot feel the same way toward dishonor as toward honor, toward pain as toward joy. Whoever does that is perhaps a good stoic, but he is not a Christian! We can see very clearly from the agony in the Garden that our Lord was not affected by an insipid apathy when he acknowledged the unappealable decision of God and made it a part of His human existence. Indifference does not mean uniformity or mediocrity. It does not by any means say that all must be the same, or that no one should stand out from the group. God has called all men to be Christians, but we cannot and need not judge what concrete form this call will take and how it should be carried out. God can demand sacrifices of us that he does not demand of others—sacrifices that are not necessary for them, but are for us, precisely because He wills to save all men. Many men seem to arrive at no real choice at all in most things. They keep things, and perhaps do not even protest when they are taken away from them. But we must belong to that strange breed of men to whom it is given, though in different degrees, to be Christians by choice and not just Christians by birth. Certainly, that is something exceptional. We cannot help it if other men, and even we ourselves, find us a bit strange; for it is not a common thing that a person freely gives up something that he could just as well have without offending anybody. So the second part of the Foundation of the Spiritual Exercises is not something that is immediately self-evident. We should pray on it again and again, so that we might achieve in some degree the attitude proposed there. And we cannot act as if this attitude is the normal thing for every Christian who is not living in conflict with God. Looked at from the human point of view, it simply demands too much of us; but we will only know in death everything that we must leave behind—then, when God takes everything away from us, even ourselves.

Note

With regard to indifference, St. Ignatius mentions a few examples. They sound very simple, but they are very characteristic: the drive to live (health   sickness), the drive to possess (riches—poverty), the drive to be somebody (honor—dishonor), the drive to exist (long life—short life). One could say that he lists quite adequately the points in which man seeks to assert himself in the different dimensions of his human existence.

4. Our Practical Attitude toward Sin

(47)

Note

With the present meditation we enter into the so-called "first week" of the Ignatian Spiritual Exercises. In this week, we will meditate on sin, judgment, and hell. We want to develop these themes very carefully, deliberately, without rushing headlong into the matter. Nor should we presuppose too much in ourselves, since these meditations are anything but easy.

If it is certain that we are sinners and have not yet escaped the situation in which our eternal salvation is threatened at every turn, and if it is certain that sin in the individual person excludes his own recognition and admission of the true sinfulness of sin (the "Father, I have sinned" is already the decisive point of any conversion!), then, theologically speaking, we can be quite sure that it cannot be taken for granted that we can understand and personally realize the following meditations. Since we are sinners (perhaps also, since we have not attained that state of freedom in which the ultimate choices affecting our human existence are made), we must expend great effort to come to a true knowledge of sin.

Therefore, we want to move along slowly and begin where we are right now. We do not want to deceive ourselves. In a certain sense, we will best make progress if we consider first of all those things that hinder us from seeing what St. Ignatius wants us to see in these first meditations.

I. Our Practical Attitude toward Sin in the World

If we look at the world, we will doubtless explain many of the things that we see there as brutality, meanness, treachery, malice, uncleanness, and so forth. We will admit without hesitation that it contains much stupidity, boorishness, proud egotism, and I know not what else. The more we look through the world and experience what men are like, the more we study world history and note its shallowness and repulsive vileness, the more we are repelled by the world.

And yet everything that we experience in this way, if we look, as it were, with Christ from the mountain of the wilderness of His temptations into the world, and everything that we tend to write off as Godforsakenness and hatred of God—if we look at all this a bit more closely, how ambiguous it appears! Then it seems as if all that is only the shadow for a light that is itself the foundation of this darkness; then it seems as if world history needs evil in order to make any progress whatever. Then many things might seem to us as unavoidable gateways or as a price that must be paid. Or, in another way, how many things do we consider as unimportant, as a mere expression of the destitute state of corporeal man, rather than as sin! Do we not think that men sin because they are suffering, rather than that they suffer because they have sinned? Nevertheless, we must confess in deep faith: Sin really exists. It is present and operative in those things that we have mentioned. It is not true that an all-pervading understanding could forgive everything. This is so even if a "deeper understanding" (which would only have human depth) might be tempted to say that the more one understands, the more one forgives. But God does not forgive everything! He can be merciful toward sin and He can forgive sin, but He will not allow it to be talked away—which is what we are inclined to. That is more like us! Therefore, when we meditate on sin we must not think that everything will be crystal clear to us. What we must do is open ourselves up for the revelation of God.

II. *Our Practical Attitude toward Sin in Ourselves*

It is very different if I take a look at my own life. Certainly, we guide our lives according to many moral principles, and do it perhaps very intensely. But that is a long way from saying that we truly believe that we are sinners or could become sinners. Basically, we think that we are pretty good Christians, very respectable and harmless. Perhaps we are irritated occasionally over something that we have done; seldom are we irritated at ourselves. From time to time, we are annoyed that we do not keep our resolutions, but normally we do not feel interiorly that we could ever be so bad that God would utterly reject us. When we compare ourselves with the objective divine law, perhaps we would admit that such and such that we do is not just right; but that God is really offended by us in this—well, we say it with our praiseworthy, even good and abstract thoughts, but not really with the innermost center of our hearts. But that is precisely what we must do, if we look into ourselves! At that sight we must say: Sin is also there and not just on the outside; it is also for me a very real and terrible possibility. It is clear that we must try to say this to ourselves again and again, and that we must pray earnestly for the full realization of this knowledge.

III. *Our Attitude toward Our Personal Human Existence as a Real Possibility for Sin*

This consideration of sin brings us to the realization that we are personally existing, that we can dispose of our lives as we ourselves wish. One characteristic of this freedom is its finality, which is the exact opposite of the ability constantly to re-do. It is also characterized by its totality. The possibility of sin (it is sin that damns man forever) shows that a basic decision can take place in us that reaches down into the deepest recesses of our being—there where all of our essential parts and developments are rolled into the one undifferentiated unity of the "heart." This basic decision can and must express itself in everything that a person does; therefore, it can also be made definitely reflective and consciously known. But precisely because of its totality, it cannot appear adequately reflective in any one (therefore necessarily partial) act. Hence, a certain fear and trembling of ultimate uncertainty necessarily remains with regard to what we have made of ourselves through the use of our freedom. Since we are creatures, a final disposition of oneself of this type in the depths of human existence is at the same time a disposition that is caught up in what cannot be arranged; that is, we attempt something whose results do not simply depend on us. We act within the possibility of a death that has been imposed on us—but it is precisely in this death that we attain perfection through the use of our freedom.

To be sure, we know that we can sinfully choose, totally and irrevocably. We can cleverly speculate about this possibility of sinning. But in the concrete realization of our own human existence, we are always running away from ourselves in this regard. Does not the statement we made above seem improbable when we take a good look at ordinary, everyday people?—especially when we see how they waste their lives in a rather primitive fashion, and how they seem to be a mere product of their surroundings—a bundle of biological drives? And yet, man is of such a nature that he goes into eternity with himself. Each man has an importance that the pagans of old would only concede to their heroes, while they despised the vulgar crowd. We know that every man is a person, not just abstractly or in *actu primo,* and that he must realize his human existence as a person. Personality is not something that happens just now and then in an exceptional case; rather, it is the normal thing. But at first sight it certainly does not seem so. And because we do not understand personality in this way, it is very difficult for us to realize that each person, no matter how dull or how unattractive, has a radical and eternally valid disposition over himself—even though we do not know when and how that actually takes place. I am not only *de facto* a personal reality of this type that can sin, but I must be so. I cannot run away from my nature. I cannot give God's ticket into my human existence back to Him and then renounce all claim to myself. And, therefore, I am on the way toward an absolute decision. My life-course will reach the end of its journey sooner or later, and then it has become eternity.

IV. *Priesthood and Sin*

We who are priests must deal with sin by our very profession. People say to us that the salvation of other men is dependent on us in some way. Certainly, we cannot cause salvation by ourselves. Men themselves and the grace of God do that, and not anyone else. But nevertheless, we are important for the salvation of others; this is so true that we ourselves will be lost if we do not dedicate ourselves to the task of saving others. It is eternally true of Jesus Christ that He "came down from heaven for our salvation." He has come into the world as the Redeemer from sin. The Incarnate Son of God is inseparable from the Crucified Who overcame sin. Since there is sin in the world, therefore, in my priestly existence I cannot abstract from the fact that that is the way it is, and that that is the way it must be.

In this meditation, we should become aware of the strangely dreadful fact that, in following the Lamb of God who took away the sins of the world on the cross, we are destined to busy ourselves explicitly with something that most people prefer to pass over in silence—and we must do that from the very depths of our being. We are here to forgive sins! On this account, we must have a profound understanding of sin. In this day and age, there is a danger that we falsely understand the mission of the Church and the apostolate to mean that it is our job to say to our fellow men: "Friends, if you just follow our directions, then everything will be okay in this world of ours." In a certain sense, that is right. Life would certainly be more bearable if men would follow these directions. But ultimately, despite all social problems and the fight against Communism, we are here so that through us men can find their eternal salvation in God. One "I absolve you" pronounced over one sin which, from a sociological point of view, perhaps is not very important, is basically more important than anything else we could do for the betterment of human existence. Until we are convinced of this fact, until this attitude pervades our whole being and enters, so to speak, into our bloodstream in such a way that we truly live from it, and that hearing confessions, visiting the sick, teaching catechism, serving the poor and afflicted are just as important to us as giving learned speeches, solving social problems, dealing with the mighty in this world, then we are far away from the call of the priest. Therefore, it is very important for our priesthood that we make the "first week" of the Spiritual Exercises earnestly and profoundly.

5. The Essence of Sin

Note

1. Before we take up the two fundamental themes of St. Ignatius in the "first week" of the Exercises (the three sins and one's own personal sins), we are going to undertake a more theoretical consideration of the essence of sin.

St. Ignatius built his sin-meditations completely on salvation history. He offers neither an abstract theory nor a mere speculative analysis of the essence of sin; rather, he proceeds according to the concrete reality of salvation history. The matter that St. Ignatius proposes to the retreatant might seem very simple, but it gives testimony to the uncommonly profound theology of the saint. Right here he shows that he is a Christian existentialist of the first order. For he was not primarily a philosopher or a theologian, but a holy man. At any event, it is worthy of note that he gives the first place in his *"Suscipe"* to human freedom, while he places the other powers of the soul after freedom, and so determines man, as it were, from his freedom. If we look at the common teaching of the scholastics of the time, it is not so obvious that he should do this. But that is the way it has been in the book of Exercises for the past few hundred years—and some people will probably say: "Would to God it were different!"

2. With regard to this meditation, we should read the first three chapters of the Epistle to the Romans, or chapter twenty-five on the last judgment in Matthew; perhaps also Galatians

5,13–26, and maybe even 6, 7, and 8 in the Epistle to the Romans. We should also read in this connection the rules for the discernment of spirits proper to the first week (nos. 314–327). These rules should be read not just because they are proper to those in the first week, but because they contain the psychological background for the salvation history we are going to meditate on.

If we want to go further into this matter, we could practice the First Prelude contained in number 47 in the book of the Exercises, namely, the imagining of the place, which here is "to see in imagination my soul as a prisoner in this corruptible body, and to consider my whole composite being as an exile here on earth, cast out to live among brute beasts. I said my whole composite being, body and soul." When we have understood this First Prelude, when we have tried with the help of Scripture, depth psychology, and experience to understand what this means, then we will have realized that that is not some weird fancy of St. Ignatius, but a brief, deft sketch of our sinful state, of the emptiness of our human existence, of our intrinsic animality. Then we will have some insight into the Ignatian meditation on sin.

I. Sin as a Personal Act

A certain type of false, vulgar Catholicism is always in danger of considering sin a mere contingent event: an event in our life that occurs once in a while; an event that, if a person does not go to confession or do some other uncommon thing, God for some strange reason holds against us, even though our sinful deed took place a long time ago. On the other hand, the Protestant is always in danger of considering sin a constitutive element of man's essence. Now the truth lies between these two positions. We say this not only from theoretical reasons, but also because in this matter it is easy to see how difficult it is for a person to see himself as a sinner in his meditation. Sin is not a metaphysical state of finiteness, of being at the end of the line, of falling off from the absolute demand of love. (This is more or less the Protestant position, which goes on to draw the conclusion that man is always and necessarily a sinner. However, anyone who has never run the danger of holding this view probably knows very little about sin.) As a matter of fact, sin is not a contingent act which I performed in the past and whose effect is no longer with me. It is certainly not like breaking a window which falls into a thousand pieces, but afterwards I remained personally unaffected by it. Sin determines man in a definite way: He has not only sinned, but he himself is a sinner. He is a sinner not only by a formal, juridical imputation of a former act, but also in an existential way, so that in looking back on our past actions, we always find ourselves to be sinners. When we have understood this, we are very close to understanding our own human existence.

Sin occurs in actions that do not have to be posited. Therefore, there are differences in sinfulness, especially the essential difference between mortal and venial sin. There are differences that must be judged objectively according to accepted moral teaching; they must also be judged subjectively. Sin is not just a dialectical opposite of grace; it is not a trick of God's love that He uses to show us our poverty and creaturehood so He can then show us how merciful He is. Sin in itself does not demand grace! And therefore, Christian existence is not a dialectical unity of sin and grace; rather, it is a road of decision from darkness to light, according to which the situation of each one of us must be judged.

It would be a false way of making the Exercises if a person tried, working from misunderstood ascetical principles, to attain a type of sin-consciousness that is not ours and cannot be ours. It is possible that the literal meaning of the book of the Exercises cannot be adequately realized interiorly by a person whom God has protected from many sins (in this regard, think of mortal sins that are such both objectively and subjectively). We must be truthful with ourselves! For if we are not, then we will find ourselves in a Protestant absolutizing of sin, and in a sin-mysticism in which we tend to think: the deeper a person throws himself into hell by means of his own actions, the more he is *the* object that God seeks so that He can forgive him. The forgiveness of sin and confidence of being justified do not stand in a dialectical relationship to sin!

If that seems too obvious, then our idea of sin and our idea of the sinner is too naïve and is too much influenced by individual norms. Just as sin exists and just as we *become* sinners by our own free actions which leave a spatio-temporal determination in our lives, so also *are* we sinners ontically; this is true of us in a much more essential way than it is true that a wall, after being painted white, remains white, or that a frog, after jumping into the water, is a frog that actually jumped. Our acts penetrate our personal human existence in a specifically different way, even when they are no longer noticed on the surface of our consciousness. In this connection, we can ask ourselves how far away from ourselves we must be, if we do not notice from within us that we are sinners, or at least that we can really be sinners, and if this situation dawns on us only, as it were, from the outside because our actions do not conform to some formal regulation.

II. *Sin as Guilt*

1. *The Attitude of Unredeemed Man toward Guilt.* Our human existence is caught between the sinfulness of all creation resulting from Adam's sin plus our own personal sinfulness on the one hand, and the redemption of Christ on the other. Therefore, it is necessary to pass a right judgment on our own sinfulness looked at from the point of view of its origin. This will reveal a make-up that tends to place suffering and misfortune *before* guilt. Not theoretically, but at least practically, men are tempted to think that guilt follows misfortune, and not vice versa. Actually, suffering and misfortune follow guilt, and this result is

not at all a vicious circle. In judging ourselves and the course of our lives, we are always tempted to consider our guilt as the result of bad luck, or of a lack of talent, or of exterior circumstances. By this basically false type of arguing that we use in trying to excuse ourselves before God, our conscience, our life, and the world, we manifest not our innocence, but only the way in which the unenlightened man, as yet untouched by the grace of God, considers his own guilt, that is, he will not admit it. He prefers to repress it.

The position of unredeemed man with regard to guilt is further characterized by the fact that he confuses guilt with fate. It is common knowledge that classic Greek tragedy does not consider guilt as the radical act of a free, responsible, human personality. Its attitude is rather that fate is something that happens to a man. Certainly, he feels himself guilty in some way or other, but even more pressing is the complaint that an absolutely just and holy God must have mercy on the tragic fate of man. Or, in another vein, the unredeemed man absolutizes himself, falsely makes a person out of himself to such a degree that he does not believe and does not desire that his guilt be forgiven—and it is precisely in this attitude that he commits the most serious sin. Perhaps we do not experience anything like this in our own souls. Nevertheless, there is such an attitude toward sin.

2. Toward a Clear Knowledge of Guilt. With the light of natural reason we can discover a moral philosophy. Philosophical ethics also has its theological aspect. Sin can only be known as a violation of the holy will of God the Creator and Lord of the world. Therefore, there is no such thing in this world as a "philosophical sin," or, if this idea does pop up, it has nothing to do with the Christian concept of sin. A man who has this idea of sin is caught up in a primitive notion that perhaps makes it impossible for him really to commit a sin. Nevertheless, it remains true that the real knowledge of guilt, that is, the sorrowful admission of sin, is the product of God's revelation and grace. Grace is already at work in us when we admit guilt as our own reality, or at least admit the possibility of guilt in our own lives. Grace is already at work when a man has the humility to hand himself over to the power of grace, when he tells himself that he is so dependent on the grace of God that he must possess it if he is to remain free of sin. On the other hand, a purely natural knowledge of guilt—one that is completely independent of grace (if this is philosophically possible)—would be suppressed if God's grace and the light of revelation were not there to help us. This type of knowledge only "notices" guilt, or formulates it in such a way that it becomes a condemnation, not a liberating and saving confession. Without grace, we would not stand firm in the truth of the existence of sin for a long period of time. We would say: "Why, we can't be *that* foolish! Guilt is merely the product of our disturbed imagination and of our existential *Angst* that has objectified itself!"

God's revelation of guilt takes place especially in the apocalypse of His grace and mercy. Only in this way! Therefore, if God did not tell us about sin in the revelation of His grace, then we would either deny the existence of guilt, or else we would utterly despair. There is no neutral position between these two. Thus we can only get a clear knowledge of guilt, both of its essence and its actuality, from the cross of Jesus Christ. (Therefore, St. Ignatius does not present a metaphysical consideration of sin in the first week of the Exercises. The first meeting with the theme of sin takes place before the cross of Christ and only there.)

3. *The Essence of Guilt.* What is meant here is the guilt of mortal sin which is a free act that we alone are responsible for, that we cannot blame anyone else for, that is more properly ours than any act of faith and love. We can only posit acts of faith and love if we receive them in their possibility and actuality as a gift of God in virtue of His supernaturally elevating and effective grace. But despite all speculation, we cannot push sin off onto God, even though the philosopher is always tempted to consider the creature as a marionette of the absolute. That is pre-

cisely what man is not! And sinful man is always tempted to say that fundamentally He is responsible for sin on Whom everything depends. But if he takes that kind of a position with regard to sin, he has betrayed the special characteristic of his creaturehood.

Guilt is contracted through the deification of a finite reality, through the identification of my absolute worth that can only be related absolutely to God, with things that cannot be posited absolutely. In the absoluteness that has been given me from above, I desire to assert myself radically in the realm of the finite. In this deification of a finite reality, there is an attack against the true meaning of my freedom, which is my capacity and my necessity of the infinite. I do not have the courage to make a leap into the infinite, to relativize everything finite, and so to surpass the finite. I remain standing on the edge of the abyss and desire to have it easier and more pleasant in this life by exhausting the possibilities of tangible things. This attitude necessarily implies a turning away from God and His essential characteristics—His immensity, power, dominion, truth and beauty, love and holiness, and so forth. Sin is also a radical offense against the sovereign will of God. Therefore, we should not act as if the objective structure and the known essence of a thing exhaust its reality. In addition to that, there is also the element in it that is willed and freely planned by the will of God. By my sin I offend against that, too!

It is most certainly true that God wills the objective order of the nature he has established and that an offense against nature is an offense against its Maker. But in the matter of sin, there is an inexplicable something left over that is also an offense against God's free will and His powerful dominion over things. This is even more the case with regard to the concrete order of our human existence, in which we are dealing directly with His Person and His Holy Spirit. We are not just dealing with His law, we are also dealing with His personal Self, with the God who is near! Not just with an order that He has created, but with an order that He has supernaturally established and communicated Himself to. Where sin actually takes place in this world, it offends against the infinite love of God, against the goodness that God Himself is in our midst; it is an attack against the uncreated grace, against the heart of God. Our sin actually pierces God! Therefore, it is essentially the loss of grace and a falling out of the life of God.

Even though it is true that from many points of view there can be no such thing as absolute evil, still sin must be considered an *absolute non-value.* All other value-deficiencies can have some meaning, can be built into a larger system that brings out their meaning. A person can give up a lot of things and still nicely arrange the totality of his human existence. He can put a plus sign before an algebraic equation. But he cannot do that with sin. If I consider sin a phase of development, if I say that it is only one of God's "tricks" so that He can throw more grace into the world, if I try to make a beginning with sin before God has said: "Your guilt is forgiven," if I should try—apart from the cross of Christ—to philosophize about a *"felix culpa,"* then I have done away with the absolute non-value of sin.

And now let us tell ourselves: There is no such thing as sin! In order to find ourselves in this meditation, we must summon up all our mental powers and make a few objections: There is no such thing as sin! Where does sin come from, if there is only the one, holy God Who creates and sustains everything? How can sin really exist, if it is supposed to be mere negativity? How can it be so bad, if it is only a lack of value? How can it be condemned by God? If we tell ourselves then that this falling off comes about because of our freedom, then the problem is simply posed once more: How can a freedom whose power is received from God effect such a falling off? Why is this act so bad, if it necessarily brings forth some positive good no matter how small? From this we can see how we would not remain true to the real existence of sin, if the crucified Christ did not say to us: Sin does exist, in spite of all improbability; it is present in the world

41

according to the testimony of your conscience in the Holy Spirit! It is here, even though it is committed in the darkness of this world and from our weakness.

We never know where we or the world with its history should be forgiven; we can never say with an absolute judgment: Here is sin, it happened right there! We cannot even say that about ourselves because we can never, with perfect reflection, grasp ourselves as agents. But we must tell ourselves: What we Christians call sin can happen in this world, has happened, and is happening right now. I, who am pleased with myself, who am so identified with myself that I must love myself, can sin. That is something frightful! Theoretically, we never challenge this truth, but in the fulfillment of our human existence we forget it again and again. And if we do admit it existentially, then that is only because God's grace has touched us, and because the light of His mercy has penetrated into our darkness. Accordingly, then, our first meditation on sin can and must begin at that place to which St. Ignatius with his main themes is leading us: under the cross of our Lord.

6. The Three Sins
(45)

Note

1. In this meditation, St. Ignatius mentions the Augustinian triple-division of the powers of the soul which was a part of the traditional inheritance of the time. He speaks of "memory," "intellect," and "will." We today would say: the spirit in its self-presence, in its self-intuition, and in its self-activity. This last division does not seem very logical, but even St. Thomas Aquinas speaks of a "*causa sui.*" We must realize that this description has to do with the presence of a spirit whose inner constitution is essentially transcendence toward God; therefore, it already has a certain type of presence of God, grasp of God, and capacity of doing the will of God. Obviously, St. Ignatius does not want us to esteem these powers of the soul in such a way that they would be mere external instruments that can be applied to some thing and then would have nothing more to do with it interiorly. We should see this "image of the Trinity" as perverted by sin, we should experience ourselves as sinners in this Trinitarian triple-division, and we should try to see the contradiction contained in our essence when its image of God is marred by sin.

2. If we run through St. Ignatius' meditations, then we see that all of them (the Foundation is not really one of them) are directed immediately toward historical events, or at least toward

things that can be imagined. St. Ignatius is a man who thinks concretely and who has little time for things that can only be treated abstractly. He wants to move the whole man; he knows that, when a man has encountered reality, his true knowledge always occurs in a "conversion to the phantasm," or in a "conversion to history." Therefore, we always find in St. Ignatius' writings a union of idea and concrete image. We could almost say: a union of history and myth. What he says with an image is not only a dressed-up idea and an artificial image, it is also a turning toward the concrete truth that appears representatively in history.

We must consider further that in our historical development, we always find ourselves in others and ratify others in ourselves. We are not so creative that we can produce something, as it were, out of the empty depths of our abstract essence; rather, we truly find ourselves by associating with others. Therefore, we can only discover that we are sinners if we meet our sinful, original portrait in history.

3. The purpose of this meditation is that we grasp the sin-situation in which our own sins occur. What we are considering here are not things that took place in some distant past, and about which we might give a report as we would of events of long ago; rather, we are meditating on facts that are constitutive of our actual situation right now. Therefore, I must consider events that co-determine my concrete human existence today. In fact, they co-determine me to such an extent that my own sin actually represents an identification with that historical past that remains as the present. In this matter, we can realize the negative side, as it were, of that anamnesis that we existentially and cultically realize in the Mass of Christ's sacrifice on the cross, that is, the anamnesis of the origin of our sin which is still present with us and which actualizes itself anew every time we sin.

If this meditation is supposed to close with a colloquy before the cross, then it is not meant as a pious, Christian conclusion that is tacked on to a meditation on a historical event that really has nothing to do with Christ as such. Rather, we are invited by the matter of this "colloquy of mercy" (nos. 52 and 54) to choose right in the beginning a place before the cross. We are invited to consider our situation from this vantage point, and so to see all the events in the history of sin as phases of that salvation history that leads only to the cross of Christ and is solved only by it. This means that we are also considering our solidarity in sin and salvation. The events of non-salvation also lead to the cross. Ultimately, they can only be interpreted and understood from the cross. We are all in the same battle! Our situation in the history of salvation is especially determined by the cross and by the first sins.

There is a danger for us as modern rationalists of dissolving these things into airy abstractions. And we can hardly do otherwise if we are going to speak about them in concepts. But in the Exercises, it is a matter of "seeing" and of transposing oneself right into the heart of the history of sin—that sin that has not disappeared, but has remained as our present state. Moreover, at this point we should so prepare the meditation on our own personal sins that we can recognize them as a type of participation in the first three sins: the sin of the pure spirits, the sin of man in his original state, and the sin of redeemed man. We should recognize the consequences of sin in these first three sins, especially the helplessness that characterizes them. In the history of sin, we should recognize that, as opposed to the more abstract sin-mysticism of Protestantism, salvation is not a dialectical opposite of sin. It is, rather, an incomprehensible grace that saves us; for God did not have to come to our aid—He could have left us in our lost condition.

I. *The Sin of the Angels* (50)

In order to evaluate the sin of the angels properly, we must have an adequate, theological idea of what the angels are. In a very true sense, they belong to the world, even though they are not corporeal. They do not just take an occasional trip into the world with either a good intention or a bad one. According to St. Paul, they are the "principalities and powers" of creation. And together with visible things they constitute the one world. Therefore, the history of the angels is necessarily also a part of my own history, an element of the concrete situation within which I must form my spiritual-personal existence and effect my salvation. Hence, the sin of the angels is a threat and a danger for that salvation.

We should realize at this point that sin also occurs in pure spirits. Despite the drag of the flesh, our ultimate determination is that we are spirit—the open transcendence toward the infinite that is God. This fact makes us essentially related to the angels. We cannot distinguish angels from men the way we distinguish the living from the dead. Men and angels belong together, not only because of the one supernatural grace, but also because of the open transcendence toward the one same goal.

The meditation on the sin of the angels says to me: you are a spirit that can sin. Very often we are tempted to consider the body, the earthly, the passionate, and perhaps also the sexual in the narrowest sense, as the real area of sin, and thus have a false notion of sin. At this point, we are not going to develop further how this attitude flows, on the one hand, from the fact that the sexual relation must be a radical way of carrying out the personal world-relationship of a corporeal-spiritual being, and on the other hand, that this personal relationship is necessarily that area within which sin can occur. But at any rate, the strangeness of sin, the free rejection of God, broke loose there where the created principalities and powers sit in power over the whole world. Therefore, this world is not determined by the sinful situation just here and there (a point which could easily be overlooked), but everywhere. If there is such a thing as the sin of the angels, then there is simply nothing left in this world (which constitutes a whole) that is immune to sin. Further, the sin of the angels is malice within the framework of the Christian world. This sin, too, is directed against Christ. It is the total performance or realization of the concrete essence of the angels. Now we do not have to split our heads over the problem of whether or not the angels sinned against a revelation of the Incarnation of the Logos that was made to them, or whether they failed in some other way. If we are all destined ultimately to the same happiness, and if the angels, too, adore Christ, then He belongs in some decisive way also to them. This way cannot be exhausted by a mere additional recognition of an objective value. If they are subject to the Logos in the flesh, then that fact must have a real-ontological and an essential meaning for them; it must be something that fulfills precisely their spiritual autonomy, which is characterized by simplicity and totality. (An angel cannot just by-the-by adore something and serve someone, but he is present to himself in this adoration and in this service.) In other words, Christ is the existential fact that counts for the personal existence of the angels. But that can only be if the angels also received their supernatural elevation because the Father always wanted to set up His Logos as a creature, and therefore from this fact proceeded to project the totality of reality. And thus, if the angels sin in the use of their being that was given in this way, then the Christological relationship of their essence cannot remain unaffected. This means that they must have taken a position with regard to Christ in their sin, and in the complete existential act that is implied in their sin.

The consideration of these things should not remain bogged down by abstract concepts. We must gradually come to realize how deeply rooted our sin-situation really is: It reaches down into the immense abyss of a sin occurring in a pure spirit—a sin against God and against His true love for creation that is manifested in Christ.

II. *Adam's Sin* (51)

From the very beginning, St. Paul draws a parallel between Adam and Christ. It is, therefore, evident, to some extent at least, that Adam sinned as a "Christian." Just how explicit his "Christianity" was to him is another question! A man's sin is always of such a nature that it is involved in the reality of this world; it is always an act of the spiritual core of his human existence that is necessarily a part of what we have called "the world." Now the Incarnate Son of God belongs to this world from the very first and in the first plan. By his sin, therefore, Adam rejects the love of God that is manifested in His creation —a creation whose alpha and omega is Christ. God could certainly have created another world; but the world He did create is directed toward Christ. If we read St. Paul's Epistle to the Colossians along with the other texts bearing on this matter, then we cannot really divide and distinguish between the Logos as immanent in the Trinity and the Logos as incarnate because of the loving freedom of God (that is, the Logos of the economy of salvation). Temporal sequence does not enter into this. Therefore, Adam's grace—the grace before the fall—must be considered the grace of Christ.

We encounter our original sin in the sin of Adam. His disobedience is the source of our sinful insubordination. To turn a deaf ear to God who is calling to His creatures—those products of His love—is the basic characteristic of every sin.

The penance of our first parents is also continued in us, and this not in the sense that we can and must repent for original sin (we can only repent for personal sins), but in the sense that the one history of sin begun by Adam pervades the life of every man as a history of penance, and that each one of us is affected personally by the results of Adam's sin. It is clear that the first father of the one human race has a place and a meaning that is radically determining for that race. In this body of suffering, I must continually come to terms with a situation that was caused by Adam. Every sin of mine is a real (not in a merely external, abstract-conceptual sense) ratification of Adam's sin, and my turning to Christ is always at the same time a turning away from Adam.

III. *Sin of the Redeemed Man* (52)

The meaning of the Ignatian statement in this part of the meditation (that is, no. 52) is not that a man redeemed by Christ is damned by God because of a single mortal sin, but rather that he exposes himself to eternal damnation by every mortal sin. St. Ignatius desires that the exercitant recognize the true import of one sin committed in the presence of the Christ. We could make a number of meditations just on this point. But here we want especially to consider that every sin essentially (however much a person must also bear the consequences that he alone has brought down on himself because of his sin) as a free act of the creature always brings with it the experience of the resistance of reality against that creature. However strange it may sound, this opposition is a constitutive element of the inner structure of the free act. Even man's freest act is also always passion in the metaphysical sense. Only God can produce something outside of Himself which, as originating from Him, is merely an act of His and does not burden Him further. We act in such a way that our deeds are constituted by association with other things. Therefore, they are always a risk. We act in such a way that something enters into our action that we cannot adequately grasp.

Now if I am supposed to meditate here on a man who is lost because of one single sin, then I should not cry out in astonishment: Is God so fickle that He damns one man because of a single mortal sin, while He makes saints out of others after they have committed many mortal sins? Instead of that I should say: The man whom I am supposed to imagine damns himself because of his own sin. If, as spiritual creatures, we always and necessarily reach out for the infinite in our free actions, then by our performed or realized godlessness we can strike at the ultimate and the irrevocable. Moreover, when I consider a redeemed man who is lost because of one mortal sin, I should also say: The occurrence of a mortal sin really produces damnation, it has an iron grip on a man as long as he remains identified with his sin; and the final form of his existence, resulting from this identification of person and act, can enter at any point in his life. Every moment of my life can be a saving-moment or a damning-moment for my human existence. No matter how true it is that man lives in time, still that time is not a garment sewed from many disparate patches; it is not to be conceived of as though moment B has no intrinsic connection with moment A. When we act in a personal way, we gather our whole life together. Somehow we possess our human existence totally in all the changing moments of time. I can actually put my whole life into each one of its moments—and in each of them either wholly gain it or wholly lose it. I can be a man who right now so sins that he is eternally lost, even though he only sins right now. When St. Ignatius says that I should consider how a man is lost because of one mortal sin and how I still remain in the order of redemption despite my many sins, then I should call this thought to mind in all seriousness: If one mortal sin can always bring on eternal damnation, then how infinite God's mercy has been with me—and how incomprehensible! And what terrible dangers we are exposed to because of our sinfulness!

These remarks are an attempt to keep you from thinking that the meditation on the three sins is too simple. We must impress on ourselves the importance of the great events in our history. These events must become, as it were, the archetypes of our essence, because they reveal to us the fundamental events of life. We cannot say: "That's all kid-stuff—everybody knows that!" It is precisely what is so familiar to us that it has got lost because of its familiarity—it is this that must become pressingly tangible for us. Only in this way will a theoretical knowledge become a forming truth of our life.

7. On Personal Sin
(55–61)

Preludes

1. If I am supposed to imagine in the first prelude of this meditation how my soul is imprisoned in this corruptible body, then this is not meant primarily as an exercise of the imagination; rather, it is supposed to be an interior realization of my true situation that goes beyond the application of the senses. In any event, the decaying, sick body is the visible carrying out of sinful existence. Today this is not just our theological point of view; it is increasingly also the psychological and medical point of view. Sickness is not just an accidental development; it is the connatural manifestation of the spiritual decay that is posited with sin. It is not only an external appearance, but it is also that which interiorly belongs to the situation of the sinner; it is the expression of his existential wasteland, of his exhausting falling-back-upon-himself, of his self-incarceration, of his not being able to do more, of his being delivered into the hands of strange powers, of his being banished into a suffering that can no longer be controlled by the spirit, but signifies the decaying, the recalcitrant, that which can no longer be dominated, the presence of death in us right now.

The person who can put himself into this situation in such a way that he clearly sees what he is in his life, has truly reached the frame of mind in this prelude that is necessary to make this meditation properly.

2. "I ask . . . for a growing and intense sorrow for my sins . . ." Everyone can make this meditation about himself: We are all sinners. Certainly, a person should not try to work himself into a false consciousness of sin. Nevertheless, in this meditation I should try to bring in all the possibilities of sin that are slumbering in me. Religiously, we would be very jaded if we would not admit how close we are to sin, and that we have very often only avoided it because we were afraid, because we were trapped in the social pressure of our milieu, but not because we were good and holy.

I. A Look at the Record of My Sins (56)

At this point, it is worthwhile to take a good look at our own lives—not just to study our past or to prepare for confession, but, first of all, to get to know the person in me that I now am, the person that I have become by my own sin-history (even if God in His mercy forgave me a long time ago: Perhaps my sinful past is not yet properly integrated into my present—and then, in my search for God, I must turn back to it); secondly, to see myself—what I can be and what I, through my sins, at every moment can become. I consider my human existence, how it develops in time. There I see the sequence of my sins: the different phases of my life that were given to me to become continuous eruptions of the love of God. Bit by bit, I have misused them and filled them with my fickleness, my laziness, my inner stubbornness and Godlessness.

I look into the room of my life, a room that should belong to God. Yes, this place, this house, this street, this store I have corrupted with the existential lie that is my life, with my foulness and treason. I have made everything into something other than it should be. I consider my surroundings, the contacts I have cultivated, my occupation that takes up so much of my

53

time. I should be amazed at my capacity to corrupt all these things. All times and places, all men and all things crowd in on me—in a thousand and one things I see myself as a person that is somehow closed off from God, that did not have enough love, that did not have enough courage to let himself go, that did not break loose to find God. Perhaps I can then get a clear picture of my sins: a picture of acts that should not have taken place and that I alone am responsible for. These are truly *my sins;* I am the one who has become *this* man. And these sins are still with me, at least as forgiven sins. Perhaps the man that is looking at me from out of my past, is the same man that I am today. Who knows whether or not I have found God's mercy, whether or not I am near God in the depths of my being—or whether or not I have already begun to be lost? Who knows?

II. *The Seriousness of My Sins* (57)

Next I should consider the utter distortion, the hatefulness, the wallowing meaninglessness and meaningless-making of my sins. St. Ignatius characterizes sin as loathsomeness and malice. It is both. In a most terrifying way, it is rottenness and corruption, brittleness and cowardice; it is a masquerade; it embraces all that is hard, offensive, and opaque in the man who is left to himself.

III. *Who Am I that Sins?* (58)

"What am I compared with all men?" Here I can consider my existential weakness amidst the mass of men. The comparison with the many makes me take note of a special element of sin: Through sin, I become an "everyman," a number in a collective, and I lose my own personal worth that would be capable of being with God forever. By sin, I make myself a worthless piece of junk that should be cast into the garbage pit. The present-day impropriety of the impersonal "one" is basically the just reward of my guilt.

2. "I will consider what all men are compared with the angels and saints of paradise." In comparison with the sinner, the saint is not just another unimportant name to pass before the crowd. Men who have attained God and sanctity have also each attained an authentic and original infinity. In that state, each one loves God and possesses Him, and is therefore truly something that pales every attempted comparison. The angels and the saints have become "complete persons." They are not just potentially persons, but they have realized their whole human existence. What they are, they are as the result of their love of God. The lost sinner receives the judgment of his deliberately willed meaninglessness. He was too cowardly to win stature and to be more than a part of the masses. I may and must compare myself with the masses in order to see, as it were in a mirror, who I really am.

3. "I will consider what all creation is in comparison with God." If I truly love God, I cannot keep myself at a distance from Him. But for one who loves, such a distance would only be another kind of blessed nearness, the humility of the creature that says to God: "*Tu solus sanctus*," only a blessedness in which a man finds God as his own life. But when man is a sinner, then he is alone, in the wilderness, among brute beasts, drinking deep the loneliness of despair. By sin, I put myself in the situation of the rejected, of those who must fall back upon themselves. Almost without noticing it and with the feeling that everything is not so bad after all, I bring about this danger. For a time, a man can think that he can make it alone. But eventually the truth becomes unmistakably clear: It is terrifying to be alone before God without God.

4. "I will consider all the corruption and loathsomeness of my body." From a theological point of view, we are constantly suffering from our bodiliness and our concupiscence; we are sick, tired, and very limited. In my great weakness, I encounter not

only the sin of my first parents, but also my own guilt. (Our own times emphasize this situation so much that we must be continually warned and reminded of the words of Jesus, that in certain circumstances a particular sickness is in no wise the expression of personal guilt.) I must experience my own helplessness as the truth of that which sin effects in me. This truth is my tendency to fall apart, my ugly lack of completeness, and the lack of the identity between idea and existence which I find in myself.

5. "I will consider myself as a source of corruption and contagion from which has issued countless sins and evils and the most offensive poison." As a sinner in all truthfulness, I am "a source of corruption and contagion." Such an expression may seem an exaggeration, but when we stand before the crucified Lord and discover that the cross, where the incarnate beauty of the Father nailed to the gibbet wretchedly wastes away, is nothing but the result of sin, then perhaps we will clearly see that there can be no exaggeration when it comes to speaking of the absolute senselessness of sin. And only before the Christ, Who is the palpable mercy of God, can we summon up the courage required for such a confession.

IV. *My Sins in the Sight of God* (59)

"I will consider Who God is against whom I have sinned." Each image that I possess of God's attributes bears the mark of my sinfulness. His wisdom stands in opposition to my ignorance, His tremendous power to my weakness, His justice to my iniquity, His burning love to my perverted love.

V. *A Cry of Wonder* (60)

Then I will consider sin in the light of the continuing goodness of the world and the saving love of God. This light will only emphasize my wickedness at first, but at the same time it gives me the possibility of being saved from myself, if I only have the courage to abandon myself. At this point, St. Ignatius once again mentions the history of salvation and how it embraces all visible things, the saints and the angels—all from Christ and toward Christ. I stand somewhere in *this* salvation history as a sinner. And the bolt of divine justice and retaliation is still restrained. The world, as it were, holds its breath and waits. This situation is still the same, but the restraint of creation, a result of God's mercy, will not continue indefinitely: Eventually and like lightning, God's holy will will break into the *whole* of creation. What I am at that moment as the result of my previous free choices, I will remain for all eternity. If I am a sinner, then all creation, which mirrors God's loving goodness, will become the fire of hell for me. But God and His creation are still good to me. They wait, they allow the drama of my history to go on. I can still make the colloquy of mercy.

VI. *Colloquy of Mercy* (61)

"I will conclude with a colloquy, extolling the mercy of God our Lord, pouring out my thoughts to Him, and giving thanks to Him that up to this very moment He has granted me life. I will resolve with His grace to amend for the future. Close with an Our Father."

To speak out, to thank, to praise the grace of Christ, to ask, to renew former resolutions, to try to change the attitudes of the heart—all of this deals with the future. St. Ignatius says simply: "I will resolve to amend for the future." Before God's mercy and His judgment, I am only a poor, weak child that must hope in Him and constantly strive to be good. Our will toward God, our good resolutions, the direction of our lives, and absolutely everything in us must be completely humbled in a meditation such as this. Everything we are, except sin, is a gift of God and comes down on us from the Father of light! In this situation, the Our Father that St. Ignatius suggests at the conclusion is very fitting: In this prayer, we have the word of the Father in heaven who forgives, of His will to give grace, of His creatures that make up the Kingdom, of the arrival of this Kingdom, of the bread of life, of forgiveness, of deliverance from all temptation, and of the liberation from the chains of evil. May the answer to these requests be given to each one of us.

8. Venial Sin and the "World"
(62–63)

Note

The third meditation of the "first week" of the Exercises should consist "in repeating the First and Second Exercise" (the one on the three sins and the one on personal sin). In this repetition, I should "pay attention to and dwell upon those points in which I have experienced greater consolation or desolation or greater spiritual appreciation." St. Ignatius considers the movement of the spirits, toward consolation or desolation, a sign that the dynamic of the Exercises is having its effect in the exercitant. Where a person experiences greater consolation or desolation, there he should dwell and pray more, while things that cause neither consolation nor desolation can be left aside.

At the end of this meditation, the exercitant should make a triple colloquy, addressing our Lady, then Jesus, and finally the heavenly Father, in order to ask three things: "1) A deep knowledge of my sins and a feeling of abhorrence for them; 2) an understanding of the disorder of my actions, that filled with horror of them, I may amend my life and put it in order; 3) a knowledge of the world, that filled with horror, I may put away from me all that is worldly and vain."

While the first request concerns the two meditations that have been repeated, the second and third requests introduce two new ideas into the Exercises: the concept of the "disorders of life," which are nothing but the *"peccata quotidiana,"* the venial sins in the accepted sense of moral theology; and the concept of the "world." The introduction of these two ideas gives us the right to consider this repetition-meditation as a completion and development of the foregoing.

I. *Venial Sin*

The presence of venial sin is obvious. In fact, it constitutes the moral disorder of our everyday life. We should take these sins, that we confess each week in an off-handed manner, very seriously. It is true that they do not realize the essence of serious sin that separates man from the grace of God, and in which he exercises such a total disposition over himself that he really becomes lost. But they do distract him from his eternal goal and injure him in many ways.

A few familiar phrases will suffice to bring out the harmful influence of venial sin on our whole life: Venial sin leads to the formation of false attitudes, and so to the corruption of character and the dulling of conscience; it lessens one's personal happiness, the state of a calm human existence that knows how to live in peace with itself. There is more: Venial sin hinders the development and growth of the life of grace, and so the personal penetration of our nature's free movement toward God; yes, in a very true sense it is an offense against God, an obscuring of the living relationship to God. Not the least of the bad effects of venial sin is that which concerns our apostolic mission. Perhaps it is easier for many of us, looking at the matter from the point of view of our responsibility for others, to see these "mere" venial sins as factors which essentially weaken our apostolic effectiveness. A person can have more or less talent, can live in circumstances that turn the Lord's vineyard into a stone-quarry in which he must nevertheless continue to labor. But very often we ourselves are responsible for the fact that our apostolic labor is much less fruitful than it should be. This means especially that we should take venial sin seriously in all of its various forms, beginning with freely chosen faults and going on to certain manifestations of our character for which we are hardly guilty, but which nevertheless show how far removed we are from that which we should be.

Some of the things we would do well to meditate on are: impatience, coarseness, uncleanliness, cheap literature, talkativeness, laughing at the faults of others, petty egotism in everyday life, petty enmities, oversensitiveness, wasting time, cowardice; lack of respect for holy things, for other men, for the life of their souls; disrespectful talk about women, harmful spite portraying itself as a clever joke, stubbornness and obstinacy, moodiness that others must put up with, disorder in work, postponement of the unpleasant, gossip, conceit and self-praise, unjust preference for certain people that we find quite pleasant, hastiness in judging, false self-satisfaction, laziness, the tendency to give up learning any more, the tendency to refuse to listen to others, and so forth.

The fight against venial sins must correspond with their particular nature: If a particular sin is a matter of carelessness that can easily be overcome, if a person truly wants to overcome it and can muster the courage to demand asceticism from himself, then a particular examen, conscientiously used, will bring quick results. But if a venial sin is deeply imbedded, if it is a spontaneous and almost reflex action of a falsely formed character, then a relatively external ascetical training is not sufficient. In such cases, the best remedy seems to be to have a great deal of patience and to let ourselves be educated by life itself. A person must observe very carefully until he has found the critical starting point. Very often, a person can only struggle indirectly against such faults, even when their symptoms are directly perceptible.

The main problem here is to discover the particular way of existence of one's own "I." No person should dare to say that he has sufficiently penetrated the meaning of his own self.

61

Therefore, the effort to attain self-knowledge in order to reform one's character must necessarily last a long time. Normally, this is a lifetime job. Certainly, we should never give up. Recurring falls should not be passed off lightly. We should, for example, be alarmed if we find that we are constantly coming into conflict with those around us—even if we discover that the others were in the wrong, or if we feel that everything we touch turns into a failure, or if we suffer in any other way that does not seem to be normal. In this regard, people often reproach themselves for things that hardly approach a venial sin. But this can still be a secondary symptom pointing to something more deep-seated.

Sometimes venial sins that we most frequently and seriously repent of are the least relevant to what we are; on the other hand, certain things that we theoretically admit without suffering from them, can be our real but repressed faults. At best, a person can attempt a radical diagnosis of these secondary results. Usually, it is not a good idea to attempt this alone, but in coöperation with and under the direction of a good spiritual director. For these particular types of "disorders of life" come within the sphere of psychopathology. Much more could be said here that must be passed up. At any rate, a person should not minimize the importance of personal defects. Nevertheless, at times these defects must just be accepted and suffered through, since there is such a thing as a truly Christian suffering at the hands of one's own defects. And finally, venial sins should not remain unnoticed, since they lead ultimately to serious conflicts and to serious sins.

II. *The World*

The concept "world" is very ambiguous. Here it means just what Scripture says of it: It is not an imaginary picture dreamed up by illusionary ascetics, but it is the world of scandals on which the Lord called down His terrible "woes"; the world of darkness into which the light came and was not received; the world which cannot receive the spirit of truth, which, according to St. Paul, has a wisdom all its own that is not our wisdom; the world which does not know Christ, which hates Him and His, but which has already been conquered by the Lord. It is the *"Kosmos Houtos"* ["this world"] of St. Paul, whose spirit we have not received, from which, according to St. James, the Christian must keep himself unspotted. In other words, in this concept we do not mean the world as it left the hand of God good and pure, but the world as it is right now—that world that has been poisoned by the sin of the angels, the sin of Adam, and our own personal sin.

There is an attitude that, even though it has not degenerated into an open breaking of the divine law, still is not in accordance with the order of grace. There is something from which sins spring forth, even though we could not say here and now that this seedbed is sinful (though ultimately it could be traced back to sin). A basic position that maintains that where one cannot obviously find sin, there only God's good and ordered world is to be found—a world that is to be simply enjoyed and loved, does not correspond with the reality of Christian human existence that is stretched out between Adam and Christ, and between damnation and salvation. Just as we find prejudices in our personal lives that are false, even though they are not sinful in themselves since a true disposition of the self was lacking in them, in a like manner there is a zone in the world that, according to Scripture, is the "old world." Hence, I can and must pray to know this world so that, with a feeling of abhorrence, "I may put away from me all that is worldly and vain."

A separation of this kind, however, is no simple matter. For I am, as it were, shot through with the "world." I am in it, but I may not be of it (Jn 17,11ff.). A person can mistake the "world" for God and all His creatures. For it exists not only where my sin is; it also exists in my incalculable past. Hence,

63

getting away from this "world" demands constant vigilance, discretion in all things, a humble and radical mistrust of self. Through this dynamic, continual, constantly growing, and self-correcting getting away from the "world," the existence of the priest—which must in some way be identified with this rejection of the world—will be, not only for those on the way toward damnation, the resolute sinners, but also for the children of Adam who live in the shadow of the history of sin without any fault of their own (they are children of the "world"!), a scandal, a provocation, perfect stupidity—giving the impression of fanaticism and exaggeration. There is no regulation in the ideals for priests that we—except for obvious sin—as much as possible should think, act, and live like everyone else. Whoever would attempt this kind of a reconciliation between factual reality and the God Who has been given to us, does not possess the spirit of Christ, nor, because of that, the spirit of the priesthood. This does not mean that a priest should be morose, misanthropic, resentful—and at the same time deep-down hanker for the joys of this world. Rather, he should be a very happy and selfless man. All the same, he must expect the opposition and hatred of this "world" for himself and all he stands for; for the "world" is inflamed with a burning hatred of God, his Christ, and his Church. We, too, must continually admit to ourselves that we are children of this "world" in many things—a strange mixture of old and new—Christians who must put on the spirit of Jesus Christ more and more in order to be crucified to the "world." St. John's admonition applies to us also: "Do not love the world!"

Note: The Triple Colloquy (63)

The first request should be directed to our Lady. We are with her in the communion of saints and of prayer—the Mystical Body of Christ. Mary has a very special place and function in this body. Prayer to Mary is a part of Christian piety. St. Ignatius is a witness to that here with his triple colloquy, in a simple but theologically relevant way.

Then we should say: "Soul of Christ, sanctify me . . . ," turning to our Mediator, the Incarnate Word who affirms in Himself before God the present world-structure. He is the Lord, the Victor over the world. He has given to everyone who does not belong to the "world" the power to become a child of God.

Finally, I should direct myself to the Father Who has loved us so much that He sent His dearly beloved Son into the darkness, the emptiness, and the sin of this world. He alone is the all-holy One, the Lord, the Judge, the absolute center, according to Whom everything else must pattern itself. In His deep, unsearchable designs, He must have mercy on us so that we can know Christ and learn to love Him in grace. When we have been caught up in His mercy, we no longer belong to the "world," and the struggle with venial sin has become nothing but a valid following of Christ.

9. Asceticism for the Modern Priest

Note

Number 64 in the book of the Exercises requires another repetition of the preceding meditations so that "the intellect, without any digression, may diligently think over and recall the matter contemplated in the previous exercises." St. Ignatius does not want the exercitant to go through the matter just once in order to get some more or less profound thoughts that will be forgotten when he goes on to new material. He is very much concerned that his "exercises" be truly understood and experienced as such; hence, he wants them to be taken in such a way that they actually change the exercitant. For this end, the repetition of the meditations is very appropriate. Whoever would believe that he has done enough when he has satisfied his curiosity, that is, when he has gained a certain rationalistic or abstract knowledge of the Exercises, has missed the whole point of the Spiritual Exercises of St. Ignatius. Therefore, it would be perfectly in order if, under the influence of God's grace, we would simply repeat the preceding meditations, in a more interior, concentrated, and personal way so that we can relish what was said there in our own personal core. Still, we would like to fill out the picture a bit more.

The sin-meditations are not only reflections on the past; they should also point out the way for the future. In the colloquy with the Crucified and in the Triple Colloquy, I should ask myself what more I can do for Christ, my Lord; and I should pray that I might know interiorly how I can improve and better order my life so that I can put the world away from me and further my following of Christ. Thus we are remaining within the framework of the Ignatian Exercises if we include a few ideas about asceticism, character-formation, self-training, and penance.

I. *The Present-Day Situation*

Our age is characterized to an alarming degree by its mediocrity. (A person can say this without being a *"laudator temporis acti,"* who esteems only the past and finds it better than the present in almost every way, and thus offends against his loyalty to his own time—whose child he is.) In former times, the differences between men—even in the Church and in the priesthood—were much greater than they are today. Great saints and mighty sinners stood shoulder to shoulder; and the sinners had to be threatened with fire and brimstone before they would repent. In our times, however, mankind seems to be characterized by an insipid mediocrity in which light and darkness flow into a sort of gloomy gray. This is especially evident in the field of asceticism.

In many ways, life is more difficult for us than it was for those of earlier times. Certainly, there are a number of things in the ascetical life that no longer "appeal" to us, that have been replaced by other burdens that our forebears did not have to carry. One might say that we, as opposed to former generations, have weaker nerves, are not as healthy as they were, have been deeply marred by war. Perhaps that is all true, but in any case it is not sufficient to explain our mediocrity.

Obviously, we cannot fall into a reactionary traditionalism that would impel us simply to continue or renew what was done in the good old days, so that we would then, for example, pattern our prayer, work, and use of free time according to the old maxims. But we must always remember: Times of radical change such as ours, in which new ways must be found, in which one must grope around to find out how to proceed in the Church, in theology, in pastoral care, in the spiritual life, are always in danger of sacrificing that which is true and proper to Christianity in the old traditions. Certainly, the spirit of Christianity must continually form itself anew and differently in each age; it must enter into the present "style" of thinking, speaking, and existing —each generation of Christians must inevitably face this problem. Whether or not the present style is essentially better or worse than the style of any previous age must remain an open question. Historicity does not always and necessarily mean progress from good to better. Therefore, it is also our task to find new ways.

Form and content are not just related to one another exteriorly in an unimportant manner. They determine one another mutually so that the two cannot be adequately separated. Therefore, in times of great change we must take care that we do not unintentionally substitute new contents under the guise of new forms; we must be careful not to throw overboard much that belongs to the heart of Christianity, whose loss would at least be a narrowing that could bring in its train bitter results. That this danger is real and not just a theoretical possibility is shown by the fact that the ordinary, the "just about" right, but never the noble, has become the norm in our day—a norm that is not unfrequently found among priests and religious. Among the latter there is also a lot of theory and little action, a lot of organization and little glowing living. Today where do we find "holy follies"? Does a spiritual director these days have to restrain his clients from such deeds? Where are the truly shining, incarnate ideas? Where are the priests willing to lead a poor life? Where are the volunteers for the front lines of the Kingdom of God?

In Germany—it may be different in other countries—one has the impression that there is a general tendency to bring about a bourgeois restoration: In general, people are smugly content, are happy that they have a car and can take a summer trip. Today, the German with his "*Wirtschaftswunder*" gives the impression in other countries of being a snob. Nor is the German clergy completely free of this spirit. There will be no finger-pointing at individuals, but still we priests should not say to ourselves: Dear God, I thank You that I am not like those clerics with large incomes—who live very comfortably from a prosperous tithing system, who feel that they are God's overseers and accordingly see to it that their churches, especially exteriorly, are kept up nicely, and who are careful that their influence in public affairs is respected. We should not cast any stones, but we should beat our own breasts. In any event, we must keep our eyes open in order to see what dangers await us.

If we were to express these dangers that concern us here in a few short phrases, then we could say: We do not have enough "spiritual life," we do not practice enough asceticism. Now that we have reached our real theme, in the following paragraphs we would first like to say something about the nature and necessity of what is called the "spiritual life," and in particular deal with its ascetical structure. Then we would like to propose a few suggestions concerning the present-day practice of asceticism.

II. *Nature and Necessity of Asceticism*

1. *Asceticism in the Broad Sense.* The "spiritual life" is life with God and toward God. We are leading this life when we forget ourselves for God, when we love Him, praise Him, thank Him. "Spiritual life" in grace means that we realize the inner divine life in ourselves; it means waiting for eternity in faith, hope, and love, bearing the darkness of human existence; it means not identifying oneself with this world, living according to the prayer contained in the Didache: "Let this world pass away and let the grace of God come."

All that is certainly an unforced gift of the free grace of God: especially with regard to the presuppositions and situations in which God has placed us, and which open up for us the area of our freedom even though our freedom cannot control them; we mean, for example, our time and inclinations, our character, what we have inherited, our fellow men, the social and religious milieu in which we were born, the "other things" given us by God in order that we might find Him; and this free gift is also our own performance or realization, that is, the "spiritual life" that we put on and actualize in ourselves is at the same time the freely given grace of God.

But while praising grace we should not forget that it does not always rush over us in a wave of victory, sweeping aside all obstacles; nor is it a simple and unhindered growth; neither does it develop our "spiritual life" only to the extent that we suffer all in silence, leaving everything else in the hands of God. Generally speaking, the "spiritual life" is grace precisely because it must be painstakingly cultivated day by day; it requires constant training and drilling. In short, the "spiritual life" is also (even though not exclusively or even predominantly) *work, planned exercise,* and *conscious development* of the believing, hoping, and loving life in us according to the laws of nature and grace, and according to the motives of a total dedication to God. This aspect of the "spiritual life" is what we mean by "asceticism" in the broad sense.

In these exercises, each one of us should ask himself whether or not he is an ascetic in this sense, or whether, until now, he has remained an amateur Christian, perhaps protected by grace, perhaps kept more or less on the right path by reason of his surroundings and moral code. Perhaps the greatest gifts of grace come to us where we have not sought them; perhaps God gives grace to us even though we do not bother much about it; perhaps he runs after us, pursues us through the events of our life in such a way that much later we can say to God's mercy: God has been able to bring good out of all the stupidities of my life; my laziness and indolence, my reluctance and tepidity, my stubborn attitude have not kept Him from remaining by my side and putting up with me day after day. That may very well be! But it does not free us from the obligation of doing something ourselves in an orderly fashion. This "something" may be different in youth and old age, but it must have its place in a man's religious life. (An older person who has reached a certain maturity through his experiences of the grace of God, can allow himself a certain freedom in the systematic development of his "spiritual life," that we cannot allow ourselves and which would be very dangerous for us.)

2. *Asceticism in the Strict Sense.* Asceticism in the strict sense is a part of the asceticism spoken of above, but only that part which is specifically Christian. This asceticism is Christian self-abnegation in the true sense—an abnegation which gives up positive values in this life, and not just useful things that are a mere means to the end (*bona utilia,* for example); it also gives up (preserving, of course, the proper relationship and subordination to higher values) personal values (*bona honesta*), such as marriage and the freedom to develop one's personality by disposing of material possessions that make for independence.

a) *The Meaningfulness of This Asceticism.* Asceticism in this sense, at least basically and in its actual practice, cannot be deduced from the mere natural order. Nor does the natural law even suggest it. Values of intrinsic worth should not be given up in the natural order except under the pressure of circumstances. To give them up in this order would be impossible ontologically and perverse ethically. All resentful disdaining of earthly goods from the point of view of the world—because a natural ethic considers them to be cheap or dangerous or common is by that very fact objectively false and suspect, from a psychopathological point of view, in its basic motivation. Moreover, it would undermine the true meaning and the genuine realization of Christian self-denial.

From a purely natural standpoint, it could happen that a person, by reason of special circumstances (which themselves

71

contain the necessity of attaining a certain good, and this necessity at the same time excludes the attainment of another good), would actually be hindered from attaining an incompatible good. An example would be to give up different aspects of the present standard of living in order to train one's nature to act in harmony and in order to take the offensive against concupiscence. But this is not the meaning of the asceticism that is specifically Christian. In this regard, a person might pose the question whether or not the choice of the evangelical counsels for most men is really the "better way" to bring order into the drives in the personal whole. It is a simple fact that the evangelical counsels create new dangers. (One would be forced to draw some painful false conclusions if one wished to interpret the "heroic deeds" and the "excesses" that have occurred in the history of Christianity in this way. We cannot explain the radicalism and immensity of the penance found in the lives of the saints by appealing to a motive of self-discipline; nor can it be explained by "pious folly" or "influences of a general, historical, spiritual nature" which really have nothing to do with Christianity.) But if penance is not discipline, then we are forced to object, against every such attempt to establish asceticism, that specifically Christian asceticism (for example, the evangelical counsels) can never be established with this type of an argument. For such discipline, asceticism belongs strictly to this world. And this explanation forgets that Christian asceticism, as an essential part of Christianity itself, must necessarily partake of the scandal of Christianity and its separation from the world. Therefore, it can only be truly understood from an understanding of Christianity itself.

Since asceticism is a virtuous striving for Christian perfection, and since this perfection must be formed by charity, asceticism itself can only adequately be grasped from the standpoint of charity. For this, however, neither the difficulty of the renunciation nor the example of Christ would suffice; it would just avoid the question. For example, a suicidal offering of one's own life would certainly be "hard," but, as a fundamentally immoral act, it could never be a true realization of the love of God. And why did Christ choose poverty, chastity, and obedience as the concrete ways of realizing this love?

There must be an objective inner connection between self-denial and love. This connection consists in the fact that the renunciation of values that, from an earthly point of view, are unrenounceable is the *only possible* representation of love for the eschatological-transcendent God; for the God who is not only the ultimate meaning and guarantee of the world, but also who wished to meet us directly in love as Himself. The revelation of such a love, which must always also be a quest for a return of love, is necessarily an intrusion into the isolation that the world would like to preserve; it is a rupture in which the world, even insofar as it is willed and governed by God, is reduced to a thing of only secondary importance—to something provisional, and our existential focal point is placed outside of it as the area of the tangible and the accessible.

Every naturally good act can be elevated by grace and informed by charity so that it is a co-realization of the redeeming divine love. But this does not mean that the transcendence of this love "appears" in the naturally good act. Precisely because it is naturally and morally good does it have a meaning in this world —a justification and an intelligibility in itself. God's transcendent otherness cannot be made manifest in itself in such acts. Therefore, He remains silent above the order of grace and its meaningful direction that surpasses the dimensions of this earth. Our confession of the transcendent God and of the relativity of this world, wrought by His direct gift of self to us, can only "appear" through the sacrifice of this world; this is a manifestation of faith and love that surpasses the world and its goods, even when these are of a personal nature. At the same time, it is nothing but an anticipation of Christian death—practice for it and its affirmation. For in death the totality of man's reality is absolutely put in question by God. There, in the most radical way, man is asked whether he allows himself to be disposed of in the obscure, incalculable beyond and by this "allowing" deny himself; whether he wants to understand the radical sacrifice of all "other things" from the cross of Christ as a true falling into the love of God.

If Christian asceticism in the strict sense is thus a mere anticipation of Christian death, nevertheless the throwing of oneself into the merciful hands of the transcendent God only becomes *visible* in the *freely chosen* anticipation. For death and only death is the complete sacrifice of this world, and thus the most radical possibility of faith, hope, and love. But it is also a "must" that is imposed on us by God. Our freedom can accept it in sin or redemption without affecting its outward appearance, that is, without removing its "obscurity." Asceticism, therefore, as the free sacrifice of values that should not be given up from an earthly point of view, is the only way in which our confession of the eschatological-transcendent God can "appear" in a palpable way.

b) *The Necessity of This Asceticism.* That we actually make the renunciation of values that should not be given up from an earthly point of view an expression of our love for God, and in this way may and indeed must anticipate our death, can only be explained ultimately by a positive call of God (either of a general or a private nature). Supernatural love could also be realized in naturally hidden and so unapparent morally good acts (as redeeming love); and it could also be realized in the silent, patient bearing of suffering and death (as transcendent love). (Certainly, asceticism would be at least meaningful, if not absolutely necessary, as a "preparation" for such suffering, so that then death—as in the case of Christ—can become the absolute culmination of our freedom precisely in absolute weakness.)

But the clear, positive will of God in this matter is manifested in the structure of the Church. She is the primordial-sacramental tangibility of the eschatological presence of the salvation of God in the world. Accordingly, God wills that she make the eschatological transcendence of the love that constitutes her inner nature

74

palpably apparent. This occurs sacramentally especially in baptism and the Eucharist, where a man partakes of the death of Christ and actually announces it until His reappearance; it occurs existentially in specifically Christian renunciation. Christian asceticism, therefore, is an unsurrenderable part of the Church's essence. As a life lived according to the evangelical counsels, it is not only the normal, persisting, and existence-determining norm for individuals, but it is required at all times in one form or another from all members of the Church.

Because the Church is not an ultimate guarantee that the world will make magnificent progress, because she is rather one that puts her hope in that which is yet to come, because she is the community of those men who have the courage based on faith, hope, and love to look for that which really counts in that which is yet to come, who do not try to construct the kingdom of God in this world, but wait for it as a gift of God sent into this world (a gift that will signify the eschatological elevation and transformation of this aeon), who, moreover, must visibly live their faith, hope, and love before the whole world and so become witnesses—for these reasons, there must be a self-denying, specifically Christian asceticism in the life of each and every one of us. Each one of us has many things to give up that would not be sinful to keep, that could be meaningful, beautiful, and a positive enriching of his human existence, because—especially if he is a priest—he must represent the Church, because he must live as an example for the world in a way that shows that he truly believes in eternal life, and that he does not belong to the children of this world who just happen "also" to believe in some kind of a future life.

Take a good look at the modern pagans that make up the greater part of the so-called Christian nations! In their eyes, we are at best men with a certain world view that we are more or less convinced of; for, as they say, it is our calling and we preach because we get paid for it. How can we convince the men of today that we really believe, that the Gospel is the center of our lives,

75

that it is not just a front, unless an honest enquirer sees that we truly give up things because of our faith—things which would be utterly nonsensical to give up if we did not actually believe? We should not imagine that we can fool anyone in this matter. We are carefully scrutinized. A full measure of asceticism will be required to win the trust of the modern man.

III. *Toward the Practice of Priestly Asceticism*

"Asceticism in the broad sense" and "asceticism in the strict sense" have a lot in common. Here we will first say a few things about the latter, and then a few things about the former.

1. Celibacy is a part of priestly asceticism in the strict sense. We must not deceive ourselves about the difficulty involved in the renunciation of marriage! Rather, we should tell ourselves something like this: With confidence in the grace of God, I am giving up something that it would be senseless to renounce, if there were no such thing as the love of God, and if, according to the word of Christ in His Church (which is the elevated symbol of His truth), there were no place for a renunciation of marriage as a witness of one's faith—a renunciation that testifies to the world that in God's name there are men and women who wish to accomplish something in their human existence that goes beyond earthly values, no matter how sublime these earthly values might be.

But celibacy is only one area of priestly self-denial. This self-denial must embrace the whole environment in which the priest of today finds himself. It must include the opposition he encounters, the fact that he is often not taken seriously, the anticlericalism that does not just arise from the fact that we are old-fashioned or domineering or acting in any other way that is not essential to the priesthood and justly offends others. (Anticlericalism is very deep-seated in the unredeemed man; so much so that, from the dark corners of his being that protest the arrival of God's light and try to entrench him against His grace, he also rejects God's messengers who bear witness to His supernatural grace.) Nor should we forget that obedience to Church authorities requires a great deal of self-denying asceticism.

2. With regard to asceticism in the broad sense, we could mention a number of things. But the most important thing here is the cultivation of the proper attitudes, especially the desire to develop a truly personal, spiritual life. Religiosity is always in danger of going from an outburst of the heart to a mere institutionalism. This tendency to exteriorization and anonymity threatens not only our pastoral work where we can very easily become mere functionaries of the Church, instead of becoming men clothed with pneumatic enthusiasm; but it also threatens our own, as it were, private spiritual life. Unfortunately, there are too many clergymen who make their daily meditation in a routine fashion, and in like manner also dispatch of their other prayers and pious practices—and so, after twenty or more years of religious life, still give the impression that their inner process of maturity has not yet begun. We should not lose ourselves in activity (which occasionally camouflages itself under the name "regularity") to such an extent that we no longer even notice that there is precious little in us of a truly personal relationship to God.

We should seek to obtain and maintain the attitude of "working out our salvation in fear and trembling." And we should also seek perseverance in the boundless trust in the grace of God! That might sound like a cliché, but if we examine ourselves a bit closer, then we will notice that we simply do not believe existentially that God is greater than our hearts, and that grace can really accomplish miracles. Sometimes we hesitate before a difficulty like a timid horse before a hedge and imagine that we cannot get over it, even though we could often overcome it if we just had a little trust in God.

Mistrust of self, realizing the possibility of self-deception, also belongs to general asceticism. Can we be truly and honestly dissatisfied with ourselves and not just with our actions, which we very often repent of only because we have not cut the figure in the eyes of the world or even in our own eyes that we would like to have cut? Do we really believe that we can deceive ourselves where instinct and feeling seem to give such a clear direction? The will to accept something like this in one's own self belongs to the Christian, and especially to the priestly, existence! In this connection, we might also ask ourselves if others can say anything to us, if we really accept the directions of superiors, spiritual directors, confessors—and that merely because of their authority and not because the directions are clear to me, because I can say to myself: If I felt otherwise, that could only come from the fact that my attitude toward obedience that has developed over many years is basically a false attitude; in fact, it has become so much a part of me that I do not even notice its falsity. Such a free submission to the criticism of others, which is only a part of Christian obedience, can bring us hours of bitter conflict. But the religious who refuses to obey in matters that do not please him not only does not desire true obedience, but he also robs himself of an important, almost irreplaceable, possibility of surpassing himself. Whoever truly desires to get outside of himself needs some sort of an Archimedean point beyond himself, his feeling and the measuring stick that is identical with himself. (Here ·the measuring stick of objective principles is not enough. In addition to these, there must be a personal encounter with a concrete human Thou, and there must be fraternal correction and direction.)

Moreover, the desire for and the courage to bear loneliness and quiet belong to the general ascetical attitudes. According to Schopenhauer, young people are tempted to run away from loneliness and quiet because they can easily stand everything else but themselves. The man who desires to serve God must be able to stand himself. He should not always flee from himself in useless gabbing, busywork, and distraction—not even in feverish labor for the Kingdom of God which can easily be, in our case, an escape from a true interior life.

We should also like to point out that a priest needs more and more of that ascetical attitude that leads him to exercise himself in acts of penance that are freely taken up. Certainly, the most important, the decisive, the greatest, the most self-denying acts of penance are always those that are imposed on us from without —our duty and our destiny. But whether or not we can bear these with Christian hope and courage, whether we can bear them without a sense of defeat and without complaint, depends to a great extent on whether or not we have trained ourselves in renunciation and self-denial by the use of the much criticized "works of supererogation."

Finally, we would like to call your attention to the directives in the Code of Canon Law for the spiritual life of priests, especially to Canon 125. Granted that the sequence of works mentioned there is in many respects historically conditioned, that is, the Mass, private prayer, visits to the Blessed Sacrament, the rosary, exhortations, and so forth. But in all these things, we can question ourselves with regard to the concrete formation of our spiritual life. If asceticism is something planned and deliberately willed, and if we are determined to take to the oars when the pressing wind of the Spirit leaves us for a time, then we need a concrete, practical program in our spiritual life—always taking into account, of course, individual differences and varying circumstances.

10. On the Sacrament of Penance
(44)

Note

In a general way, Christian existence manifests a sacramental character. That flows from the nature of the Incarnation of God and from the nature of the Church. In the Incarnation, God Himself entered into the history of the world. We can no longer reach God by leaving the created world or by abandoning time, space, and history; nor can we reach Him through the transcendence of our spirit toward the Absolute. He can only be reached concretely right where we ourselves are—in our flesh and blood. All grace as a participation in the inner life of God is now grace that comes from the Incarnation and therefore grace of Christ. It does not come straight down from heaven—straight from the other world to this world, but it comes from definite historical events: from the birth of Christ, from His earthly life, and from His cross. It is for this reason that the continuation of the incarnational salvation-act of God is essentially spatio-temporal, corporeally tangible and historical; in fact, it pertains to the Church and her sacraments.

This general sacramentality belongs, as it were, anonymously to all the salvation events that occur in the life of each individual and in the Church as a whole. Every act of a justified man, even though it is the most interior and the most spiritual act, is, since it occurs in time and space, bound down to this world, and it is an event of the general sacramentality of the Church that is necessarily involved in the corporeal world, even though it might only occur in a "private" manner. The public and official appearance of the general sacramentality of the Church occurs where God's salvific action and man's answer to it embrace certain vital activities that have a special reference to the official Church in a way that goes back fundamentally to the institution of Christ Himself. We call these official salvific acts the sacraments in the strict sense of the word. It is easy to see that the institutional Church has a special interest in those general and frequent events that are of great importance for all men and for the constitution of the Church.

To these events belong not only the so-called "first justification," baptism, by which a person comes to the Church for the first time, but also the so-called "second justification," by which the already-baptized sinner is once again justified and again becomes a member of the Church in the full sense—a member of that Church whose task it is as the holy Church to justify sinners.

St. Ignatius wants the exercitant in the Spiritual Exercises, which were originally thought of as a radical second conversion, to receive the sacraments of penance and Holy Eucharist. And rightly so! For even though the Exercises require a great deal of personal, individual effort, still they are the acts of Christians, which acts, given the concrete situation of their general incarnational-sacramental structure, press on toward their full realization in the actual reception of the sacraments.

Since the "first week" of the Exercises seeks to stir up *metanoia* in the exercitant, that is, the admission that he is a sinner, it seems fitting to say something here about the sacrament of penance.

I. *The Confession of Sins as an Act of a Man before the Church*

We who are priests should never forget that every sin committed within the Church has an essential ecclesial characteristic. It is not possible for man to live just for himself alone. Each man exists only inasmuch as he is a constitutive part of the whole community. It is even less true that a Christian could live only for himself. By his actions and his omissions he is always the Church. And least of all could a priest live just for himself to such a degree that he would only come in contact with the Church in his official duties and other than that have nothing to do with the community of salvation. Our personal history is a sanctified human existence in which a part of the Church as the medium of God's grace is fully realized. When we as baptized members of the holy Church, which in her historical tangibility and visibility is supposed to be a witness to God and to His saving and victorious grace in the world, when we sin in this Church then we are not only acting against the salvation of our own souls, we are not only damaging the love of God and His holy law, but we are also acting against our own membership in the Church. We injure the body of Christ. We distort, to the best of our abilities, the mission of this body—its tangible and visible holiness. A historically demonstrable holiness of the Mystical Body of Christ must be the lasting testimony for the fact that God has really taken pity on the world and that He has come with His grace into the darkness of the post-Adamite world in order to win the victory, and not just to put in an occasional appearance. In a very special way, we priests are called on to take part in this holy task of the Church so that by the manifestation of our holiness, we become witnesses to the grace of God. Each of our sins, and in their own way even our venial sins, are therefore an offense against the Church.

Even though a sinner, despite his sinfulness, always remains a member of the Church in a very true sense, still he does not belong to the Church in the same way as the justified man does.

If he did, then the Church would only be an externally constituted, sociological institute of salvation. It would certainly not be the Mystical Body of Christ that is made to live by the presence of the Holy Spirit. To be sure, the Church is also a visibly constituted community—a community from which the Spirit of holiness can never be completely lacking. Otherwise, she would be the Synagogue and not the Church of the end-time.

When, by our sins, we have injured the life of the Church, which is the witness of the spirit of God, then we must come to the Church and confess them. We tell her of our guilt that we have brought upon ourselves not only in her presence, but also directly against her. We priests must also do that even when we only have venial sins to confess, because even by means of these sins we disturb our priestly membership in the Church. In this connection, we can think of the non-dogmatic but very true teaching of St. Thomas Aquinas that the acts of the penitent form a constitutive moment in the sacramental process of the sacrament of penance. According to St. Thomas, the sorrowful confession and the absolution of the priest taken together make up the salvific, historically tangible sign of God's mercy. The sinner who comes to the Church to confess his sins does not merely blurt out his sins so that the priest can have the "proper matter" necessary to decide whether or not this penitent is worthy of absolution. What really takes place in his confession is the liturgy of the Church of sinners. This Church is separated, as it were, in her double function in the sinner and in the priest: She is present there as the community of those who need to be saved, and as the bride of Christ that comes to men in the power of God. Both functions belong to the one Church: the man who confesses his guilt and the priest who receives this confession in the name of the Church.

When we confess our sins in the *Confiteor* to the angels and the saints, to our brothers and sisters, that is not just a pious custom by which the sinner asks others for help and humbles himself in an external and arbitrary way in front of his fellow men. For this self-accusation flows from the nature of the Church and of the guilt contracted by those within this Church. If the Church today for very good reasons has restricted the practice of public confession so that confession now takes place before one confessor, this still does not change the fact that we truly come to the Church and confess our guilt to her—that guilt that we have contracted against her and through her against God.

II. *Absolution and Intercession as an Act of the Church for the Sinner*

When we confess our guilt, we separate ourselves in a certain sense from the Church. As a sinner, I must explain that of myself I am not what I should be because of my reception into the Church, that is, a part of the tangibility of the already apparent grace of God. In the very act of admitting that my membership in the Church has become a lie, I remove the false appearance that my membership had up to that moment. Thus, by admitting my guilt, the truth of my existence receives, as it were, the tangibility that belongs to it by reason of the Incarnation. Now the Church can speak out her words of forgiveness which restore full peace with God, and which save me in her community on earth so completely that by that act God grants His justifying salvation also in heaven.

When we approach the Church as contrite sinners, we are sure of her prayers of intercession. She prays for us every day while she calls on God's mercy at her altars, in the prayers of the saints, in the daily carrying of the cross of her faithful ones. In fact, we cannot even approach her in sorrow unless God's grace has already touched our hearts. We could not even count on the grace of contrition if the Church as the holy bride of the Lord did not continually intercede for us, and if she were not His very body that is together with Him as the act of redemption in the presence of God, so that as a mediator she can win grace for the individual member. We should also consider that prayer for sinners is a lifelong task of the priest!

III. *Remembrance of the Cross of Christ*

St. Thomas Acquinas says in the third part of his *Summa Theologica,* where he treats the sacraments, that each sacrament is a commemorative sign (*signum rememorativum*) of the redemptive act of Christ, an efficacious sign here and now of grace, and a prognostic sign of the final redemption. If we apply this truth to the sacrament of penance, it means: In this sacrament, the event of the cross of Christ, which is God's judgment on sin, enters into our life in a historically tangible way. Because we truly undergo a change of heart in this sacrament and take our place under the cross, we are proclaiming the death of the Lord until He comes again. The forgetting of self and the detachment from self that is an essential part of penance is then really my way of realizing in myself Christ's self-immolation on the cross. But my penance can only achieve that if it is elevated by God's grace to a supernatural act. As a supernatural act, our penance is not a purely natural or ethical act plus supernatural elevation. It is the continuation of the life of Christ in the specific type of penance in which a man condemns himself by his confession, and, so to speak, separates himself from himself (the Pauline "*krinein*" has both of these meanings!). But this division within the self is not at all easy to understand. It is only because we have grown up with the practice of going to confession that we feel that we can bring it off without too much difficulty. But when a person has truly sinned, and when he has become identified with his perverse deed, it is most difficult for him to condemn himself and at the same time believe that God will be merciful to him.

Actually, we can only realize this condemning division within ourselves if God deals with us and grants us the grace for it. But

85

it is precisely in this way that the unity is achieved between the sacramental continuation of the cross of Christ in the tangibility of the sacrament of penance, and the personal realization of it in the heartfelt sorrow of the sinner. Thus, the cross of Christ remains as the judgment of grace in our human existence. It reveals both the absolute absurdity of sin and the still greater grace of God. Each of these makes an historical appearance when we commemorate the cross of Christ in the sacrament of penance. And this judgment of grace is also, as Tertullian said, an anticipation of the future judgment. The sacrament of penance is a prognostic sign of the arrival of the final Kingdom of God in the life of each and every one of us. We must go forth to meet this eschatological judgment of the thrice holy God Who searches our hearts. We cannot now know with absolute certitude whether or not, in that fearful judgment, we will be found worthy of mercy or wrath. What we can do is let it enter into our present moment in a sacramental way out of the future in faith, hope, and love, so that it meets us as a revelation of grace.

IV. *Confessions of Devotion*

What we have said so far should suggest the value of frequent confession. For the defense and explanation of the frequent confession of devotion, there are no arguments that prove that it has been commanded or that it is a necessary means to the end—provided, of course, that we do not bring in the positive law of the Church, which is very discrete in this matter. And we should not act as if such a position were a proven fact. We cannot make a case for the frequent confession of devotion by claiming that in it the forgiveness of sins is easier or more certain than in a truly contrite examination of conscience when a person repents "privately" for his sins. Nor can we say that the confession of devotion offers the graces necessary for everyday living, since the Eucharist is the normal help for the struggle with our daily faults. Even the direction of souls need not be carried on exclusively in the confessional. However, that grace and the judgment of grace should appear in the most tangible way for the Christian, is something that lies deep in the very heart of the incarnational nature of Christianity. So even though the frequent confession of devotion is not a real obligation, still it is a meaningful continuation of the incarnational structure of Christianity.

We testify by our frequent confessions that the grace of God is the freely given grace of Christ. When we wrestle all alone with our conscience, someone might think more or less explicitly that this is a matter that basically concerns only the transcendent God Who is always merciful. But this is just the way grace does not work! Grace is an event; it is an unexpected and unowed, an incomprehensible and incalculable gift that is not always and everywhere offered to us; it is only granted when a person undergoes a change of heart—and that only as long as the aeon of Christ persists. The grace that brings about a quiet, repentant examination of conscience is also the grace of the Incarnate Son of God, and because of Him finds its full concretization only in sacramental expression. Theologically, the most important aspect of the confession of devotion is to make perfectly clear an awareness of the incarnational structure of grace, and personally to realize this awareness in a confession of one's sins that enters into the very heart of Christian existence.

In addition to this, we can add a number of pastoral and ascetical considerations. For example, that, with the practice of frequent confession, we examine our conscience better, we are more serious about our sorrow for our sins, we submit ourselves to an external and objective control that is very healthy, we receive an admonition that puts a little more pressure on us, and so forth. We should also consider the following: If priests only go to confession when they have mortal sins to confess, then sooner or later lay Christians will imitate them. Eventually, this would mean that everyone who goes to confession, by his very going, publicly declares himself to be guilty of mortal sin. This, then, would be a characterization of the sacrament of penance that, even though it would not be contrary to its nature, still would only mean a reintroduction of the administration of the sacrament of penance that was current in the early Church, and that was found to be unsound from a pastoral point of view. For this practice brought it about that real sinners put off their reconciliation with the Church until the moment of their death.

A Protestant bishop addressed his Lutheran pastors recently with these words: "We must once again make the practice of penance something living and operative in our church. But we will never achieve that if we pastors do not learn to go to confession. We should go regularly, even when we are not conscious of a serious sin that would exclude us from the Kingdom of God." Therefore, it has really become possible in our day and age for Protestants to realize that a sacrament of penance, which is explicitly directed by the authority of the Church, is lacking, and they are making efforts to rediscover it. With this situation facing us, would it not be very strange if we began to neglect frequent confession out of carelessness and a desire for comfort in the spiritual life?

11. Death, Judgment, and Hell
(65–71)

Note

St. Ignatius closes the "first week" of his Exercises with a meditation on hell. Since St. Ignatius suggests in other sections of his little book on the Exercises that the exercitant should seriously consider the problem of death and judgment (for example, in the Annotations, in the rules for meditating, in the rules for making a choice [nos. 186–187]), we should like to include the themes of death and judgment in this meditation on hell.

In the first prelude, we should try to represent to ourselves someone who is dying or one who is already dead. Or we can use the prelude that Ignatius suggests for the meditation on hell. He asks the exercitant to speak out as follows: "I will ask for that which I desire. Here it will be to ask for an interior sense of the pains which the lost suffer, in order that if I through my faults forget the love of the Eternal Lord, at least the fear of punishment may help me not to fall into sin" (no. 65).

I. Death

The death that a man must undergo is ambiguous in a terrifying way. First of all, it is a participation in the death of Adam, and as such the revelation of sin and despair. And secondly, our

89

death is also the participation in the death of Christ, and hence a participation in the advent of redemption from sin. In this sense, it is the incarnation of that faith that saves. Looked at from the outside, and this can be true even of the experience of a man who is dying, both of these meanings seem to be the same. According to the way each person accepts and endures this ambiguous and puzzling fate, whether in despair or in faith and love —therefore does he die either the death of the first sinner or the death of our Lord.

Our death is a culmination of the unrepeatable *onceness* of our personal human existence. The Epistle to the Hebrews (9 and 10) applies this *"hapax"* (onceness) to the death of Christ. Also, with regard to its onceness, man's death cannot be practiced ahead of time. We cannot study death perfectly before experiencing it. Man goes through it once either rightly or wrongly without the chance of correcting himself. This is so true that what we call heaven or hell is the result with absolute finality.

Despite this onceness, there is such a thing as a real preparation for death. St. Paul says that we die our whole life through (2 Cor 4,7ff.). It remains true that death is just the way life was, and that a person only concretizes in this death the full meaning of the "detachment" spoken of in the Foundation of the Exercises. Therefore, in a very true sense death is actually anticipated in every moral act in which the higher and more distant goal is preferred to the lower, nearer, and more pleasant one.

Through the intrusion of death from without, and through the rupture of existence which essentially characterizes death, indifference is, as it were, forced on us whether we like it or not. Now absolutely everything is taken away from us. Now, even if we are in a good hospital and have all the necessary drugs, we are suspended with Christ between heaven and earth and are excluded from human society. But death is especially the end from within myself: It is my final act.

We can also consider the weakness involved in death in an Adamitic or a Christian way. Death is either that impotency which is the ultimate result of the sin that took hold of Adam, or it is a participation in the self-divestment of Christ that was never so great and so extensive as it was in His death on the cross.

We might think of the loneliness of death. A dying man is pitilessly lonely. No one can do anything for him. We can share our life with others, but not our death! But the loneliness of death is especially a being-alone before the hidden, living God: It is either the blessed abandonment of Christ, or the unholy expulsion into the outer darkness that is eternally impregnated with hate.

The onceness of death implies also its finality. In death, I am really at the end of the rope. There just is no life after death in the sense that my human existence then "keeps right on going" more or less the way it is now. Death means a radical and questionless existence with or against God. Therefore, the finality of death is the last decision. To this extent, man's death is also his judgment.

II. *Judgment*

These words "*krinein*," "*judicare*," and "judge" say a lot all by themselves. "*Krinein*" means to be separate and also to decide; "*judicare*" means to reveal the true situation; "judge" means to put something in right order. "Judgment" has a terrifying ambiguity for us even though we are not actually being judged. We can well say that, "It is a terrible thing to fall into the hands of the living God," if a person tries to hide himself from God as Adam did in paradise. However, if a man dies the death of Christ, then we can well apply to the judgment the words of Jesus: "He who hears My word and believes in Him Who sent Me has eternal life and will not come to the judgment!" And everyone who dies with Christ can say: "Father, into Your hands I commend my spirit."

This judgment will only bring to light that which is "known." It will only reveal what is in our hearts, what is already present in the very depths of our being—and is present in us in such a way that we really become aware of ourselves through it. Nevertheless, the judgment, looked at from a human point of view, will come *very suddenly.* In Matthew 25,37ff. we find the words of Jesus in which he lets the just and then the unjust ask the eternal judge: "Lord, when did we see you hungry . . . ?" If we do not water down these words of the Lord, then they say that the judgment will really bring out that which is hidden from us and that which we have hidden from ourselves in the past—and this will be so with regard to the simple deeds of our daily lives (cf. Gal 5,13ff.). This judgment will show us these deeds as that which they have always been, even though we have tried to repress their truth with superficiality or downright bad will. It will also show us our deeds as that which remains present, as the eternal face of our human existence, as that which can never disappear and is gathered together here to form a unity, even though the actual deeds were performed at different times and in different places.

When we consider this judgment, we can say with St. Paul: "If we judged ourselves we would not be judged" (1 Cor 11,31). If we separated ourselves from the lie that tries to masquerade as our true nature, if we separated ourselves from our twisted characters and from the values that we have substituted for those that God made, if we separated ourselves from this wicked world and freed ourselves for God by the practice of indifference and of the "more" of the Foundation, then we would not be judged.

III. *Hell*

1. *Prelude.* "The first prelude is a composition of place, which is here to see with the eyes of the imagination the length, breadth, and depth of hell" (no. 65).

2. *Application of the Senses.* Very often, the "application of the senses" that St. Ignatius recommends for this meditation is either misunderstood or understood in a much too simple fashion.

The point here is not to sketch a fantastic tableau of hell in the baroque style, since that is not what hell is in reality, and for this reason it will not be taken seriously. But if it is possible in this one order of creation for a creature to be lost forever, then we must be able to make an application of the senses. To be very honest, perhaps this sounds a bit simple in the writings of St. Ignatius, but the reason for that is not that St. Ignatius was a shallow thinker; rather, he was not the type of man who easily indulged in lengthy psychological descriptions.

St. Ignatius does not seem to know about the "pain of loss," and he also seems to concentrate the punishment of hell in the realm of the senses. Actually, he experienced the presence of spiritual reality not just in theoretical thinking. He had the rare ability to perceive the presence of the spiritual directly in his sense experience. He did not live in a world of rationalistic phantasy. He knew the way to true imagination, to the unified totality of human knowledge that can "imagine" concrete reality as it is. For man is such a unity that there can be no real separation between intellect and sense.

Perhaps the "application of the senses" can be described in another way—the way Ignatius conceived of it as a function of the power of imagination. In order to achieve this, let us put ourselves right into the middle of the extreme loneliness of one who is left completely to himself, where no one helps him, where he cannot tell his troubles to anyone, where he must carry on alone and forgotten. He does not perceive God's justice anywhere. There is darkness everywhere, and his own internal luminosity (that is, the whole of it, both intellect and sense) is oppressed by emptiness. Because he has never loved anyone but himself, this lonely person is locked in the prison of his own darkness, and can never emerge from it. He must conduct an eternal monologue with himself: a dead conversation, since all true speech lives only in a loving going-out from the self and being with the other. Even the loving call of God does not affect such a person; the call is there, but not for him, because God cannot reach a heart that is totally and finally closed. We should try to taste the inner bitterness and emptiness of such a person (insofar as this is possible, since we are not lost, and therefore can only put ourselves in his position in a very limited way). We should try to feel the burning chains of contradiction in which he is so entangled that he can never escape, yes, and never will try to escape, since he has made his final decision and will always be identified with it. Now he knows himself as he truly is, and realizes that his present dreadful state is the fruit of his former evil choices. We should experience within ourselves this foulness and the gloominess of this self-incarceration!

This is the kind of application of the senses that Ignatius wants us to make use of in the meditation on hell. This does not give us a picture of hell filled with illusions. A true application of the senses does not approach its object from the outside, but enters into its interior and, as it were, identifies itself with it in such a way that it experiences it in the totality of the power of imagination, which is a unity of sense and intellect. If our belief in hell is not supposed to be so abstract that it ends up by being unreal, and if it is supposed to be a living, human belief, then our theological knowledge of the condition of the damned must be applicable to human existence as it is—a unity of body and spirit. Thus, it must be subject to the power of imagination.

There is not much more to say on this point. Even the particular suggestions that St. Ignatius gives, for example his "worm of conscience," are indications that he does not want fantastic flights of phantasy to take place in the "application of the senses."

3. *The Meaning of the Meditation on Hell.* This meditation should put a little more humility in our love of God. I should note the questionability and the weakness of my love of God, and beg God to protect me through the fear of hell from ever forgetting Him or denying Him. I can forget this love and I can reject God. I am never sure of myself. I only become sure when

94

I hand myself over completely to the grace of God day after day. But I can only accomplish this gift of self and this getting out of myself when I am interiorly aware of my uncertainty, when I apply the meditation on hell to myself with complete existential urgency. I must realize that hell is not just something in this world that is far removed from me, but that, as the absolute state of being lost, it is my true, existential possibility that I can actually become through the misuse of my freedom. We do not fall into hell by accident. Our sin itself is infernal loneliness, darkness; it is something nonsensical, suffocating, and dead—and what we call hell is only the final culmination of sin. The possibility of hell that is involved in man's every free act is the logical conclusion of the free rejection of God's mercy. I am not asking myself in this meditation whether the real possibility of hell with which I myself must reckon has become an actuality for many other men. Rather, I should say with St. Theresa of Avila: That is the hell into which I can fall! And if I can entertain the hope for all other men that they have escaped damnation, if I can think well of all other men, as a pilgrim on this earth I have the obligation to accept in humility this fact as far as I myself am concerned—that hell can gush forth out of my heart and out of the core of my own nature.

As long as I am a wayfarer on this earth, I can only approximate a full existential realization of the meaning of hell as a possibility for myself. I can only hope to realize existentially the hopelessness of hell when, proceeding from my own experience of sin, I try to apply my complete knowing power to finding out what sin finally is when it fully becomes itself. When the belief in hell has reached this intensity within the totality of my personal, human existence, then it necessarily signifies that "interiorly taste and relish" of the fallen state that St. Ignatius seeks as the fruit of the meditation on hell.

If this meditation is to be a truly existential experience, then it cannot stop at the application of the senses. Because I have every chance in the world not to end up in hell, I must place myself with all the seriousness of the hell-meditation under the cross of my Lord. There, where I can see the love of God portrayed as nowhere else, and where I am challenged to return that love, with piercing fright I should feel the fickleness of my love. When I offer my love to God in temptation and want I should say: "I will see to it that I will love You even when I don't want to love You any more. I will remain true to You then out of fear of myself."

I know that I can abandon my love, that I can let it fall away from me in the heat of temptation. I also know the basic reason for this state of temptation of my love: It does not proceed from me alone—it is a gift from without. Even as a love that moves me, it is always something given, even in its most personal aspect. When I am able to love God to such an extent that my love is really capable of creating an eternity of bliss, I am still moved by God, and I am still under his influence. A true knowledge of man's love of God always implies, therefore, an awareness that it is a gift of grace, and that it is always subject to temptation. Where this love becomes a reality, it must also be very humble. Only by encountering opposition and strangeness do we come to realize who we are and what we should be; and we also attain that "chaste fear" of ourselves that is supposed to be the fruit of this meditation.

The continually present background of this meditation and its final end must be the One who is our measure: the crucified Christ. He is the one Who stirs up our love. He is the one Who sends us His love day after day. His cross and His terrible death, that is also our judgment, speak to us in urgent tones that we can be unfaithful to our love, and that we can sink into the bottomless emptiness of our own self-love.

12. The Enfleshment of God

Note

With this meditation, we enter into the "second week" of the Exercises. St. Ignatius reserved a lot of time in his "four week"-long Spiritual Exercises for meditation on the hidden and public life of Jesus. Here we can only undertake a few basic meditations. In order that the import of the meditations on the life of Jesus might make a real impression on us, we will begin with a few theological considerations, even though there is a danger that they might seem to get involved in theological speculation and so rather removed from prayer.

Let us ask ourselves very simply: What do we Christians mean when we profess our belief in the Incarnation of the Word of God? To express that truth for every age is the constant task of Christology—a task that is never finished. We pose this question fully aware of the fact that it is too much for us. And in our answer to it, we will treat more or less at random certain parts of the complete answer that we cannot give in full. In our treatment, we will presuppose a knowledge of the Church's answer instead of just repeating it. This should not be taken to mean that the old formulas that give an answer to this problem should be cast aside or considered false. God forbid! The Church and the faith of the Church are always the same in the course of her history, otherwise we would only find happenings of an atomized history of religion, but not *one* history of the one Church and of the same faith.

Since this one Church had and still has one history, the old formula is not the end—it is also the starting point. The spiritual movement from it and back to it gives us the only guarantee, or, perhaps a bit more cautiously, the only hope that we have really understood the old formula. For all understanding takes place through this fact, that the understood does not remain frozen fast, but is set loose into that nameless mystery that supports all understanding. If that is so as a general rule, that is, if true understanding always implies the previous openness of the knower to the ineffable mystery, and if this mystery is not just the remains of the understood that is not yet completely mastered, but is really the condition of the possibility of the grasping of the particular—is the incomprehensibility of the primordial all that surrounds us (we can name this "all" anything we want), then it is not surprising if this must occur where the grasping fate of the incomprehensible Word is supposed to be understood.

The Word of God became man. In order to get some understanding of this sentence in this short space, we will not attempt to say anything about the subject of this sentence—the Word in Himself. Although this is unavoidable, it is still very dangerous. For it could happen that someone might distort the true understanding of the Incarnation, if he does not think clearly about the "Word of God" who became man. Since the time of St. Augustine, scholastic theology has been accustomed to consider it obvious that each one of those uncountable Three that we call the Persons of the one Godhead could become man, provided only that He should will it. With this presupposition, "Word of God" in our sentence does not mean much more than any divine subject, any divine hypostasis: "One from the Trinity became man." Under this hypothesis, therefore, we do not have to know anything more distinct—only what pertains to the divine "Word," in order to grasp this sentence.

But if, following a tradition that antedates Augustine, we have serious doubts about this presupposition, then the failure to try to understand the predicate from a precise understanding of the subject will not be passed over as quickly as possible. For if it is essential to the Word of God that *He* and *He alone* is the one who begins and can begin a human history, provided that God wants to assimilate the world to Himself in such a way that this world is not only His product that is quite removed from Him, but becomes His own reality (as His assimilated "nature" and "surrounding world" that is necessarily given with a nature), then it could be that we only understand what the Incarnation is when we know what the *Word* of God is, and that we only properly understand what the Word of God is when we know what the Incarnation is. But we are not going to begin with this point in our attempt to understand something about this mystery. We will begin with the predicate of the sentence.

I. *God Became MAN*

The Word of God became man. What does it mean to say: "He became *man?*" We are not asking here what it means to say that this Word *became* something. We are looking at *what* He became. Man! Do we really know what he is? Someone might say that "man" is the best known part of this statement. Man is what we are; it is what we experience every day, what has been experienced millions of times in the history to which we belong, what we know from within ourselves and what we know from the outside—from our surrounding world. In addition, we might also add the following: Relying on this limited knowledge of man, it is possible to distinguish his essence from his personal self-possession; then it is possible to call his essence (that is, the content of his being, his "what") "nature," and to call the subject, dwelling in the nature, "person." Then our sentence means: The Word of God assumed an individual human "nature" and thus became man. But from what we just said about man, do we really know what "man" and consequently what "human nature" is?

Naturally, we know a great deal about man. Every day differ-

99

ent sciences make numerous statements about him, and each of the arts, in its own way, speaks out on this inexhaustible theme. But does that mean that man is already "defined"? To give a definition, to give a limiting formula that adequately lists all the component parts, can only be accomplished when we have a real object that is composed of ultimate parts, which parts must themselves be limited and perfectly understood. We will pass up the question of whether or not a definition in this sense is strictly possible. At any rate, as far as man is concerned such a definition is impossible. A deficient definition, though, might be that man is: indefinableness that has fulfilled itself.

There are many aspects of man that can be defined. We can call him a *"zoon logikon,"* a rational animal. But before we rejoice in the absolute clarity of this "definition," we should consider carefully what "rational" really means. If we do this, we stumble onto something literally boundless. For we can only say what spirit is if we express what man is concerned with and what concerns him. And that is something limitless, something without a name. Therefore, man is in his essence and in his nature a mystery. This is so not because he is the infinite fullness of this mystery that is inexhaustible (that is, the primordial form of that which is mystery for us), but because in his true essence, origin, and nature he finds himself as a conscious reference or relationship to this fullness (that is, the form of the mystery that we actually are).

When we have said everything about ourselves that is definable, then we have still really said nothing unless we have at least implicitly said that we are essentially turned toward the incomprehensible God. This basic reference, which is therefore our very nature, is only understood if we freely let ourselves be seized by the incomprehensible. The free acceptance or rejection of the mystery that we ourselves are as the poor reference to the mystery of fullness, constitutes our human existence. The pre-given object of our accepting or rejecting free decision is the mystery that we are; and this mystery is our nature, because the transcendence that we are and that we exercise brings together our existence and God's existence—and both of them as a mystery.

In all of this, it should be noted that a mystery is not something that has not yet been made known, something that stands beside some other fact that is known. If this is what a mystery is, then it would be no different from something that has not yet been discovered. Rather, a mystery as something which is absolutely impenetrable is just there, it is a given, it is something that cannot be produced. It is not something second-rate, something not yet mastered; it is the ungovernable ruling horizon of all understanding that makes all understanding possible while it is constantly present and silent. Thus, mystery is not something temporary that will soon be abolished or that could exist in another way. It is necessarily and essentially a characteristic of God (and from Him also of us). This is so true that the immediate vision of God that has been promised to us as our perfect fulfillment is really the immediacy of incomprehensibility, and therefore also the removal of all appearance. For the present, we have not yet reached that. For, in that vision, we will see through Him, not through the weakness of our own poor transcendence, that he is really incomprehensible. The vision of the mystery in itself as received in love is the bliss of the creature, and makes out of that mystery a burning bush of eternal love.

Where are we now? We are getting closer to our theme. For, if that is what human nature is, then we understand—always, of course, within the framework of the basic mystery that God and we are—then we understand more clearly what it means to say: God assumes a human nature as His own. This undefinable nature whose limit or definition is its limitless reference to the infinite mystery of fullness, has arrived, if it is assumed by God as His own reality, at that point where it was always headed by reason of its own essence. The full meaning of that nature is to give itself away completely, and it only fully realizes itself by burying itself in the incomprehensible. This happens in an un-

101

surpassable manner when this nature, by giving itself completely to the mystery of fullness, so empties itself that it becomes God Himself. Therefore, the Incarnation is the unique case of the perfect fulfillment of human reality—which means that a man only *is* when he gives himself away.

Whoever has the proper theological understanding of the meaning of *obediential potency* for the hypostatic union, that is, the assumption by the Person of the Word of a human nature, knows that this potency cannot be a particular capacity in man along with his other possibilities, but is really identical with the essence of man. Whoever understands this must also admit theologically that it must be possible and justified to describe this essence in such a way that precisely *as such* it is potency. And this is what we have just attempted to do.

This attempt does not mean to imply that the possibility of the hypostatic union as such can be deduced *a priori* without its actual revelation by God; nor does it mean to imply that this possibility must be realized in every man who has such an essence. The first possibility must be rejected: 1) because it is a characteristic of man's transcendence that a limitation of its possibilities would be false, and that therefore at least a hypothetical extension and culmination of the possibilities given with his transcendence is justified; and 2) because every such perfection remains hypothetical as long as it has not been proved (which in our case is certainly not possible) that this transcendence would have abolutely no meaning unless it attained its fulfillment in the hypostatic union.

Even though this transcendence actually is unlimited openness to the *free* mystery of God, a necessity for fulfillment by a hypostatic union cannot be deduced from it. Therefore, we can conclude that: 1) a clear knowledge of that possibility, even though we might discover all the relevant data discoverable by man, will still remain impossible; and 2) this potency does not have to be realized in every man. For the fact of our creaturehood and our sinfulness and our radically perilous situation reveal in the light of the Word of God that this potency has not been actualized in us. Nevertheless, we can still say: God assumed a human nature because it is essentially open and assumable, because it alone (in counter-distinction to the defined or limited non-transcendent) can exist in a state of complete possession by another, and in that way attain to the full perfection of its own incomprehensible meaning.

Man has no choice. Either he understands himself ultimately as utter emptiness that is seen through by others with a cynical smile; or else (since he is certainly not the fullness of being that can justifiably rest content with himself) he is discovered by the infinite—and thus becomes a person. If this is what man's essence is, then he only attains the unsurpassable fulfillment of his essence—toward which he is always going—if he prays and believes that somewhere a similar essence has found its "*ek-sistence*" in God in such a way that it has given itself perfectly to mystery and questions the questionless, because this "*ek-sistence*" was assumed by the Questionless and assumed as His own answer. Thus, it is not so strange, if we may use the word, that there is such an event as an enfleshment or hominization of God. For this "strangeness," as a perfect whole (that is, man's openness to being), is already present in the mystery of the primordial knowing power of each and every man. The only really difficult question is how and where and when this "someone" can be known, and what earthly name he will bear. But whoever seeks this "someone," in whom as fulfillment he finds the eternal mystery of fullness of his own essence, and seeks him in simplicity and honesty, will easily note that only in the Person of Jesus of Nazareth dare he believe that this happened and is happening for all eternity.

The rest of us are all far from God because we think that we alone know ourselves. Jesus was aware that only the Father knew His mystery, and in that way came to know that only He understood the Father. In order to guard against any misunderstanding, it should be noted that the Christology we have been

103

developing is not a Christology of consciousness opposed to an ontological Christology treating the substantial unity of the Word with His human nature. Beginning with the metaphysical insight of a true onto-logy that sees true being to be spirit as such, our Christology tries to formulate the ontological counterpart to the ontic statements of tradition, to which they are necessarily ordered, so that we can better understand the meaning of the Incarnation. Then the true statements of tradition do not give the mythological impression, that God came down to earth disguised under the appearance of a human nature that remained quite external to Him, in order to straighten things out because His job of directing them from heaven was not going very well. And something else: Any idea that this humanity-divinity happens wherever there are men, that it is not the unique wonder, would mean that this historicity and the personal element in this event would be reduced to the level of nature—that which happens always and everywhere, and so this truth would really be mythologized. Further, an idea like this would oversee the fact that this humanity of God, in which He as an individual is present for each man (it is for this reason that He is a man and not to divinize nature), in itself is not graced with more nearness to God or with something different than that which is actually intended for every man—that is, the "beatific vision."

II. *God BECAME Man*

The Word of God *became* man. This is the statement that we want to understand better. But can God *become* something? This question has always been answered in the affirmative by pantheism and all the other world views that consider God an essential part of history. But at this point the Christian and the theistic philosopher find themselves in a more difficult position. They profess God as the "unchangeable one" Who just is, the "pure act" Who, in the absolute security of His infinite reality, possesses from eternity to eternity the fullness of His own being, without having to become and without having to seek anything else. And precisely when we accept the fact of our changeableness as a true grace, in that moment we necessarily also confess the unchangeable God. For only because He is infinite fullness can the becoming of nature and the becoming of our own spirit have any meaning whatsoever. It is for this reason, therefore, that the confession of the unchangeable and unchanging God of infinite perfection is not just a postulate of philosophy, but also a dogma of faith.

Still, it remains true: "And the Word became flesh." Not until we have come to terms with this are we truly Christians. It would be very difficult to deny that traditional scholastic philosophy and theology get very obscure when it comes to this point. They explain that the change and becoming take place only in the creature that is assumed, not in the Word who assumes. Thus, everything is supposed to be crystal clear: Without any change in Himself, the Word assumes a created reality that does change even while it is being assumed. And so all change and history and suffering still remain on this side of the absolute abyss that separates the unchanging necessary from the changing, conditioned world. But it still remains true that the Word *became* flesh, that the history of the development of this human reality was His own history, and that our time became the time of the Eternal, and our death became the death of the God Who does not die. It remains true, therefore, that the application of different predicates, which seem to contradict one another and of which a part cannot be applied to God, to two realities—the divine Word and the created human nature—should not make us forget that the created reality is the reality of the Word of God. Nor should it make us forget that, after this separation of predicates and after this attempted solution, the whole question begins all over again. This question is one of realizing how the statement about the unchangeableness of God can be reconciled with the fact that what took place on this earth in the development and history of

105

Jesus is the history of the Word of God Himself, and is *His* own *becoming*.

If we take a good look at this fact of the Incarnation, then we simply must say: God can become something; the Unchangeable can be changeable *in another*. With this statement, we come to an ontological principle that a purely rational ontology perhaps could never discover as one of its basic starting points or fundamental principles. What this really means is that the Absolute, while retaining the perfect freedom of his infinite non-relativity, has the possibility to become the other, the finite. God has the possibility in the very act of divesting *Himself*, giving Himself away, of positing the other as His own reality. The primordial phenomenon that we should begin with here is not the concept of an assumption that simply presupposes what is to be received and then attributes it to the assumer; for in such a situation it is never really assumed, since it is rejected by God's unchangeability (which is conceived undialectically and as completely isolated for itself alone) and can never affect Him in His unchangeability. But the primordial phenomenon that we find in our faith is rather the self-divestment, the becoming, the kenosis, the genesis of God Himself who can become by positing the other that He Himself becomes, though He, the origin of all, does not become. Because He pours Himself out and at the same time remains infinite fullness (since He is love, that is, the will to fill that which is empty, and since He has the means to fill with), the other comes into being as His own reality. He constitutes that which is different from Himself because He retains it as His own; or, put the other way around, because He truly desires to have the other as His own, he constitutes it in its own true reality.

God Himself goes out of Himself as the fullness that gives itself away. Because He can do this, because His ability to become in an historical way is His basic and primordial possibility, for this reason He is defined in Holy Scripture as love—a love whose lavish freedom is simply indefinable. And therefore, His power to create—the ability to produce the other out of nothing without losing anything of Himself, is only a derivative, limited, and secondary possibility that is founded on this primordial possibility, even though the former could be actualized without the latter. Therefore, the possibility of being assumed by God, of being the material for God's own history, resides in the very essence of the creature. God always projects the creature by means of His creative power as the grammar of a possible self-expression. Perhaps this could be a starting point for reaching an understanding of the fact that only the Word of God became man and only He could become man.

The immanent self-expression of God in its eternal fullness is the condition of His external self-expression, and the latter is only a continuation of the former. Even though the positing of creatures is the work of the Godhead without distinction of Persons, still the possibility of creation has its ontological basis in the fact that God, Who has no beginning, expresses Himself in Himself and for Himself, and thus posits the original, divine difference in God Himself. And when this God expresses Himself outside of Himself, then this expression is the expression of this immanent Word; it is not just any word that could be attributed to one of the other Persons. Only from this standpoint can we better understand what it means to say: The Word of God "becomes" man. Certainly, there are men who are not the Word of God. Certainly, men could exist even if the Word had not become man, just as the less can always exist without the greater, even though the less is based on the possibility of the greater and not vice versa.

If the Word becomes man, then His humanity is not something pre-given; it is something that becomes and originates in essence and existence, if the Word divests Himself and to the extent that He does so. This man, precisely as man, is the self-divestment of God, because God externalizes Himself when He divests Himself; He manifests Himself as love when He hides the majesty of His love and reveals Himself as an ordinary man. Otherwise, His humanity would merely be a garment, a masquerade, a sign that indicates the existence of something, but does not really reveal anything about the one who is there. The fact that there are other men who are not this self-divestment, this "other-existence" of God Himself, does not negate what we have just said. For the "what" is exactly the same for Him and for us. We call this "what" human nature. But the fact that this "what" in His case is stated as His own self-expression and for us it is not, brings about a radical difference between us. And the fact that He states as His own reality just what we are opens up our essence and our history to the freedom of God. It says what we are: the sentence in which God could expose Himself and express Himself into the emptiness that necessarily surrounds Him. For He is love, and therefore He is necessarily the wonderful possibility of the free gift of self.

At this point, penetrating man to his most profound and obscure mystery, we could define him as that which proceeds from the freedom of God when God's self-expression, His Word, is spoken with love out into the emptiness of Godless nothingness. Someone has termed the Logos the abbreviated Word of God. The abbreviation, the cipher of God, is man, that is, the Son of Man—and in the final analysis, men exist only because there was supposed to be a Son of Man. Actually, we could say that when God desires to be non-God, then man begins to be—that and nothing else! This, of course, does not mean that man is reduced to the level of the vulgar and the common; it really means that he is brought back to the mystery that always remains incomprehensible. Such a mystery is man.

Now, if God Himself is man and remains man for all eternity, then theology may not make light of man. For if it did, it would be making light of God Who remains the impenetrable mystery. For all eternity, man is the expressed mystery of God—thus participating in the mystery of His supporting ground. Hence, man must always be accepted in love as an inexhaustible mystery —presupposing, of course, that we do not think we can grasp the full meaning of God's self-expression (man) by ourselves, or that we can understand man in any other way but by seeing him in the blessed obscurity of God. It is only in this obscurity that we can grasp that this finite man is the finiteness of the infinite Word of God himself.

Christology is the end and the beginning of anthropology, and this anthropology in its most basic form, that is, Christology, is theology for all eternity. This is the theology that God Himself proclaims when He speaks His Word as our flesh into the emptiness of Godlessness and sin. This is the theology that we ourselves then pursue in faith, provided that we do not think we can find God by simply ignoring the man Christ.

We could say of the Creator presented in the Old Testament that He is in heaven and we are on earth. But of the God whom we confess in Jesus we must say that He is right here where we are, and can only be found here. If He still remains infinite, then this is not intended to say that He is "also" infinite somewhere else. It simply means that the finite itself has attained an infinite depth, that it is no longer opposed to the infinite. It means that the finite is that which the infinite has become in order to open the way for everything finite (of which He Himself has become a part) to attain the infinite, or rather, in order to make Himself into the entrance, the door to the infinite; and by becoming a finite existence, God Himself has become the reality of that which is nothing.

Because the Word creates in His Incarnation in the very act of assuming and dispossessing Himself, the axiom for every relationship between God and creatures is operative here in a radical and unique way. This axiom is: Nearness to God and distance from Him, the subordination and the independence of the creature, are not opposed to one another, but increase together. Therefore, Christ is more of a man than anyone else, and His humanity is the most independent, the most free, not in spite of the fact that it is assumed, but because it is assumed and posited in being as the self-expression of God. The humanity of Christ is not the "appearance" of God in such a way that it is the appearance of an emptiness or vapor that does not have its own value in the eyes of the one appearing. By the very fact that *God* Himself ex-sists outside of Himself, this very existence of His has its own value, power, and reality.

This consideration brings out the fact very well that every idea of the Incarnation that turns the humanity of Jesus into a "disguise" used by God to make His presence in the world known is—heretical. It is this heresy, which was rejected many times by the Church in her fight against Docetism, Apollinarism, Monophysitism, and Monothelitism, and not the truly orthodox Christology, that is held today to be mythical and is rejected as mythology. It must be admitted, of course, that this kind of mythological thinking about dogmatic Christological statements can be present in many Christians who hold on to verbal orthodoxy. This situation usually stirs up a protest against mythology. For the idea that God should change Himself into a man, or, in order to get some attention, would gesticulate (because He is invisible!) with a human reality that is not truly a complete man possessing freedom and independence, but a puppet used by an actor to make a few statements—that idea is mythology and not the dogma of the Church. Unfortunately, this description is more or less applicable to the catechism, not as it is printed, but as it exists in the heads and in the thinking of many Christians. And at this point, we could ask whether or not those who feel that they must de-mythologize Christianity think of her teachings in the same way as the pious mythological Christians, even though both groups know the right dogmatic definitions. Thus, it could come about that the non-Christians in their eagerness to demythologize would pounce on the imagined heresy of the Christians, thinking that their view is the true dogma of Christianity.

Conversely, it is also true that many who reject the orthodox definitions of Christianity, because they misunderstood them, may existentially realize in themselves the true belief in the Incarnation of the Word of God. For whoever looks at Jesus and His cross and His death and really believes that the living God is speaking His final word to him in Jesus, and whoever believes that Jesus frees him from himself and his condemnation to death—that man believes something that is true only if Christ is what the Christian faith proclaims Him to be, and that man actually believes in the Incarnation of the Word of God, whether he knows it reflectively or not. This is not a denial of the meaning of the correct definitions that are the ecclesial-sociological foundation of the common faith. Only the heretic (not the Catholic!) who identifies those who have the true faith with those who profess the correct definitions, can deny *a priori* that a person can truly believe in Christ even if he rejects the approved definitions of Christology.

In fulfilling his human existence, a person cannot realize in himself existentially every position that is theoretically thinkable. Therefore, whoever accepts the ultimate truth about his life from Jesus, and whoever confesses that in Jesus and in Jesus' death God is telling him the ultimate meaning of his life and death—he thereby accepts Jesus as the Son of God Who is professed by the Church. How he formulates this experience to himself is of secondary importance. Moreover, many persons have encountered Christ without knowing that He is the final and blessed answer to their life and death, and without knowing that He is the Jesus of Nazareth in whom all Christians believe.

Created freedom is always a risk of the unknown that lies buried in that which is clearly seen and willed, whether this risk is recognized as such or not. When the will goes after something definite it pays no attention to that which is *completely* unseen and *perfectly* other. But it still does not follow from this that the unstated and the unformulated is therefore necessarily not seen or willed. We must not forget that God and the grace of Christ are in everything as the hidden essence of all desirable reality. Therefore, it is not so easy to seek after something without running into God or Christ. Thus, whoever (even without an explicit verbal revelation) accepts his human existence and his humanity (and that is most difficult!) in patience, or better, in

111

faith, hope, and love (no matter what he might call them) as the mystery that resides in the mystery of eternal love, and whoever carries on with his life in this valley of death, is in effect saying "Yes" to Jesus Christ whether he knows it explicitly or not. For the man who lets himself go and jumps, falls into the abyss that is there; he does not fall into the abyss he thought was there. Whoever completely accepts his human existence (this is unutterably difficult, and it is at least questionable whether or not we really do it) has accepted the Son of Man, because God accepted man in Him. If Scripture says that that man has fulfilled the law who loves his neighbor, then this is the ultimate truth, because God Himself has become this neighbor; and when we love and accept our neighbor, we are loving and accepting God Who is both so close and so far.

Man is a mystery. No! He is *the* mystery! He is this not only because he is needy openness toward the mystery of the incomprehensible fullness of God, but because God spoke this mystery as His own reality. For how could God, provided that He wanted to express Himself into the emptiness of nothingness, and provided that He wanted to shout His own Word into the deaf desert of nothingness, how could He possibly say something unless He created someone to perceive this Word and then actually spoke his Word to him? This brings about one result: the self-expression of God and its perception. That this happens at all is a mystery. A mystery is something completely unexpected, incalculable, astonishing, *and* self-evident at the same time. Mystery is the only thing that is truly self-evident, because ultimately it is mystery that makes the conceptual and the abstract intelligible, and not vice versa. Thus, the Incarnation of God is the absolute mystery and also the most obvious mystery. We might almost think that that which is strange and difficult in this mystery is not the mystery itself, but the fact that this obvious and absolute mystery occurred and is occurring in Jesus of Nazareth. But if the desire for the nearness of God, which alone in an unknown way makes everything else bearable, sees how this nearness manifested itself, not in the postulates of the mind but in the flesh and in the hovels of the earth, then only in Jesus of Nazareth, on Whom the star of God rests, can one find the courage to bend one's knee and tearfully pray: And the Word became flesh and pitched His tent among us.

13. The Following of Christ

I. *The Essence of the Following of Christ*

We pointed out in the last consideration that the innermost determination of the world is that it is the "surrounding world" or the "living space" for God Himself Who "becomes" in the world. This is so true, as we saw, that the very possibility of the world is founded on the possibility of the Incarnation, even if this primordial possibility of God were not actually realized in a non-incarnational order of things. Therefore, the ultimate reason why every man exists is that, by his life and existence with the Incarnate Word, he might make it possible for God to undertake the adventure of His love outside of Himself. In order to achieve this, God really does need humanity, because finite man (and this is what God Himself became) is essentially related to and dependent on the other human "Thou." This means that all of humanity is concentrated around the Son of Man as its source of ultimate meaning. Humanity is "the fullness of Christ."

Now if the concrete life of Jesus of Nazareth and nothing else is the appearance, the manifestation, the presence of the Word of God Himself and His life, and if in this concrete life of Jesus the inner life of God is revealed to us in an unsurpassable way, then a personal entering into this life of Jesus of Nazareth is a participation in the inner life of God; then the gaze into the face of Jesus of Nazareth is changed into the face-to-face vision of God, even if both the encounter with Jesus and the consequent vision of God only make their presence fully known when the confinement of our poor body is split wide open by death. "Jesus said to him: Have I been with you for so long and you have not known me, Phillip? He who sees me also sees the Father. How can you say: Show us the Father?" (Jn 14,9).

Grace, which is an existential injection of the one graced into the inner life of God, is not just any kind of divinization of man with its own metaphysical justification. It is not something which, though "merited" by Christ, remains fundamentally independent of Him and can be produced by the will of God—which will is trans-historical, coexistent with every moment of human history, and prone to interfere in that history directly. Grace is not that. It is a concrete assimilation to Christ and a participation in His life. Therefore, ontologically and not just morally, it is the *grace of Christ*.

We should not reduce this participation in the life of Jesus to some sort of a moral relationship. Moral influence coming from Jesus must be made possible by and based on an ontological influence. By reason of the Incarnation of the Word and the whole history of the life and death of Jesus, each one of us is already personally involved in the life of Jesus. In fact, the whole world including the life of every human being is really affected and determined by His human existence. In a narrower and historically more perceptible sense, after being affected by Him we were incorporated by Baptism into that community which is His Body, and by this sacramental-ontological determination of our historical existence, we were drawn even further into His life. Something similar to this occurs in the other sacraments: They indicate and at the same time strengthen the "pull" into the rhythm of His being that has irresistibly laid hold of every creature according to its ability to be the surrounding world of Christ. This remains true even if we do not perceive it, and even if our way of expressing this reality is clumsy and inexact. Still, our entrance into the blessedness of the inner Trinitarian life

115

of God really only takes place when we are drawn into the concrete historical life of Jesus as it is present to us now.

Thus far we have only considered our participation in the life of Jesus insofar as it is something pre-given before our free choice with regard to it; that is, insofar as it is a pre-given determination of our "nature" as opposed to our "person." Thus this life of our Lord that is always necessarily affecting us is seeking a free response from us—a free response that will affirm that life and become one with it so that the grace that is revealed in Him might truly become ours.

We can turn a deaf ear to this "call." We can prevent Jesus' rule of life from becoming our rule of life. We can try to the best of our ability to eliminate the life of Jesus from our life, but we will never really succeed. For even when it is rejected, it remains a constitutive of man. The only thing that would be accomplished by such an attempt is that it would literally change heaven into hell.

But if we listen to this "call," and if we accept his life in faith and love, then what we call the *following of Christ* takes place. To be sure, this *following* can be realized at different levels of self-reflection. At one level, it depends on whether or not Jesus has entered into a man's life, as it were, anonymously, or whether Jesus' own portrayal as found in Scripture and the preaching of the Church is known to this man. At another level, it depends on whether or not he has interpreted the existential realization of the following of Christ rightly or wrongly, and whether he has related his interpretation rightly or wrongly to his "historical knowledge" of the life of Jesus.

If we think it is possible for a real following of Christ to take place even when an "historical knowledge" of the life of Jesus (which is transmitted by Scripture and the teaching of the Church) is not actually present, this does not mean that the value and the meaning of the Gospel is in the least diminished.

If the Word of God wanted to reveal Himself in such a way that He entered into the world as the tangible and public epiph-

116

any of grace, and not just as an anonymous historical force, and if He remains in the world in this way until the end of time, then our life with the Word that has so revealed Himself must attain the same level of publicity that He has; it must relate itself explicitly (with the help of Scripture and tradition) to the "historical" Jesus; it must understand itself as a part of His "fullness"; in a word, it must be "ecclesial"! However, the necessity for this understanding cannot be deduced from a positive direction of God. And it is more than something merely fitting that is required by the "dignity" of the Incarnate Son of God, that He should not only be recognized in this world by a few followers as the center of all creation, but should be revered and loved publicly right now as the King of the universe. Rather, only a constant relationship to the "historical" Jesus, only a repeated meditation on the mysteries of His life, and only an unceasing listening to His words can produce the kind of imitation of Christ that knows what it is doing and so can grow to fruition.

Only by looking at Jesus of Nazareth and by listening to His word that comes to us "from outside," can we come to a clear understanding of what we have always been: persons whose reason for living and existing is the life of the Incarnate Word of God Who offered Himself publicly to the world in Jesus of Nazareth. Otherwise, we would not even be aware of our following of Christ, and consequently we would only be indirectly and implicitly responsible for our free acceptance or rejection of Him; our following of Christ would also be in constant danger of misunderstanding itself, and so of losing itself—for we must not forget that our reflective knowledge is not just reflective, but that it has a formative influence on what takes place in the depths of the soul. If this is the case, then we must *consciously* follow Christ; then we must knowingly pattern our lives after the life of the "historical" Jesus of Nazareth. It is with this end in view that St. Ignatius proposes the meditations on the mysteries of Jesus' life.

What we need here is a theological concept of the imitation of

117

Christ that will enable us properly to evaluate the "second week" of the Exercises. Therefore, as the result of the preceding considerations, let us keep these two points constantly before our eyes in the following meditations:

1. The imitation of Christ does *not* consist in the observance of certain moral maxims which may be perfectly exemplified in Jesus, but which have an intrinsic value in themselves independently of Him and can be known as such. The imitation of Christ consists in a true entering into *His* life and *in Him* entering into the inner life of the God that has been given to us.

2. The call to follow Christ does not reach us in words that come from the outside, and that put us on a path really contrary to our own nature. Ultimately, this call is the necessary development and unfolding of what we have always been: free persons determined by our very nature to live with Christ.

II. *The Formal Structure of the Following of Christ*

We can conclude from the nature of the following of Christ that we have just described that it must necessarily be a decision to find one's own way of following Him.

In the Incarnation, the Word of God assumed a human nature that is essentially related to the other human. Thou. In order to find himself, a man needs communication with other men. Man only attains his full perfection by finding acceptance from others and by loving them in return. This is also true for Christ! We are forced to say of Him: By reason of the fact that the Word as man loves other men, He fulfills and perfects His own essence. In His own true history, He becomes what He is supposed to be in His humanity, and He only accomplishes this by being our brother and by letting us exist in our own right. This fact has not always been as clear as it should have been. For in the history of the Church there have been attempts to copy the life of Jesus in the most literal way, for example in the Franciscan dispute about the nature of Christian poverty.

The true following of Christ, therefore, which is a life with Him, consists in allowing the inner structure of His life to work itself out in new and different personal situations. Only when we really carry on His life in our own way, and not by trying to produce a poor literal copy, is the following of Christ worth living, does it really interest God, and does it have the power to win eternity with the elevated Son of Man Who sits at the right hand of God. Because this kind of a continuation of the life of Christ preserves the inner structure of His life, and because it is carried on in His Spirit, it is the authentic following of Christ!

This continuation of the life of Jesus that is new and different for each one of us must be discovered by each individual in the form that is valid for him. Just as an historical situation cannot be deduced from universal historical principles, so also my way of following Christ cannot be deduced from the general norms for following Him. The discovery of the right way to follow Christ is always the result of individual personal decision. And the personal responsibility for this decision, which cannot be pushed off on a moral book or a spiritual director, is an essential element in our imitation of Christ. Therefore, we must risk the loneliness of this kind of existential decision. We should not try to push this responsibility off onto someone else—a tendency that is often at the bottom of the search for the "ideal spiritual father."

Obviously, the intention here is not to propagate a narcissistic introversion that seeks only to develop its own being. Since man can only save his soul by losing it, he can only fully develop his own being if he cultivates it by serving others, and by selflessly coming to the aid of others.

It also follows from the nature of the imitation of Christ that it consists essentially in *obedience*, even though self-decision and self-responsibility play a large role in it.

Even if the following of the Lord must be realized by each person in his own way, still this following must have certain definite characteristics that stamp it as the following of *Christ.* It must have some basic traits that all who want to enter into the life of Christ must recognize and obediently adopt before they give it their own individual style. Of course, the demand placed on us by his unique life, which is the incalculable epiphany of the sovereign grace of God, cannot be deduced from the general laws of our existence as the natural law can. Still, as an historical fact this demand is the "new law" of Christ that is binding on all. He revealed this law to us by His life and words, which we can see for ourselves in the history of His life.

The decision that each person must make in order to find his own way of following Christ is itself an act of obedience. It is a listening to the particular imperative of God that put me in my present situation so that I might continue the life of Christ in it; more exactly, it is a following of Christ Who appeals to my personal freedom and indicates to me my place in His total plan.

Therefore, ultimately, personal decision and subordination to authority, which are involved in the imitation of Christ, are not opposed to one another: Both of these attitudes represent essentially inseparable constitutive elements of the one dedication to the Lord. Still, their relationship to one another is polar and dialectic. Harmony between them cannot always be found easily and painlessly. In fact, the tension between them is something very typical of Christian existence. Nevertheless, Christ wills that we follow Him in obedience, but certainly does not will that we just trot along in His footsteps, which would really be a lot easier. Every one of us has a mission to accomplish in the name of Christ that no one can take away. Both of these attitudes, obedience with regard to the general law of Christ and the courage to be oneself—which is really only a more radical form of obedience, proceed in exactly the same way from the essence of the following of the Lord. The difficulty lies in the fact that both of these attitudes must be realized in the same person; but, on the other hand, it is precisely this realization that constitutes the loftiness of our Christian existence.

III. The Material Structure of the Following of Christ

Before we point out the universally valid principles contained in the meditations on the mysteries of His life—in order to go beyond that and see the particular imperatives applicable to each and every one of us in his own way, we want to indicate ahead of time a few basic characteristics of Jesus' life.

That which is amazing and even confusing in the life of Jesus (and the reason why we do not notice it any more is that we are accustomed to ignore it) is that it remains completely within the framework of everyday living; we could even say that in Him concrete human existence is found in its most basic and radical form.

The first thing that we should learn from Jesus is to be real men! The courage to do this—to live from day to day under the threat of sickness and death, to be exposed to one's own superficiality and to the superficiality of others, to be a member of the masses, and so forth—is not at all easy. (Humanism and Renaissance are fundamentally only an escape into a utopia that is just apparently heroic!) But if the Word of God assumed a concrete human existence in Jesus, then this must clearly be so great, meaningful, important for the future, and so full of possibilities, that God did not become anything else but a man just like this when He wanted to go outside of Himself.

Moreover, in His life Jesus is a man of scandal. This is something that we are always tempted to protest against! If we look at His life through the eyes of an unbelieving historian, then we meet a man Who was born in a miserable corner of the earth, Who begins His life unnoticed by others (even His parents did not understand Him!), Who is pushed around by the politics of the time, and Who, after a short public life that is hardly very important, dies in agony on a cross. There is nothing magnificent in this life! In a certain sense, Jesus did not even live at all, at least not in the way we would expect a spiritually rich human life to be lived. He passes up everything that we consider necessary to make our lives abundant and full. To be sure, He remarked that the lilies of the field are clothed with more beauty than Solomon in all his glory, but at the same time He said that they were only grass that would wither on the next day. He passes up marriage, art, and even friendship, for the men He gathers around Him do not really understand Him, so that He really remained very much alone. He does not pursue politics or science. He did not solve any of the social problems of the time. He showed no resentment toward these things. He did not despise them. He just did not busy Himself with them. The only thing we can really say about Jesus is that He was a very pious man.

Most likely, we would have imagined the human life of God in quite different terms. Naturally, the Incarnate Son of God should have been pious. He should have shown us how to pray to the living God correctly. But in addition to that, He should have had time and care for many other things. We should have expected that He would compose a magnificent literary work; we should have especially expected that He would reform the world politically and socially, that He would establish in some visible way the Kingdom of God.

We would like to find some traits in Jesus' life that would make Him a bit more congenial. But we find none of this! What Paul said of Jesus is very true. "He humbled himself." The Word of God truly hid His glory in His humanity. Obviously, He was not concerned about manifesting His divine majesty in His humanity. But if the Word as the first and last spiritual principle of all creation reveals Himself in Jesus, is present in Him, then does not the metaphysician have the right to expect that all of creation would, as it were, be gathered together in Him so that

He might really be the quintessence of the world, the concentration of everything that is good and beautiful? Jesus, however, passes up everything. At the most, He allows Himself a simple pleasure occasionally: a banquet, familiarity with John, a look at the temple—but even in this case, it is his disciples who call His attention to the beautiful building. He is silent and passes by like one for whom everything in a certain sense is already dead, or at least very provisional. All of those things are the "other" for Him; they are not the Kingdom of God, and therefore He does not consider them essential.

It is difficult for us to accept the fact that Jesus really cannot do anything else but save souls. We really would not have anything against that, even if He did this very intensively. But we would like to see this zeal combined with some other things that are very dear to our hearts.

Certainly, we should follow the Lord, that man of scandal, with discretion. In a certain sense, we need the world. There are many things that we can and should incorporate into our lives, and there are many things that we should enjoy with gratitude to God—to borrow a phrase from St. Paul. (In fact, it is our duty to continue the life of Jesus in many areas of human endeavor where He was not "allowed" to go in accordance with the will of His Father). We should not be filled with resentment. We should not conduct ourselves like those "ascetics" who make their renunciation of the goods of this world easier for themselves by converting the objects of their renunciation into something bad. We should not be fanatics. We should follow Christ in joy and happiness. In order to be able to do that properly, we should have many different experiences of this world—sin only excepted. The dialectic human situation of using and leaving the things of this world that we already spoke about in the conference on the Foundation, applies also to the following of Christ. And yet, as Christians—and especially as priests—we must take the scandal in Jesus' life very seriously. This is and remains the basic form of His history that irresistibly forces us to make a decision.

What we said earlier about standing apart from this world, what Paul means when he says, "You have not received the spirit of the world . . .", what St. John means when he demands, ". . . do not love the world and what is in it!", and especially what Jesus demands when he warns us not to receive our glory from ourselves—all of that is presented to us in the figure of Jesus of Nazareth in a most concrete form, and forces us to come to a decision. (Thus we arrive, more or less *a posteriori*, through a study of Jesus' life, at the same result that we tried to reach *a priori* in the meditation on priestly asceticism.) As an official of the Church, the priest should represent her in such a way that she does not seem to be a Church of political power, or a Church of cultural progress, or a Church of the worldly millennium. The priest should be a witness to her as the continuation of the life of Jesus of Nazareth Who speaks only of serving the Kingdom of God, of obedience to the Father, of carrying the cross, and Who, as a matter of principle, passes up everything that is not God and the salvation of souls.

Once again, this must be understood and put in practice with discretion. The Church laudably promotes culture. She also needs money; her houses of worship should be beautiful. The Church should be a leader in learning so that her voice will be heard in the world, and so forth. All that is really quite obvious! But we are always tempted to be scandalized at the hiddenness of Jesus, just as He was a scandal to the Jews and a stumbling block for the Gentiles. This temptation lies deep inside of us. Therefore, in this regard we should always keep this clearly before our eyes: Jesus demands a renunciation, even in Christian world-affirmation, that is composed of a truly interior poverty animated by faith. This attitude produces a fullness of life that only Jesus can give.

In our meditations, we should consider in a more concrete way what we have just proposed in a rather abstract form. We

124

should consider the poverty, modesty, confinement, and simplicity of Jesus' life, and then ask ourselves if we have the courage to submit ourselves to the law of His life, so that we might follow Him as He wants us to.

14. The Kingdom of Christ
(91–100)

Note

The meditation on the Kingdom of Christ is the fundamental meditation of the "second week" of the Exercises. It clearly shows that the Ignatian retreat is supposed to be orientated toward a decision.

In the "first week," the retreatant is supposed to have become mistrustful of his former life, and he is supposd to have aroused within himself the will to make a decision. He is supposed to have prayed for the courage, while being aware of his eternal destiny, to make a right choice on which will depend his salvation or damnation. Now he is supposed to ask himself if he has discovered the major problem in his life, if he is oppressed by a special difficulty that requires a fundamental decision. St. Ignatius wants the exercitant to stir up in himself the courage to make a *binding choice* that will truly affect his life, even if it is only in a very small matter. In the Exercises, he is primarily interested in finding the concrete way in which God wants the exercitant to follow Christ. This can be hidden in something relatively small. A choice such as this naturally implies the possibility of other alternatives that are also choosable. The choice here is not between good and evil, but between different means that in themselves could be used to attain the end. In this situation, it is not at all easy to decide what I should choose here and now.

According to Ignatius, this choice should be made in the "second week" if at all possible. To achieve it in the "second week," he brings the exercitant face to face with Christ, the concrete norm of Christian living. The purpose of the meditations on the life of Jesus is not just to discover the general principles of the "new law" of following Christ; rather, the purpose is to discover the imperative in the life of Jesus that applies to me alone, and then to make the choice to carry it out in my life. Accordingly, St. Ignatius does not confront the exercitant with the whole life of Jesus. He shows him particular events so that through this kind of exposure he might be able to find his own concrete form of following Him.

In order to allow this "exposure" to become thematic, and in order to make it subject to an impartial judgment, Ignatius offers a guideline in his "Rules for the Discernment of Spirits." These rules are supposed to be read during the "second week," and their application to the particular problem of the retreatant is one of the most essential parts of the Exercises.

The introductory position of the meditation on the Kingdom of Christ indicates that the decision should not be made here. The result of this meditation should be an unconditioned readiness to make the choice God is asking. To achieve this, Ignatius has the exercitant make a complete offering of himself to the Lord, and pray that He might tell him what to choose in the following meditations by the example of His life and the inspiration of His spirit. The purpose, then, of the meditation on the Kingdom of Christ is to arrive at a complete willingness to follow Christ.

To be sure, Christ is presented to the exercitant in a very definite light. In this meditation, he is supposed to encounter in Christ the man of scandal; he is supposed to dedicate himself completely to the Lord insofar as the Lord is clearly against everything that the "world" (in the biblical sense), both the world inside of us and the world outside of us, seeks. Still, the

127

meditation on the Kingdom of Christ is primarily interested in the *presuppositions* of a true choice. The proper attitude and the right circumstances for a choice will be produced by the encounter with the scandal-giving Christ the King. But because we are easily deceived in essentials, and because very often with regard to the essential meaning of the cross in the life of Christ we are deceived, it is very difficult to acquire that attitude. It is for this reason that Ignatius places us before the suffering Christ, before the Lord Who perseveres to the bitter end so that He must be a scandal and a fool to the world. This is the Christ Who demands an absolute decision from us.

In the second part of the meditation, the two points of the Foundation recur again: On the one hand, the *Tantum-quantum* of using the proper means, on the other hand the *more;* the former is calculating, appraising, taking no chance on an adventure of love, the latter is an unconditioned desire for that which is greater—not just for that which is required. Ultimately, though, both of these attitudes belong together, since many Christians will not go beyond the *Tantum-quantum* which really contains within it the *more* of a greater and more perfect love. This must be so if Christian life is to be lived at all. In any event, the goal of the meditation on the Kingdom of Christ is to produce a definitive readiness to follow Christ, and it explicitly includes the choice of the difficult, the laborious, the humble, and the poor as an essential element of this following.

For the motivating principle of this meditation, Ignatius chose a parable, in accordance with his times, of a great king who organizes a crusade and calls on his subjects to follow him in this undertaking. Naturally, everyone knows ahead of time that subjects are obliged to follow the call of their king (think of the knights of the time), and that there will be dangers, suffering, and deprivation; but they also know that there will be a battle which will end in a glorious victory.

The historically conditioned characteristics of the parable can actually be reduced to a form that is valid for all men, which we might even call its metaphysical-anthropological background. For man's existence is essentially a battleground of decision, a risk, a unique history that leads to a final goal; it is not primarily ordered to abstract principles, but to the concrete Thou, and therefore it is forced by its very nature to ask where the true Lord of the battle is. This kernel in the notion of kingship will always be valid, even when the monarchial state is no longer in existence). One can also fit the parable of the king into the framework of salvation history. This can be done from the image of the carrying of the cross. There is a Kingdom of God and a kingdom of Satan, this aeon and the coming aeon. Both of these compenetrate one another, ever since the total framework of decision was given in the advent of Christ. The cross of Christ is already the victory over the lord of this earth. We can be sure that our Lord has been victorious.

The relationship of God to the world is not completely other-worldly, but it is history that He makes with us through His Incarnate Son. What happens in this world is not a meaningless repetition of the same thing, it is not a circle that is hopelessly enclosed within itself, but it is a true history of salvation and damnation, dependent on personal decision, that was made possible by the Incarnation of God. The Church herself is not a static dispenser of salvation which was once founded by God and now does the same thing over and over again, that is, baptize individual men, accompany them through life in order finally to deliver them at the gate of heaven; no, she is the real continuation of the history of Christ, she carries on his decisive battle, and must continually produce his victory in others.

Another universally valid application of the parable of the king can be drawn from the basic idea of a king. This idea leads us immediately to Christ as the Son of Man Who is the absolute Thou for each one of us, and to Whom we are ordered. He is the culminating point of mankind that I seek from the bottom of my heart, even if I have never heard the name of Jesus. For I am essentially ordered to the concrete One that I can love and serve

E

129

absolutely. But I can only do that with regard to a living Thou—I cannot do it with regard to abstract principles! Nor can I love and serve myself alone. If I try to do that, then I necessarily make an idol out of my own reality, and therefore fall into my own finiteness, into my own vacuum and condemned emptiness.

Of course, the concrete Person to Whom we are essentially related is the living God—the only unconditioned spirit, Who gives us our existence in the act of calling us and relating us to Himself. But we only encounter this God in a concrete way in the Incarnate Word of God Whom we can never exclude from the essential historicity of our personal situation. Hypothetically, there could be an order of things in which He would not appear, but in the present order of things a person either finds the Incarnate God, or else he runs right by the living God and serves only himself and the idols of this world; in this case, he runs into emptiness and darkness, into the desert of sin. We have already considered this point. Whether or not the name of the Incarnate God is made known explicitly to all men in this life as it has been made known to us through the grace of our calling in Jesus Christ, at the present time is a question for us of secondary importance. We know that the living God to Whom we belong and Whom we serve is called: Jesus Christ. We stand before Him. He is calling us to follow Him. All we have to do is say "Yes" and put on the concrete form of His life.

Preludes

1. "This is a mental representation of the place. Here it will be to see in imagination the synagogues, villages, and towns where Christ our Lord preached."

The Lord we are dealing with remains eternally the same one Who once lived in Palestine. To be sure, He is the King of glory, the Glorified One, the one Who is raised to the right hand of the Father. But still, I can only meet Him when I know by means of a real anamnesis of an ecclesial-sacramental and contemplative-existential kind that He is the one Who lived in Palestine in His own age. Very often, we tend to think that somewhere, sometime He did this and that, but that those events have nothing to do with His present existence. This is not the way He exists now, for what He once did has now become eternity, and when I approach the King of glory then I meet someone who lived out His life in Palestine over nineteen hundred years ago. For this reason, in the Mass we relate ourselves to His death on the cross, and not just to some abstract effects of His sacrifice. If we are supposed to consider the places in the first prelude that are eternally connected with the Incarnate Word of God, then this has a very deep theological meaning.

2. "I will ask for the grace I desire. Here it will be to ask of our Lord the grace not to be deaf to His call, but prompt and diligent to accomplish His most holy will."

I. *First Part of the Meditation:*
The Parable of the King

1. "The first point will be to place before my mind a human king, chosen by God our Lord Himself, to whom all Christian princes and people pay homage and obedience."

Being chosen by God belongs to the Middle-Ages idea of a king. By the king, "to whom all Christian princes and people pay homage and obedience," is meant the Emperor of the Holy Roman Empire. With this little touch, the consideration of Christ as the universal Lord is well prepared.

2. "The second point will be to consider the address this king makes to all his subjects, with the words: 'It is my will to conquer all the lands of the infidel. Therefore, whoever wishes to join with me in this enterprise must be content with the same food, drink, clothing, etc., as mine. So, too, he must work with me by day, and watch with me by night, etc., so that as he has had a share in the toil with me, afterwards, he may share in the victory with me.'"

This description of the king clearly brings out the fact that he experiences all of the hardships of the crusade, just like everyone else. Naturally, then, all those who want to go with him must share his lot and be satisfied with it. (This calls to mind the words of St. Paul: "If we have died with him, we will also live with him!")

3. "The third point will be to consider what the answer of good subjects ought to be to a king so generous and noble-minded, and consequently, if anyone would refuse the invitation of such a king, how justly he would deserve to be condemned by the whole world, and looked upon as an ignoble knight." (This third point touches on a more human note.)

II. Second Part of the Meditation: The Application to Christ

"The second part of this exercise will consist in applying the example of the earthly king mentioned above to Christ our Lord according to the same three points." This application is not carried out strictly, but undergoes a characteristic slant toward the "more" of the Foundation.

1. "First Point: If such a summons of an earthly king to his subjects deserves our attention, how much more worthy of consideration is Christ our Lord, the Eternal King, before Whom is assembled the whole world. To all His summons goes forth, and to each one in particular He addresses the words: 'It is My will to conquer the whole world and all My enemies, and thus to enter into the glory of My Father. Therefore, whoever wishes to join Me in this enterprise must be willing to labor with Me, that by following Me in suffering, he may follow Me in glory.' "

In his First Epistle to the Corinthians, St. Paul says more or less the same thing: He must reign until the Kingdom of God that He brought into the world, that is still coming and that is still not simply identified with the Church—until this Kingdom has been laid at the feet of the Father. But before that, according to His own words, He must suffer in order to enter into His glory, because that is the fate and destiny of the whole world.

It is as clear as crystal to St. Ignatius that the crusade of Christ, the establishing of the Kingdom of God in the world, means suffering. The following of Christ is the following of the Crucified; it is a sharing in the descent of God into creaturehood, into darkness, into the abyss of sin; it is the suffering of death, or, as the Bible has it, it is the coming of the Son under the law.

This is not meant to be understood as applying to the "missions" in the strict sense! The meaning here is not that we should offer ourselves to Christ to go out on the missions. Ignatius' point is clear from the way he wants the exercitant to respond to the call of Christ the King. There is a question here of our willingness to allow the enfleshed Word of God to draw us into the history of conquering this world. Therefore, it is a matter of our readiness to open ourselves up for the coming of the Kingdom of God. This means that we must accept labor, poverty, the cross, and even death so that we might become a part of this Kingdom and its glory.

In the second point, therefore, the meditation concentrates on these labors. "Consider that all persons who have judgment and reason will offer themselves entirely for this work." This offer must be directed toward the cross of the Lord; anything else would be an idealistic illusion.

Then in the third point the "more" of the Foundation appears again—the "more than mere duty and mere reason." "Those who wish to give greater proof of their love, and to distinguish themselves in whatever concerns the service of the eternal King and the Lord of all, will not only offer themselves entirely for the work, but will act against their sensuality and carnal and worldly love, and make offerings of greater value and of more importance in words such as these: 'Eternal Lord of all things, in the presence of Thy infinite goodness, and of Thy glorious mother, and of all the saints of Thy heavenly court, this is the offering of myself which I make with Thy favor and help. I protest that it is my earnest desire and my deliberate choice, provided only it is for Thy greater service and praise, to imitate Thee in bearing all wrongs and all abuse and all poverty, both actual and spiritual, should Thy most holy majesty deign to choose and admit me to such a state and way of life.' "

This is an unconditional desire to accept the cross of Christ and to share in the scandal of His life. Of course, Ignatius formulates this offer in a way that perhaps cannot be concretely realized in the same way by each one of us. But at any event, what he says clearly indicates the direction my choice could follow, since he speaks of insults, injuries, poverty, and so forth. Therefore, he is speaking about things opposed to the world and the flesh. And the fundamental will to follow Christ in labor is also clearly expressed here—provided, of course, that, with the consideration of my life and with the help of the discernment of spirits, it becomes evident that He is actually calling me to do this. At this point, it is still an open question what the Lord wants me to do, but the fundamental desire for the "more" of the Foundation, which reveals itself here as readiness for the kenosis of the Lord Jesus Christ, must now be accepted. Anyone who hesitates here should really give up the retreat right now.

Ignatius suggests that, "This exercise should be gone through twice during the day, that is, in the morning on rising, and an hour before dinner, or before supper." Thus, he emphasizes how important he feels that this meditation is. We should not get the idea that this is just a pathetic little speech with very little content. If we take our Lord's words seriously, then the resultant choice that it demands of us—which is really supposed to be present in every Christian life, and especially in every priestly life—is shockingly difficult and dark: It is something that can determine my life for all eternity.

Our God is a God of consuming love. He wants to possess us completely! He gives us no rest and pursues us our whole life long. If we are priests, we will have to share Christ's fate whether we want to or not. But the important thing is that we consciously and lovingly say "Yes" to him—a "Yes" of the whole heart. In this matter, it can be decisive whether or not we have prepared ourselves in this meditation on the Kingdom of Christ with a whole-hearted gift of self.

15. The Annunciation
(101–109)

Note

The meditation on the Kingdom of Christ is placed at the head of the "second week" as its foundation. Following this, St. Ignatius has the exercitant meditate on the mystery of the Incarnation. A theological consideration on this matter has already been given. At this point, one might go over what we said before once again, perhaps a bit more according to the way Ignatius suggests in his introduction to the meditation on the Incarnation.

We can also meditate on the Incarnation from the point of view of its connection with the Annunciation to Mary (Lk 1,26–38), especially since Ignatius proposes a special meditation on the history of the Annunciation. Actually, it is impossible to speak of the Incarnation without at least implicitly thinking of the Annunciation to Mary. If we try to consider the truth of the Incarnation of the Word independently of the Annunciation, then we consequently fall into the danger of reducing this truth, which is essentially news and an event, to an abstract metaphysical speculation. In any event, we can only gain an existential understanding of the enfleshment of God by taking the unity of the Incarnation and the Annunciation into consideration. We can only really penetrate to the concreteness of the Incarnation by proceeding through the history of the Annunciation.

Just as it would be false to think of the Incarnation of the

Word as a hypostatic assuming by God of a preëxistent human reality, so it would be equally wrong to think that God had, so to speak, separated the human perception of His Word from concrete humanity and had achieved a relationship to mankind, as it were abstractly, through some sort of a questionable "specific" similarity. Rather, His human existence means a real childhood from a human mother. In this child-mother relationship, the Incarnation is not locked in a blind, natural process; it springs forth from the free encounter of God's news of His coming with the loving response of one woman—a response that was pre-blessed by the news itself. Thus, the appealing and commissioning news, which the angel brings to Mary, is already the ineffable expression of the living God in the Word, is the offer and the advent of His grace and truth.

The procedure that St. Ignatius suggests for the meditation on the Incarnation, the Annunciation, and, in fact, for all the mysteries of Jesus' life, that is, first to look at the persons concerned, then to hear what they are saying, and finally to notice what they are doing, need not be followed slavishly. But we should always sincerely try to get to the heart of the mystery we are meditating on. According to St. Ignatius, we should project the mystery under consideration into our own lives during our time of prayer. The retreatant should bring his own life face to face with the mystery, and so make his meditation as existential as possible. This is very important because we are supposed to reach a definite decision in the meditations on the life of Jesus.

Preludes

From now on, St. Ignatius requires three preludes to each contemplation. In the first prelude, the exercitant is supposed to try to imagine in an anticipating and global way the mystery he is about to contemplate. In the second prelude, he is supposed to "see" the mystery by putting himself in imagination into the actual historical setting. In the third prelude, he is supposed to ask for the specific fruit of the meditation that is relative to his choice. In the present contemplation, the exercitant should "ask for an intimate knowledge of our Lord, Who has become man for me [we must add: by means of the Annunciation], that I may love Him more and follow Him more closely."

I. *The World of the Annunciation*

In the introduction to the meditation on the Incarnation, St. Ignatius recommends that the retreatant carefully consider the world into which God injected Himself as man. We can do the same thing for the Annunciation. But we should not just conjure a picture of the ancient world; what we should think of is the present-day, confused, endangered, worried, and superficial world that disdains any idea of salvation. The Annunciation is meant for this world too!

With magnificent simplicity, St. Ignatius sketches the blinding multiplicity and questionability of the world for the exercitant. He tells him to consider the men on the face of the earth: "Some are white, some black; some at peace, and some at war; some weeping, some laughing; some well, some sick; some coming into the world, and some dying; and so forth." Let the exercitant take note: I belong to this world; it is my framework of existence; I am buried in its confusing multiplicity and in its apparently inescapable problematic. In my own constantly changing situation (for example, when I am hungry or full, tired or rested, sick or healthy, depressed or happy, and so forth), I am experiencing just a small portion of the problem of existence of all mankind. By being involved in the ups and downs of international life, of my own country and culture, and by trying to take an active part in these things, I really become more interiorly aware of myself and acquire more control over myself. God wanted to enter into this world where apparently everything is mixed up, where each thing only seems to appear so that it can fall back again into black chaos, where there is so much pride and baseness, where the heroism that does occur is so surrounded with banality that it usually remains at best doubtful, where everything seems to be locked eternally within itself, where there are very few ears to listen to the transcendent God. God Himself wanted to participate in this world. And He added a long chain of words to the good news He made known to Mary by means of His angel. With this news He, the living God Himself, truly became man, because it was accepted by the divine love of the woman of His new and eternal covenant. ". . . and of His Kingdom there shall be no end!"

II. *The God Who Announces Himself*

In the Incarnation-meditation, St. Ignatius wants the exercitant to turn his eyes away from the world and look at the three divine Persons—how they look down on the earth from their throne of glory and see "all nations in great blindness, going down to death and descending into hell." We can also take this procedure in a contemplation on the Annunciation. We should behold the Father, "from Whom all fatherhood, earthly or heavenly, derives its name" (Eph 3,15), Who is the originless fullness of mysterious life; then the Son, the Word of wisdom in the inner divine existence; and finally the Spirit, who as the alert love of the Father and the Son penetrates the depths of the Godhead. This Trinitarian God eternally conceived this world in such a way that He wanted to assume it with a love that is incomprehensible, as the place for His own created history, in order to participate in earthly multiplicity as the incarnate God.

In this connection, perhaps we could ponder whether or not this announcement from God, which brings His mystery unimaginably close to us, and therefore must essentially surpass every human statement about God, even when carried and made known by a creature, is already His gift of Himself in grace. If the Word is the immanent self-expression of God within Himself, Who therefore contains the complete revelation of God, this revelation must indicate the Incarnation of the Word. From this point of view, we could also note that an announcement of this

139

kind, such as the Annunciation was and such as the teaching of the Church is right to the end of the world, must always manifest, precisely as *something said,* a primordial sacramental character; that is, it must be an earthly symbol of God's grace that contains Him in some way.

III. *The Angel of the Annunciation*

Unfortunately, the holy angels play a very small part these days in our thematic spiritual life and in our theology. This really should not be so, especially if we take Scripture at its face value as the norm for both theology and the spiritual life. The Annunciation itself should be enough to encourage us to strive for a more existential relationship to these creatures of God. They also belong to the world—at least to the world that has become His Kingdom through the effectiveness of grace. The angels seem to be so hidden in the blessed mysteriousness of God that apparently we can only know about their life and their presence from revelation. Because the angels are spiritual, they must be a mystery even to themselves; because they are filled with grace, they must be perfectly committed, free of emptiness and meaninglessness, and admitted to the eternal, luminous mystery of God.

We would have more experience of the holy angels, if we were completely committed to the Kingdom of God. We should try to realize that the silence of these spiritual beings as far as our subjective spiritual life and our theology are concerned, proceeds from the fact that, because of their nearness to God—Jesus said that they constantly see the face of God—they do not possess a type of communication with other creatures that is realizable in this world only. Of course, they cannot be perceived by the senses, since they are pure spiritual beings. But they still belong with metaphysical necessity to the world-horizon of our knowing power; as personal beings created after the image of the Word, they must necessarily be endowed with the power of communication, and they must exist in such a way that they can only fulfill their own existential reality by giving themselves to another who understands. Their silence, therefore, must be attributed to our imprisonment in this world, and not to any lack of intelligibility on their part. This means that, for them, their silence is a characteristic of their supernatural endowments (we will not experience this until the veil of the flesh is torn away!), and for us it is an expression of our lack of the gift of integrity. The ability to experience the holy angels present within our world-horizon must have been a part of man's original integrity. If the loss of our conscious relationship to the angels is a result of our loss of the gift of integrity, then our attempt to re-integrate our human reality (even if only partially successful) will mean a sharpening of our awareness of the angels' working on us. Actually, St. Ignatius expects this to happen—at least to a considerable degree—in and through the use of his "Rules for the Discernment of Spirits."

It is in accordance with our Adam-caused loss of integrity that as pilgrims in this world we are more conscious of the influence of the fallen, God-hating angels. These angels are primarily responsible for the Godlessness of the world. We already touched on the influence of the fallen angels in the meditation on the sin of the angels. There we noted the hellish emptiness of the spirits of this world. Now we meet one of those angels who offered themselves completely and freely in grace to God. This angel announces the Incarnation which is also the source of his own grace. His announcing is both his service and his very nature. He is really a proclaimer of the Word—and this is what we should be our whole life long. Therefore, he is most certainly connected with our life's task.

IV. Mary

Then we can look at Mary, a member of the human race, the virgin full of grace, the handmaid of the Lord who is touched by the Annunciation, and to whom God gives a motherhood sur-

141

passing all motherhood. By uttering her *Fiat* to the holy will of God she becomes the representative of all mankind. Where the ineffability of God's becoming a creature occurs, where He posits Himself outside of Himself into that which is not-God in order to fill this empty other and make it into His own reality—there we will find no deathly lonesomeness, no silence of the finite that is open to the infinite, no brilliant glory confronting utter darkness. What do we find?—a woman who conceives the self-expressing God in love, who perfectly affirms God's message, and who abandons herself in complete freedom to God. God found at least one heart in this dark and apparently lost world in which He really came into His own, and this heart is a true motherly heart.

By accepting God's message that was brought to her, Mary became one with the destiny of her child. From that moment on, she took a unique, unexchangeable, and eternally valid role in our salvation. What took place in the Annunciation was eternally hidden in God. As a result of her humble love, Mary is our mediatrix before God, our queen, the virginal mother to whom we can always have recourse. We should try to speak with the woman of the new and eternal covenant very simply and tenderly: about her Son, our Lord Jesus Christ, about her who became a loving handmaid in the fullness of her grace, and about ourselves who want to follow Christ with her.

V. *The Message*

The Annunciation begins what John later joyously proclaimed: "And the Word became flesh . . ." This is the victory of God over all Godlessness; this is the triumph of grace over all opposition; this is the unexpected and incomprehensible revelation of the immense love of God. The magnificence of the salvation-news that was brought to us by the Incarnate Son of God is already anticipated at one stroke, when Gabriel says to Mary: ". . . you have found grace before God. You 'will conceive and bear a Son.' He will be great and will be called the 'Son' of the Most High. The Lord God will give Him 'the throne' of His father 'David'; He will 'rule' over the house of Jacob 'forever,' and 'there will be no end to His Kingdom . . .'" But the scandalous character of the Incarnation begins with this announcement: From now on, we find glory in humiliation, fullness in emptiness, riches in poverty, life in death. This is what St. Paul means when, speaking of the Incarnation, he says that the Word came in the flesh of sin, under the law, in the form of a slave, and under the power of death. His failure and His death agony begin already when He is received by Mary. At that moment, the descent and the kenosis truly begin for Him. The cross becomes His throne.

God wanted to put Himself in those things so that we might find Him in them. The desert wasteland of our human existence, our poverty and weakness, our sickness, our incarceration in darkness, our life on a dead-end street right in the midst of death —these things are now basically filled with the truth of His life, with His freedom that is true freedom, with the majesty of His power. We do not have to seek God any more in His unattainable otherness. He is right where we are. He is looking at us from every point of the compass. He is carrying our burden, has tasted the bitterness of our life, has travelled our streets, and meets us in the brothers and sisters of our own race. But that the saving victory of God's grace is concealed within our weakness so that it really confirms our distressing situation—we do not want to put up with that! Certainly, we would like to see the Incarnation of God, but in such a way that by means of it we can escape our ennui. However, it just so happens that Christian existence means being called to a life of scandal—the scandal of His coming in our flesh, and the paradox of achieving glory only through the kenosis of the cross.

From the moment of the Annunciation, Mary is intimately affected by this tension. Her fate is the same as that of her child!—not only in glory, but especially in labors, insults, and death. To be sure, the angel greets her as one perfectly graced, so

143

that her heart is filled with the joy that she sings forth in her *Magnificat*. But at the same time, her great favor of grace has its bitterly serious side. Through this grace, she became the Mother of Sorrows. From the moment she utters her "Yes" to God's holy will, she becomes suspect, and, as it were, an outcast. And after she gave birth to her child, He Himself became a puzzle to her. She must even accept being abandoned by Him. But she accepted all of that when she answered the angel: "Behold, I am the handmaid of the Lord; let it be done to me according to your word."

V. *The Annunciation and the Priesthood*

Next we can consider how the Annunciation is related to the priesthood. Mary's "Yes" is the event by means of which the Word becomes man. Here God's deed and man's deed meet one another in an unsurpassable way. The priest of the new covenant is the official guarantee that the Incarnation, which began with the Annunciation, will continue on in the world. He is supposed to realize in his own personal life, by means of the faith that Elizabeth praised in Mary, what he performs in his official capacity; that is, he is supposed to carry on the Incarnation of God by surrendering himself to it.

Ignatius wants the exercitant to close this meditation on the Incarnation with a triple colloquy to the three divine Persons. We should do this in our meditation on the Annunciation of the Incarnation, and so let the basic structure of all Christian prayer become explicit or thematic. Through the Incarnation, every word of the redeemed addressed to God is basically the ineffable call of the Spirit of our Lord Jesus Christ in the middle of our human existence; and every word of ours participates in the fullness of the Word of God Who assumed our flesh and blood in order to retain it for all eternity. Thus, every word penetrates to where the living mystery of divine being eternally holds sway. During these days of the Spiritual Exercises, we should turn over in our minds again and again this incomprehensible opportunity of our prayer. This is something we cannot escape; nor is it something that constitutes the mysterious essence of our words to God only where these words break forth in song from a mystical experience, or are forged by sublime theological contemplation. It is also part of simple everyday prayer, and it is operative where men who have become silent persevere in the questionable and obscure emptiness of God. This should be our attitude when we meditate before the majesty of God.

16. The Birth of Our Lord
(110–112; 121–126)

From a theological point of view, this meditation is only a repetition of the meditation on the Incarnation of the Word. But here we want to consider more carefully a few traits of the epiphany of grace in Jesus Christ that can give us more help to reach the decision that each of us should make in this retreat.

I. *A Birth in the Confinement of Time*

Look at the Lord and see how He subjects Himself to time! What a venture—to risk entering a certain family at a certain time with the divine life! The appearance of God in the flesh!

Often we suffer in the circumstances we find ourselves in—circumstances that are the result of former history and the factors that were at work in it. Often we are the plaything of politics and suffer greatly because of it. We look apprehensively into the future. We ask how, under such conditions, the life that we have planned for ourselves can even be possible. Afraid of life and mistrustful of its unfolding, we constantly ask ourselves if the real order is going to give us the material necessary to shape our lives. The Word of God risked entering into this dull reality to become a troublesome outcast, the member of a dispossessed family, and a citizen of an enslaved land. He is born in poverty, in a stable, because Mary and Joseph were not admitted to the

146

inn. Thus St. Paul was able to say of Him: "He became poor for your sake, even though He was rich . . ." (2 Cor 8,9). But even this poverty was not exceptional—no one noticed it. What Mary and Joseph were forced to experience in Bethlehem was probably not a great shock to them. Rather, they accepted it as the normal treatment of poor people. Nevertheless, a birth in such lowly and ordinary circumstances, at least according to our way of thinking, hardly seems suitable for the beginning of a magnificent life. All the circumstances of Jesus' birth indicate a birth that is poor, very ordinary, and terribly common; it is neither extremely poor nor of such a nature that one could predict a noble life from it. His birth is also unrecognized by others: It takes place somewhere in the outskirts, and the people of the time were busy with other things. A few wretched shepherds find it a heavenly event; world history pays absolutely no attention to it.

The very fact of being born, however, is something distressing. "To be born" means to come into existence without being asked. Contingency and being called unasked into existence are factors that belong to the reality of the finite spirit. The starting point of our life that determines it for all eternity in such a way that we can never escape it, is in the hands of another. The acceptance of this unchangeable situation is something that belongs to the fundamental facts of human and especially of Christian existence. The human reality of the Word could not have a fate different from that of creation, at least from the moment that it was provided for by the creative power of God. Even the Lord had to begin!

We can imagine the most wonderful things about the glory of this Child who was given to us, but His birth, in any event, is a descent into privation. Through His birth, he truly put on *our* history. How we can and must reconcile this fact with the prerogatives that theology rightly ascribes to Him, is another question. We should notice here that He came into the world the same way we did in order to come to terms with the pre-given facts of human existence, and to begin to die. In number 116 in his book of the Exercises, St. Ignatius wants the exercitant "to see and consider what they [Mary, Joseph, and the others] are doing, for example, making the journey and laboring that our Lord might be born in extreme poverty, and that after many labors, after hunger, thirst, heat, and cold, after insults and outrages, He might die on the cross, and all this for me." According to St. Ignatius, we are supposed to look at the life of the Lord without whitewashing it, without romantic phrases, and without a debilitating humanism. In the meditation on His birth, we should be able to see this point clearly: At His birth, the Incarnate Word begins His death march, and everything that is mentioned in the history of His birth is an early announcement of His end in utter poverty, weakness, and death.

II. *A Birth for the Fullness of Eternity*

With this perspective of the history of the birth of Christ we still should not forget that a new and eternal reality appeared in this birth. This reality is not only an eternity such as the connatural immortality of a spiritual subject, but also the eternity of a personal subject that has value in the eyes of God: Life in the "glory of God." The Child who then began His life's journey from His mother's womb remains forever as a divine reality. When we look at God now, we always see the Man whose history began with this blessed birth. Through this birth, God's kindness and His love for man, His "philanthropia," appeared (Tit 3,4–7). On the other hand, man really only becomes lovable when the happy ending of his life is guaranteed, when God establishes the beginning of this end by inserting His own blessedness into human life to carry it along. Only in this way is human living made really bearable. Otherwise, it is only a question to itself and to others—a question to which there is no answer, because there is just too much involved in it: Transcendence toward the infinite, finiteness, spirit and body, an eternal destiny and the passing fate of time, plentitude and want.

For the fundamental questions relative to our human existence, we have no other truly concrete answer but that there is a Man Who was born as a member of our race and Who was like us in all things. His human reality—and therefore ours too!—has meaning and direction, yes, and even an intelligibility surpassing our powers of comprehension, because here the eternal Word of God, the blessed self-expression of the originless mystery, was born, and because God, since He wanted to manifest *Himself,* revealed Himself as man. This is the beginning of "the end of the ages" that, according to St. Paul, has come upon us (1 Cor 10,11). Before this event, the dialogue between God and man was an open thing—no one knew which way it would go or how it would be terminated. God kept the details of its further development to himself (Eph 3,9). No one could tell from the history of the world before the coming of Christ how it would end. But with the birth of our Lord, God's final Word is spoken into the world: He establishes His Logos as the Word of the world, so that now, as it were, the Word and the call of God plus the answer of the world coincide in one God-man and for all eternity have become hypostatically one. It is for this reason that world history, that is really engaged in a dialogue with God, is closed right here. And nothing unexpected can ever really happen again. Therefore, the rejoicing of the angels and the mysterious announcement of the "glory" of God on earth accompany this birth. Up to this moment, God had refused to make this announcement and in fact could not make it, because the world lacked the peace and the inner unity that proceed from the "good pleasure" (*eudokia*) of God.

Now the only open question is the one that is directed to us: How will we respond to the final Word of God directed to the world—a word of mercy, of God's coming to her, and a word that signifies her total acceptance by God? The world-horizon

149

of our human existence is now necessarily this Word of God Who has come into the world. We cannot remain neutral to a world-horizon of this kind. It must be the source both of our disturbing restlessness and of our heartfelt joy. Now we should consider these events in our hearts as Mary did (Lk 2,19).

17. The Hidden Life of Our Lord
(134, 271)

Note

For the third day of the "second week" of the Exercises, St. Ignatius suggests a meditation on the hidden life of Jesus. He does not give any points for this meditation, but only says: "On the third day use the contemplation on the Obedience of the Child Jesus to His parents, number 271, and the Finding of the Child Jesus in the Temple, number 272. Then will follow the two repetitions and the Application of the Senses." St. Ignatius places the meditation on the hidden life of Jesus before the one on the Finding in the Temple because in this way the state of the commandments and the state of the evangelical counsels can be considered after one another.

I. *The Priesthood as a Religious Form of Life*

Celibacy in the Western Church is a clear indication that the priesthood of the new covenant is not just any kind of an office that a person fills, as he might busy himself with any occupation that does not have anything to do with his private life. For celibacy establishes and forms his very existence; it binds together the private and the public areas of human existence and

151

makes an inseparable unity of them. Thus, Christian priesthood is clearly a religious state of life. The religious element is not something merely accidental to it—it is the one ruling force in its "interior life."

This is not perfectly self-evident! Certainly, it is not something to be wondered at if a spiritually healthy, properly educated, maturing Christian develops a relatively intense religious interest. If he discovers the world and himself in the middle of it in the course of growing up, and if he becomes aware of the different possibilities for his human development, then it only seems natural that the religious dimension would occur to him as a possible and very meaningful way to develop his personality, and it seems only natural that he would experience a strong pull toward a metaphysical-religious existence. Objectively, religion is the foundation and the crowning point of all human existence. Therefore, it is perfectly normal if many young people get the feeling that they could devote their entire lives to a religious vocation. Every lively, maturing young person tends to test the existential possibilities that are discovered in this phase of life. He or she does this with an eye to seeing whether or not he could invest his whole life and all his powers in one of them. The intensity of the religious life that frequently arises in the early years usually levels off later on for most people. (We do not have to bother ourselves here with the question, to what extent the increase of religiosity in old age, when one's powers begin to wane and death approaches, is a meaningful development of the dynamism of human life intended by God.)

For some young persons, however, the development of the religious side of their being becomes something more than just the development of a normal religious attitude. In their case, God makes use of the basic religious instinct to call them to a type of life in which the religious element is the only determining factor, and not just something—which is an entirely different case—that is the most important and crowning factor of their lives. A vocation to the priesthood of the New Testament is just such a determination to a completely religious form of life. By reason of his priesthood, the priest of Jesus Christ is no mere religious official who exercises some kind of religious function that could perhaps just as well be handled by a sacristan. He cannot withdraw himself into a private life that has no religious orientation when he has received his pay for carrying out the duties of his office. On the contrary, his priestly vocation determines absolutely and completely his whole being. There is no room in his life for anything else but his priestly activity.

The maturing Christian can certainly be mistaken with regard to a true religious vocation, especially since many different tendencies, seemingly very similar, are normally found together between the ages of fourteen and twenty. He can mistake the normal religious tendency with a religious vocation. Of course, the religious tendency should continue. Naturally, it should not disappear like the morning mist immediately after puberty, but it must be nourished as the most important aspect of his life, even if it has become very weak. Yet, in an essential and even truly Christian sense, the adult lay person is completely involved in his worldly position, his family, and his job. Surely, he knows that he must remain open to God, and that he must fulfill his religious duties. But his kind of life, even if it is devoutly Christian, is still something completely different from the thematic religious existence of the priest. This remains true even though it might be extremely difficult to describe the psychological and theological differences between lay and priestly existence. (That religious integration is fundamentally only possible up to a certain degree, that a priest cannot be one hundred per cent ascetic and also in a certain sense should not even be such, is an entirely different problem. We have already touched on this point in our consideration of the Foundation of the Exercises. But if it is not proper for us to set up utopian ideals for the priestly life, still that should not prevent us from seeing the radical difference between ordinary religious interest and the religious vocation that absorbs the whole person.)

God demands essentially more from the priest of the New Testament than he does from those whom he endows with ordinary religious interest. Certainly, this general religiosity can take many different forms: It can develop in an apostolic or a doctrinal fashion; as a speculative talent it can lead to the discovery of new truths; it can blossom out in the direction of self-reformation, or it can even appear as a talent for leadership; and so forth. All that may more or less be the necessary presupposition for a special divine call to the priesthood, but it is not simply to be identified with it. This call is really a unique grace for the radical following of Christ, and for basing one's whole existence on Him, at least insofar as the call means a participation in the high priesthood and the salvific mediation of Christ.

If we take this remarkable doubleness into account—the "from above" element and the "from below" element of the priestly religious vocation, then certain false developments in the clergy can be expected as a matter of course. In one way or another, all of these developments proceed from the confusion of the common religious interest with a religious vocation. In practice, then, this leads to conflicts because of the dualism of priestly existence mentioned above.

For example, a priest who tries to fulfill the duties of his office and in the process only remains on the level of the lay Christian as far as the religious-existential carrying out of this office is concerned, is really only some sort of a religious functionary for whom his religion is just one occupation among many others. The other extreme is the overly zealous, fanatic cleric who cannot stand to see other people live differently than he does. He tries to force his own narrow, clerical outlook on others. He thinks that everyone should be like him! Frequently, he is burning with jealousy because he cannot live the way he would like to live, that is, in a way forbidden by his priesthood. He compensates for his dissatisfaction by tearing down everything nonclerical, and by demanding that everyone do what he dislikes doing.

154

The overly pious priest is like the zealot in that he does not know how to give things up in the right way. The result is that his true human growth is stunted because he underestimates the demand placed on him to direct all his powers to God, Christ, the Church, and the salvation of men. In addition to this, he tends to spoil everything else because he does not understand the meaning of true self-denial. The worldly cleric is just the opposite. He denies that his vocation is essentially different from that of lay Christians. Therefore, he hardly fulfills his most serious obligations, and so even sinks below the level of the religious functionary. Even the embittered, spiteful religious shows signs of the conflict mentioned above as a basic ingredient of priestly-religious existence. Cynically, he seeks out those thing that are not permitted in the Church or for the clergy because he wants to escape from a burden that he probably underestimated in the beginning of his religious life, and that he now feels he can no longer carry. Perhaps he argues this way without even noticing it: Just look, the others are not doing it either!

Really, only a *holy* priest is neither a mere religious functionary, nor an overly zealous religious fanatic, nor overly pious. He is not bitter in spite of the true bitterness of human existence. He does not try to escape into neurotic extravagances. He is able to persevere patiently with God and to accept from Him his vocation to follow Christ as a priest without demanding the same thing from everyone else. The holy priest knows how to give things up pure and simple, without tarnishing his relationship to the world and without belittling the value of the world. He can give up everything because he truly loves God and finds everything again in Him. We are on the way toward this type of priestly existence—with God's grace—and our concrete life is a mixture of its basic elements. And we should have confidence that the God who couples His incalculable call to the priesthood onto the common religious tendency will also bring to completion in us the good work that He began.

II. *The Hidden Life of Jesus as a Religious Form of Life*

It is possible to divide Jesus' life into three periods: the hidden life, the public life, and the passion. Each one of these periods is stamped with certain definite characteristics. There is a remarkable difference between the first and second periods. But we do not have to adduce any further evidence here to prove that Jesus' hidden life unquestionably belongs to the totality of His messianic mission, and therefore to the mysteries that are important and meaningful for the proper formation of our priestly existence. Jesus lived a completely religious life even in his hidden everyday life—a life that seems so useless as far as His mission is concerned. A retired and hidden life can very legitimately be filled with political, artistic, or scientific interests! not even marriage is excluded. But perhaps this kind of life is a bit harder to understand when the one and only ruling force is the religious. The meditation on the basic structure of Jesus' life and its existential realization has already shown us that Jesus is primarily and exclusively a religious man. This also holds true of His hidden life!

If we disregard the daily work necessary to support oneself, if we disregard membership in a certain family, adherence to a certain people, and some of the other ordinary requirements of human life that do not really determine a person in a necessary way, then the only thing that is meaningful in the hidden life of Jesus is His religious attitude. In the decades before His public life, Jesus renounced, as it were ostentatiously, a life of frequent contact with others. The resolve to remain at home and to concentrate on religious interests must also be an essential part of a priestly life! Obviously, we can still be well educated, scientifically up to date, aesthetically inclined, politically orientated, and so forth; we can also take a trip overseas, perhaps to a Eucharistic Congress, and truly enjoy ourselves; but in the midst of these things, we should never forget that the truly form-giving element of our priestly life (as opposed to its matter which can and should include these other things) is still the specifically *religious* element. Our life is a "life with Christ hidden in God" ["*vita cum Christo in Deo abscondita*"]. Without a doubt, this was the type of life Jesus led before His public appearance. If His hidden life was not primarily a religious life, then it is impossible, with the very best will, to find anything really significant about it.

III. *A Few Characteristics of Jesus' Hidden Life*

In Luke 2,52 we find one characteristic that is most important for the formation of our spiritual life: "Jesus increased in wisdom, age, and grace before God and men." Given the certain fact that Jesus possessed the "immediate vision of God" from the first moment of his earthly existence, it might be very difficult to give an adequate theological explanation of the growth of Jesus' interior life. However that may be, the fact of His growth is a datum of revelation that cannot be talked away. When it comes to shaping our own following of Christ, we must not forget that the Incarnate Son of God had to grow to maturity slowly, and was able to wait about thirty years for His "hour." In any event, this tells us that we must not rush in the development of our religious existence. Usually, one does not become a saint in one day. We should have the patience to develop our priestly life slowly! We should have confidence that God has prepared a life for us in which our truly decisive opportunities will not be easily missed. We should be patient with ourselves! We must learn to wait and to grow in waiting! If we honestly wait for God to act—which does not mean to subscribe lethargically and smugly to spiritual fatalism, then our hour will come, and it will come at the right time, even if it seems to us now that our life is going nowhere.

A general characteristic of Jesus' whole life, even of his hidden life, which at least to a certain degree is indispensable for our priestly existence, is His poverty. Independently of whether or

157

not a person has a vow of poverty, at any rate the priest of Jesus Christ cannot be like a hired employee who bemoans the fact that he does not make more money. Today more than ever before, the priest must be ready to lead a modest and in a certain sense a poor life. This necessity cannot be ultimately established by metaphysical or moral-theological arguments. It must be deduced from the life history of Jesus of Nazareth. Only when we realize that He as the Incarnate Word and the King of the world did not shrink from "vegetating" for three decades in a remote corner of the world called Nazareth, can we hope to convince ourselves that poverty does not limit the possibilities of following our High Priest, but actually increases them. No matter how convinced we are that we can do more for the Kingdom of God and the salvation of men if we have abundant material resources to draw on, these resources should not contribute to our own personal comfort and ease. For even if we are not religious and bound by religious vows, we still have to follow Jesus poor!

According to Matthew 13,55 and Mark 6,3, Jesus earned His bread as a laborer up to the time of His public life. Work is not just a wonderful chance to develop one's own personality; it is primarily vexation and annoyance—and this was the lot of Christ. One has to admit that his life is generally not very interesting. It is more a series of rather banal vexations. The laborious and at the same time apparently useless work that Jesus did simply and unostentatiously during the years of His hidden life makes a good example for our priestly work in the helping of men. We should not have any illusions about our work! In the long run, it is an irritating annoyance, a banal monotony, an exhausting nuisance that ultimately gets us nowhere. And after all of it, as an old pastor or prelate, we get the feeling—usually not without foundation—that our younger brothers in the spirit are more or less waiting for us to move over and make room for others.

In his second chapter (v. 52), St. Luke describes the hidden

158

life of Jesus as a life of obedience. As a child, Jesus was able to obey simply, spontaneously, and honestly, and not just to give us a good example. To be sure, the twelve-year-old Child in the temple shows that He obeys with an awareness of His own freedom, and He does not at all give the impression that He could not do otherwise. In this case, He not only manifests His independence with regard to His parents, but He also shows that His obedience is something that He freely embraces as a man. In this connection, we should think over the meaning of His obedience, its social and personal implications, and so forth. We already said once in the course of this retreat that man must have a point outside of himself in order to transcend himself, and that this point must be first of all another human Thou. That man can only really find God when he is able freely to renounce himself and get outside of himself—this can be termed the theological function of obedience.

IV. *Our Hidden Life in Christ*

According to Colossians 3,3, the life of the Christian "is hidden with Christ in God." From the moment we are baptized into the death of Christ, the source of our life is in heaven. According to Philippians 3,20, our "citizenship" is in heaven, and according to 2 Corinthians 4,18, through God's grace we experience the invisible more than the visible. Like Moses, we hold onto that which is invisible as if it were the most tangible—and by holding on we become strong and patient (Heb 11,1). This shifting of one's own innermost reality, which fundamentally characterizes every Christian human existence, to the supernatural, to faith, to that which is not this-worldly, finds its tangible realization in what we call religious existence in the strict sense. Therefore, it is found especially in the life of a priest.

By really living our religion, and by devoting all our efforts to it, we must, as priests and witnesses to Christ, bring it about that, according to God's will, our fellow men die in Christ and have their true home in heaven, not on earth. We cannot be successful in carrying out this fundamental Christian goal, unless our priestly existence in itself is a profession of sensationlessness in the midst of official Church business, of modesty and obedience while directing others, of seclusion and regularity in the midst of much activity. Otherwise, it is hardly possible to lead a life in which the religious element plays more than a secondary role. The courage to embrace an ordinary life like that is a measure of our faith. Certainly, too much concentration on self also has its dangers: It can develop into a lethargic jogging-along that is only an excuse for mediocrity and dullness. Sometimes by living this way a person can make everything easy for himself; he can avoid difficulties and circumvent dangers that should not be circumvented; he can thus fail to realize and achieve his own freedom by refusing to embrace the difficult adventure of a truly religious life. Instead of deriving his power from obscurity, and instead of embracing the very difficult reality of priestly existence, a person can live very comfortably. He can get along peacefully without any disturbance; he can seat himself daily at a finely appointed table and find out from his calendar what the program of the day is.

Let us take a good look at Jesus Who had the courage to lead an apparently useless life for thirty years. We should ask Him for the grace to give us to understand what His hidden life means for our religious existence.

18. Jesus Remains in
the Temple
(134, 135, 272)

Note

During the "second week" of the Exercises, Ignatius wants the
exercitant to begin considering what sort of a decision he is going
to come to. Not only are the decision-inducing meditations on
the Two Standards and the Three Classes of Men supposed to
contribute toward this, but also especially the meditations on the
Life of Jesus and the corresponding considerations that affect our
own personal lives. Now the decision arising from these considerations should not remain within the principles of the decision
(that is, indifference, the "more," "that which is more conducive
to the end"), but it should discover the definite means that the
exercitant should employ in order to follow Christ the way God
wants him to. According to Ignatius' idea, this decision would
consist of a choice between a life of the commandments and a
life of evangelical perfection.

All of us are constantly faced with choices, at least in the sense
that we have to choose between two things—of which one is
perhaps objectively more difficult and requires more sacrifice, and
the other is easier and possibly more attractive. It is very possible
actually to choose the second object. For the "more" of the
greater love of God does not always have to be concretized in

that which is actually and objectively the greater or more difficult thing. In any event, we are all called to choose "that which is more conducive to the end." But whether or not my actual call to follow Christ is also a call to choose that which is objectively more difficult, is something that must be discovered in the Exercises under the influence of the Spirit. One cannot deduce *a priori* the means that should be chosen by a certain retreatant from the attitude or frame of mind he is in when he begins to enter upon his decision.

Before entering into the considerations that are supposed to lead the exercitant to make his decision, St. Ignatius proposes the meditation on Jesus' remaining behind in the temple (Lk 2,40–50).

We should be careful not to consider the meditations on the various events of Jesus' life as an excellent opportunity to draw moral lessons. Ethical maxims are treated much more exactly in moral handbooks. The purpose here in these meditations is to place ourselves in a real, not just abstract, relationship to the event of Jesus' life being considered by means of a salvation-historical and salvation-bringing remembrance. This relationship will bring us the grace necessary to follow Christ. We must always keep this fact before our eyes when we are meditating on the life of Jesus, otherwise our meditations can rapidly becoming boring and useless. What takes place in a narrower, sacramental sense in the sacrifice of the Mass, also occurs in a very true sense in the faith-penetrated remembrance of the other events of Jesus' life: And this remembrance is not a mere speculative treatment of Jesus' history—in it, the grace of a definite mystery is revealed and offered to the one praying.

I. *Jesus Fulfills the Law*

In fulfillment of the law of the Old Testament, the twelve-year-old Jesus makes a pilgrimage to Jerusalem to worship Yahweh in the temple. Just think of it! Jesus, the only-begotten Son of

God Who is always with the Father, Who can say of Himself, "I know that You are always with Me!", who really is the expression of God and therefore is the only perfect worshipper in spirit and in truth, Who does not need any contrived ceremonies limited to time and space, Who is the only one who descends from above—this Jesus fulfills the law. We might even say that He comes in the "flesh of religion." Christianity and the Church of the new and eternal Testament are also regulated by rules, norms, laws, and precepts that affect the life of each Christian. Those things will not disappear until we have died and have completed the last descent with Christ. As long as we are journeying in darkness and in the shadow of death, the highest type of religious experience and the most intense love must be governed by certain external laws. Ignatius would say that these experiences must be subject to God, orderly, and carried out in external cult-acts according to the prescribed laws. That is not at all so obvious! Actually, God always remains greater than all external signs, and under certain circumstances He even manifests Himself to those who, from no fault of their own, do not recognize the signs He has given.

We constantly get the impression with regard to Church ceremonies and law that they are really very narrow, yes, picayune and unimportant. Perhaps we should say: Whoever is too involved in a philosophical, categorical religiosity and cannot go beyond himself to the transcendence and infinity of God, is not a truly "religious man." Such a person would not be like the religious man Jesus presents us with when He answers the question of the Samaritan woman at Jacob's Well with regard to the proper place of worship, apparently ignoring her question: "The time is coming when the true worshippers of God will worship Him in the spirit and in truth" (Jn 4,23). Of course, that was not His *complete* answer, for He institutes the Last Supper, requires baptism, and establishes a Church of explicit, legal requirements —the Church of Peter and the Apostles. But at the same time

163

He knows—and this is proved by His words to the woman at Jacob's Well—that God is always greater than all forms. This is true not only for those that He Himself observes when He, the living temple of God, makes a pilgrimage to Jerusalem with a crowd of people who, for the most part, were only interested in fulfilling the letter of the law. This also goes for these prescriptions that He has given us in His worship of the Father. At any rate, by means of His pilgrimage He reveals to us a very definite side of the religious life: the humility of even the most spiritual person to submit himself to forms and laws coming from without.

II. *The Conflict*

Unless we want to water down the Gospel account, we must admit that it tells us of a real conflict in Jesus' life between doing His Father's will by remaining in the temple and His duty to obey His parents. Jesus remains behind in the temple without telling His mother and His foster father. Later, Mary asks, "My child, why have you done this to us?" The tension we encounter here was not the result of a sin on either side, but still it was a very true conflict. We are only too easily inclined to assume that there can only be conflicts between ourselves and our fellow men, and also between us and our superiors, for example between the bishop and ourselves, between the requirements of the twentieth century and the directives of Canon Law, between personal needs and the duties of office, between the movement of the Spirit and written regulations, when malice, narrow-mindedness, tyranny, pride, or the desire of independence are at work in one way or another. With an attitude such as this, the conflicts that do occur, which should be endured with mutual respect, with patience and love, will usually only be poisoned—they certainly will not be resolved.

We should not be so simple as to think that there cannot be

any real conflicts when both sides are in the right. It was God's will that Mary and Joseph demand that Jesus go home with them, and it was God's will that Jesus should remain behind in the temple. He did not just "put up with" one alternative or the other. The principle governing this tension is essentially other-worldly: in the unappealable freedom of God! There is no instance in this world that is an adequate judge of this case. We also find conflicts such as this in the history of the Church. Of course, this does not mean that everyone can do as he pleases. Certainly, we cannot simply disregard Church law, the rubrics, the orders of our superiors, the directions from Rome, and so forth, by appealing to our own personal inspirations of the Spirit. The question is only how such tensions within the realm of one's own personal initiative *and* one's obedience to the Church can be overcome and resolved. But we do not have to solve that problem right here. The important thing is to note: There can be such conflicts, and they should be borne with humility and selflessness—as is the case here with Jesus, Mary, and Joseph.

III. *The State of the Commandments and the State of the Evangelical Counsels*

According to St. Ignatius, in this meditation we should attain a state of real indifference between the state of the commandments and the state of the evangelical counsels.

Jesus comes from Nazareth and returns. In between, we find Him overstepping the order of the fourth commandment in order to heed the sovereign call of God. His conduct on the occasion of His first pilgrimage to Jerusalem is a unity of these two things: the normal, the ordinary, that which is required by the commandments, *and* the call that comes directly from heaven. Jesus must also be true to the latter, even though it is unpredictable, transcendent, and beyond the commandments—and even though, as a personal call, it means sacrifice and risk.

IV. *A Few Additional Considerations*

Perhaps we might consider the coming of age of the twelve-year-old Child Jesus. He dedicates it to the service of God! While we only too easily think that our independence must be asserted by going against the demands of God, of the Church, and of the special community in which we live, Jesus uses His independence to carry out His Father's will.

It might very well be that Jesus' statement of "being about My Father's business" is not perfectly clear. Is Jesus saying that He belongs totally to God, or is He speaking of the temple that belongs to Yahweh? In any event, Jesus is aware of Himself as one Who is with the Father in a very special sense. Therefore, He has the courage to step outside the limits of a normal life. Apparently, He does not feel that human existence means perfect harmony, without problems and without conflicts, between the demands of human life and the demands of God. He who had the least need for it gives us an example that being about God's business, which is true religious existence, can demand absolute homelessness, abandonment of security for a dangerous loneliness, emancipation that goes against certain human values, and a painful change of relationship to one's fellow men.

We do not need any special psychological talent to perceive that remaining in the temple must have brought about a tormenting loneliness in the child Jesus. We can also very easily imagine, without going into deep theological speculation, that it must have been very painful for the heart of Jesus that He could not explain His conduct to His mother, and that she did not even understand Him when He told her what He was about.

We can also consider how the extraordinary events surrounding Jesus' first visit to the temple are terminated by His return to ordinary, everyday living. Jesus finally returns with His parents to Galilee. His emancipation in the temple is only an episode: It is a brief appearance of the totally other that immediately humbles itself by returning to that which is normal. One of the

characteristics of a true Christian life is that it avoids sensational-
ism, even when called to do something extraordinary, something
surpassing anything this world has to offer. Christian existence
does not seek ostentatious display, does not build itself up, is
not sustained by an attraction for individualism, for wanting to
be different just for the sake of being different. Christian existence
has the courage to capture the extraordinary, the new, and the
unexpected in formal expression, so that it can preserve it and
regulate it. Christian existence can even adapt the new to normal,
ordinary people, as the history of the religious orders has proven
again and again. The great movements in the history of the
Church have not been the result of that which is most human
in the Church. But they have passed into the normal life of the
Church in such a way that the ordinary person in the Church can
accept them without great surprise.

The history of Jesus' first visit to the temple also contains
an example of what we might call the *charismatic* element in the
life of the individual and in the life of the Church. Vocations
to a life that is contrary to what went before, to the already
regimented, to that which is already established by custom and
law, can occur in the lives of certain individuals. In fact, they
must occur in the Church, because the Church has not yet by any
means discovered all of her possibilities and needs. New forms
of life in the Church and new pastoral methods do not necessarily
have to be thought up around the green tables of the Roman
Curia. Naturally, that can happen too, but it is not necessary,
and in the course of Church history that is not the way things
normally took place. Otherwise, one could demand that Jesus, if
He was supposed to be subject to His parents on the one hand,
and if He was supposed to announce His messianic mission by
remaining in the temple on the other hand, should have been
directed in this by Mary, or at least should have consulted with
her. Then there would have been no conflict, and the relations
between parents and child which were doubtlessly willed by
God would have been properly observed. But in the history of

167

the Church and our life in the Church the situation is such that God demands of us that we submit ourselves to her official machinery, but at the same time He does not want us to observe it in a simple, schematic way that is traced out for us down to the most minute detail by Canon Law.

Surely, we should also realize that true charismatic impulses, which are never capricious and fond of innovations, are connected with sacrifice, renunciation, penance, humble love, and obedience to the Church and her official organizations. The Church needs the charismatic and the unexpected. God has not resigned in favor of the Church's administrative apparatus. Nor has He abdicated in favor of the direction promised to the Church through the Holy Spirit! He Himself is the Spirit Who breathes where He wills and descends upon children and fools, upon the poor and the simple, and perhaps even upon this or that theologian. But all charismatic and pentecostal gifts must remain *in* the Church: They must remain in the constitutional, legally organized, authoritarian Church. Only when the charismatic observes the proper order, and when the official Church directs and supports the charismatic, is the life of the Church everything that it should be.

We should try to open up our human reality to the history of Jesus' first pilgrimage, and we should ask our Lord for the grace to be unconditionally true to the call to be about our Father's business, so that we might be able to continue in our own lives what we have learned from Him in this contemplation.

19. The Two Standards
(136–147)

Note

1. The Decision-Character of This Meditation. The meditation on the Two Standards is the first of the so-called decision-meditations in the strict sense. At this stage St. Ignatius gives very detailed points. He wants the exercitant to reach a decision that will affect his whole life.

Our life is a chain of decisions. We dispatch many of them, so to speak, with the left hand. This is perfectly legitimate, since it would be impossible for us to be in a constant state of intense reflection. Improvisation is legitimate! But if man as a personal being, that is, as a self-reflecting being—one freely disposing of self, is supposed to choose his destiny and not just be driven and directed, then he must always examine his activity thematically so that he can take control of himself. Even if he is never perfectly successful in this, he must nevertheless seriously scrutinize his actions and judge them. He must continually ask himself this question: "What happens when I posit a free act and make a decision; what do I have to do to make my choice really personal and objectively correct?" The ultimate intensification of this problem of human existence is the particular problem before us right now: "How can I distinguish between a true call of God and a false impulse?" The meditation on the Two Standards is supposed to shed some light on this question for us. It lays before

169

us the technique of temptation and the mode of God's dealing with souls. In this way, Ignatius proposes to the exercitant a highly developed criterion of decision that is worked out in concrete detail in his "Rules for the Discernment of Spirits." This criterion should be considered from every angle in the meditation on the Two Standards and in the repetitions of this meditation.

2. *Situation of a Human Choice.* We can never make our decisions from a neutral position. We live in a world burdened with sin. The pre-given framework of our decisions has been formed by the history of sin that we already considered in the meditation on the three sins. The sin of the fallen angels, original sin, the sins of all men, and my own personal sins make up an essential "existential" that determines all my choices. But on the other hand, our freedom can never be separated from the Incarnation of the Word, or from His grace. Thus, the field of our decisions is essentially determined by the opposition between Lucifer and Christ. Not one of us can escape the uncompromising decision for Christ. This may be a very obvious truth of our faith, but we must constantly remind ourselves of it because we have a tendency to avoid the constant battle, to seek our own comfort, to make life easy for ourselves, to make no sacrifices, to make reservations. And yet, our life must constantly be involved in painful decisions. It is constantly pointed beyond this world. The separation into two camps, the camp of Christ and the camp of Lucifer, not only dominates all of our surroundings—it penetrates to the very depths of our hearts.

We have already encountered the standard of Christ in the meditation on the Kingdom of Christ. Now when it is necessary to make a very definite decision, and when it is therefore necessary to take up the right position in the battle between the two fronts, St. Ignatius presents us with the image of the two standards that are battling one another. This image has a pre-historical origin. It is constantly used in Scripture and tradition (for example, Jerusalem-Babylon; the City of God and the City of

Satan). But while tradition, at least since the time of St. Augustine, draws a clear line between the fronts of the two kingdoms—the Church here and the kingdom of Satan over there, Ignatius emphasizes the mutual penetration of both kingdoms. According to St. Ignatius, there are no static front lines between the two, but only swift emissaries who are sent to all parts of the globe. The meaning here is not that the Church is on one side and all those who are not visibly in the Church are on the other side. The kingdoms of Christ and Satan as described by St. Ignatius both embrace the whole world. Lucifer also expands his power inside the Church, for there we find pride, greed for wealth, and power. The Church is also the Church of sinners and not just the Church of saints! On the other hand, God seeks to win over men who do not yet belong to the community of the Church in a visible way, as it were officially, through the reception of baptism. This is a fact even though the grace of God is always the grace of Christ and his Church, and even though the Catholic Church with her history is the only perfect representative of the approaching Kingdom of God, and even though there is and must be a "missionary front" that is identified with the boundary of this Church. But in the meditation on the Two Standards, St. Ignatius is not considering the foreign missions. His goal is an ascetical one and under this aspect the banner of Christ cannot be simply identified with the Church, nor can the banner of Satan be simply identified with the world outside of the Church.

I. Lucifer's Standard: The Art of Seduction

1. "Imagine you see the chief of all the enemy in the vast plain about Babylon, seated on a great throne of fire and smoke, his appearance inspiring horror and terror" (no. 140).

Therefore, I should try to come to the realization in this meditation that this personal opponent of truth, of the love and grace of God and of His Kingdom, truly exists, and that I live within the sphere of influence of this adversary's power. We need

171

to be told this again and again, as it were by someone outside of us, just as we need to be reminded that there is sin in the world. In the course of this retreat, we have already discovered that it is not at all easy to see how there can be sin in a world that is completely under the control of the almighty will of God. The attempt to explain all of man's attitudes, acts, and their motives exclusively in a good way may appear to be laudatory, but fundamentally it is only a sublimated form of the temptation to deny the existence of evil. Certainly, we have the right, especially in the realm of scientific study, to strive for a more adequate synthesis, and we have the duty to approach our fellow men with understanding. We do not have to figure out ahead of time that they are all wicked, vulgar, and deceitful. Certainly, we should look for shortcomings first of all in ourselves before we accuse others; we should be obliging and modest; we should try to find traces of Christ's footsteps everywhere we go; we should not paint everything either black or white in the pastoral care of men. This is all true, but we must still reckon with the reality of evil, of the personal adversary of God and His power in the world, even if we cannot specifically and definitely put our finger on it.

2. "Consider how he summons innumerable demons, and scatters them, some to one city and some to another, throughout the whole world, so that no province, no place, no state of life, no individual is overlooked."

St. Ignatius wants the exercitant to note that the power of the devil is everywhere operative. Here we do not have to go into the theological question of how we ought to think of these evil spirits and their mode of operating. The important thing is to be very aware of this point: Their power extends over the whole world; in everything and even in the very best we find this pull and drive, this power of the "principalities and powers" of evil. There is no place where we can hide ourselves from them so that they do not see us. Everywhere we must distinguish between good and evil, and in the process of forming our decision we are always exposed to the influence of the "evil spirit."

3. "Consider the address he makes to them, how he goads them on to lay snares for men and bind them with chains. First they are to tempt them to covet riches (as Satan himself is accustomed to do in most cases) that they may the more easily attain the empty honors of this world, and then come to overweening pride.

"The first step, then, will be riches, the second honor, the third pride. From these three steps the evil one leads to all other vices."

By means of the speech St. Ignatius puts in Lucifer's mouth, he instructs the retreatant in the devil's art of seduction in order to show him how he could be tricked into making a wrong decision.

St. Ignatius presents three levels of temptation: riches, honor, pride. Certainly, the possession of material goods, which is what he means by "riches," is, from among all "the other things," the most removed from the core of the person. A sinful identification with these things will, therefore, be less persistent and less deceptive than is the case with those things that naturally have a greater affinity to the human person. But just because of the relative distance of material possessions, there is a danger that man will gradually and imperceptibly accustom himself to them, that he will become so personally involved and lost in "the other things" that he completely forgets about God. So a man could say to himself: "It won't hurt anything if I have an expensive car, own my own airplane, and take my vacation in Hawaii every summer." Of course, this need not hurt anything or anyone! But I can lose myself more and more in such things, and then pretty soon I will not hesitate to accept "the glory of this world" (Mt 4,8). And it is much more difficult to break away from this. A position in society, literary renown, or a reputation for scholarship leave me much less free than material possessions. Then the possibility of perhaps losing my

173

fame will make me fearful that I am losing absolutely everything. This means that I have attached myself to the things of this world, and that I will hold on to them at any price—ultimately, even against the will of God. It is not very far from here to an explicit rebellion against God.

There is, therefore, an unmistakable increase of intensity in the three levels of temptation that Ignatius proposes. This is not to say that the temptation to sin proceeds according to this order for every person. It is possible for sin to be realized in the realm of material goods. On the other hand, ambition and lust for power can appear in some men even though they do not have great possessions. Moreover, St. Ignatius is not particularly interested in urging the connection between wealth and pride. For if we look less at the objective order of material things and more at man's attitude toward them, then we will find a triplicity in St. Ignatius' thought that could perhaps be described as the *desire to possess,* the *desire to be somebody,* and the *desire to exist.*

We already said with regard to the Foundation of the Exercises that created reality gives man a place in which he can make his free choices. These are not necessarily between God and the devil—they can also have to do with genuine inner-worldly values. The things to be chosen are ambivalent in a neutral, not a pejorative, sense; they can be used for this or that; they possess a certain plasticity; they are waiting, as it were, for man to give them a positive value.

Now God's adversary, the father of lies and a murderer from the very beginning, uses this ambivalence as a point of departure for his deceits by making us very interested in these material goods: Man should have an intense desire to possess them, and he should be completely involved in taking care of them. A "desire to possess" of this type really is "wealth" in the broadest sense; it embraces not only material goods, but also spiritual values such as success, honor, cultural accomplishments. As the first level of temptation, this "desire to possess" does not go beyond the ambivalence of material goods. In fact, Satan emphasizes this ambivalence by pointing out the neutrality of all material things. He does this by suggesting such questions as: "Why worry? You shouldn't be suspicious! Isn't all of this in accordance with the moral law?" But the devil moves on immediately to the second level of temptation. He tries to bring a person beyond the still ambivalent "desire to possess" to the "desire to be somebody," and to a self-identification with the things he possesses. This switch goes almost unnoticed: Imperceptibly the standard of values is changed. A too close association with things takes a man's proper perspective away from him; he becomes so dependent on them that he is not even aware of this dependence, and in fact cannot be aware of it, since an awareness of this situation requires a certain distance from things—a distance which he has lost by reason of his identification with them.

The desire to be somebody leads ultimately to the desire to exist absolutely for self, and to the attempt to assert oneself unconditionally through an existential identification of self with one's possessions and capabilities. It even leads to an absolute self-assertion against God. This revolt can remain unthematic when a person "desires to exist" in opposition to pure goodness, truth, selflessness, and honesty. Thus a truly perfect Godlessness proceeds from an avaricious prostitution of oneself—from the desire to be rich. Nevertheless, it must be pointed out that there is a mutual relationship between Godlessness and the desire for wealth: Behind the desire to possess lurks a fundamental fear of life that is rooted in unbelief—in an existentially realized unbelief. This unbelief is not a mere abstraction; it consists in the fact that a person does not want his human existence to be based on God any more. Such a person knows deep down that he is not sufficient for himself, and that he cannot persevere all alone. Therefore, in the midst of this innerly threatening situation he must attach himself to material things and try to get his self-confidence from them. This simply means that he identifies himself with them.

175

II. *The Standard of Christ: His Call*

"In a similar way, we are to picture to ourselves the sovereign and true Commander, Christ our Lord.

1. "Consider Christ our Lord, standing in a lowly place in a great plain about the region of Jerusalem, His appearance beautiful and attractive.

2. "Consider how the Lord of all the world chooses so many persons, apostles, disciples, etc., and sends them throughout the whole world to spread His sacred doctrine among all men, no matter what their state or condition.

3. "Consider the address which Christ our Lord makes to all His servants and friends whom He sends on this enterprise, recommending to them to seek to help all, first by attracting them to the highest spiritual poverty, and should it please the Divine Majesty, and should He deign to choose them for it, even to actual poverty. Secondly, they should lead them to a desire for insults and contempt, for from these springs humility. Hence, there will be three steps: the first, poverty as opposed to riches; the second, insults or contempt as opposed to the honor of this world; the third, humility as opposed to pride. From these three steps, let them lead men to all other virtues."

Poverty here means the ability to leave things—a certain abandonment to trust in God. First of all, naturally, Ignatius is speaking of actual poverty. Something like insults and contempt is the natural result of detachment from worldly possessions (we are not just speaking of material goods, but also of spiritual values such as a career, a reputation, and so forth), even if it is not always expressed in the form of open ridicule. The person whose whole life is truly centered in God and who does not give himself completely to the things of this world, is, in the eyes of the world, stupid, backward, cowardly, and useless. The man who stays his distance from worldly goods and does not attach himself perfectly to them in the battle-ground of this world is always at a disadvantage to those who identify themselves completely with the weapons of this world. Certainly, good people and pious people are often more stupid than they should be; they are often less adroit and less competent than they should be. But a universally valid and necessary character-istic of the following of Christ is that those who take their Christianity seriously cannot be first in the race for worldly possessions.

The priest or layman who says to himself: My life must appear so and so; I want this salary, this much in the bank, this comfort, this success; that seems like the best job for me, and so forth—he is on the wrong path from the very beginning. And if he does not want to be "rich" in this way, but really wants to be "poor" in the Christian sense of the word, then he must expect to experience failures even in the Church, and not just in the profane world. Even in the Church, there are people who use their elbows, who push themselves forward, who try to get ahead with good means and with bad, and who identify their influence simply with the unfolding of the Kingdom of God. Whoever does not go along with them will certainly feel the consequences of it. And he exposes himself to that which Ignatius calls "insults and contempt."

If we do not want to fall for Lucifer's deceits in our service in the Church, we had better not expect a lot of outward success. And even interiorly, we will hardly be successful as we had hoped! Per-haps we will be declared saints after our death, but that will not interest us much then! At present, medals and ribbons are normally only given for worldly success. They are not generally given for those deeds that really usher in the Kingdom of God. Even in the Church, very little honor and recognition are given for selfless renunciation, steadfast perseverance, for sacrifice without looking for a reward, for an unconditional orientation toward the will of God in imitating the crucified Lord. There cannot be such recognition in the Church! True poverty of this kind naturally gives rise to humility which opens and frees one's heart. And Christian humility goes its own way without looking at itself, without expecting a reward; it knows that it is rich only in and through God, and in no other way.

Nevertheless, we must be aware of the fact that the attitudes desired by Christ and the attitudes desired by Lucifer can be mistaken for one another. Greed can hide under the disguise of poverty, and the seeking of insults and contempt can be a refined form of seeking recognition from others. One can be very proud in a shabby suit! These false forms are worlds apart from the poverty and humility Ignatius describes as the characteristics of the standard of Christ. These characteristics are only present when they are subject to the cross of Christ, when they are submerged in the daily fulfillment of duty, when they bring one in contact with the community in order to help others and to be ready to leave all judgment to Him. Only the person who, as it were naturally, chooses the more difficult way without proposing himself and his own method of working and his own form of the spiritual life as *the* only way or at least the most preferable way, can hope to have achieved in some degree the level of generosity that Christ expects from those enrolled under His banner.

20. The Sermon on the Mount
(161, 278)

Note

Even if we consider the Sermon on the Mount more of a literary composition of the evangelist than an exact account of one of Jesus' sermons, at any rate we must accept the text as it stands as a collection of the authentic teachings of our Lord that were directed to His disciples, and that have universal validity. This text contains the law of the New Testament that is inseparably bound to the Person of Christ: This law is supported and sanctioned by His existence, and really announces His coming. Even this law would only be a dead letter without Christ! This law can only be fulfilled in the power of His Spirit. This is no mere example of norms that a philosopher could arrive at by means of a metaphysical-ethical deduction. The new law of the Lord can only be fulfilled in close association with Him—by following Him.

I. *The Beatitudes* (Mt 5,3–12)

Normally, these statements of Jesus are accepted as very self-evident. But they are not at all easy to understand! It will not hurt anything to register the complaint of an, as it were, un-converted heart against them in order to bring out their full meaning. In the eyes of the world, the individuals mentioned here, the poor and the sorrowful, the meek and those believing

179

in justice, the pure of heart, the peacemakers, those persecuted for justice' sake, are anything but blessed. Nor are Jesus' words to them meant to be taken in this sense: "Yes, you are having a rough time now, but just wait, and in a short time you will be that much better off!" Rather, Jesus says that the person immersed in the depths of this poverty, of this sorrow, of this meekness, of this thirsting for a justice that seems ridiculous to the world, of this emptiness of heart, of this ability to give in to others because he does not want to hold on to the disputed object as a result of the peacefulness of his heart, of this mercy . . . *already possesses blessedness.* It gushes up, so to speak, out of the innermost core of these highly praised attitudes. To be sure, we must experience that as a result of faith, and we can only experience it if we follow Christ. Only the person who can muster the courage to accept the word of the Lord, and to be convinced that he is not a fool or an idiot if he is not rich, lascivious, revengeful—only the person who really believes in the cross of the Lord, accepts it, and makes it a reality in his life, knows that the only true happiness of this life is buried in the inner core of these praised attitudes, and that this happiness is, as it were, called into being by the faithful reception of Jesus' word.

We should try to go through each of the beatitudes with this in mind! We can only understand them as the wisdom of the cross because Christ has come and is present. For our sake, He abandoned riches for poverty, a happy life for sorrow, justice for injustice, and love for persecution. Therefore, these things, which would otherwise be black abysses of folly and confinement, truly contain hidden within themselves the only happiness of any value: the blessedness that is God alone.

II. *The Task of the Disciples* (Mt 5,13–16)

We who are priests are "the salt of the earth" and "the light" in the darkness of the "world." Let us try to put together for ourselves all the statements in the New Testament about the mission of the priest, and then try to apply them to ourselves. They apply to all of us who, through the grace of God in Jesus Christ, have become or will become priests of this new and eternal covenant. They apply to us because they first applied to the one High Priest, the Incarnate Son of God. Then we should ask ourselves whether or not our lives really offer the bread of eternal life to our fellow men, the nourishment of the truth of God and the cup of His water; and we should ask ourselves whether or not we are corrupting our brothers and sisters by our vapidity, choking their hunger for eternal life with our filth; and we should ask ourselves whether or not we are the ones that our Lord has threatened to vomit up because we are neither hot nor cold. Do we have the glowing hearts, the shining eyes, the true and honest words in which our brothers and sisters encounter God Himself, His light, His faithfulness and love?

III. *The Old and the New Commandment* (Mt 5,17 ff.)

We cannot peacefully and self-contentedly pass by the inexorability of Jesus' statement: "For I tell you that your goodness must be a far better thing than the goodness of the Scribes and Pharisees before you can set foot in the Kingdom of heaven!" We also are in danger of becoming religious legalists and champions of certain accidental Church practices—the very same thing that our Lord condemned the Scribes and Pharisees for. Generally speaking, the Scribes and Pharisees were men who had put the letter of the law in the place of God. Are we really a lot different from them in this regard? Do we not all too often make an anti-essence out of the essence of religion? Certainly, we should not be self-willed men even under the New Testament —men who completely disregard the structures, laws, and practices of the Church. But given the necessary loyalty to the established norms, this still remains true: If our goodness is only the goodness of the Scribes and Pharisees, if our worship is a cult of the letter instead of the spirit—a worship that ends with the

181

Church instead of being a service of the Church rendered to God and men, then we are not men and priests according to the will of Jesus Christ! The commandments preached by Christ are not perfectly observed when they are only observed according to the letter.

According to the words of the Lord (Mt 5,21–26), the fifth commandment of the decalogue is only fulfilled when this commandment has changed into a boundless attitude of love. What Jesus says here can be applied without qualification to all the fights among the clergy—those sad tales of jealousy between priests and religious, the self-righteousness and passion to know and to act better than anyone else, the dissembling conduct lacking in honesty, selflessness, and respect for others. Christ demands that, in the midst of all conventions, we are always penetrated with honesty and the Spirit. We should hear this coming loud and clear through Jesus' words: What are you doing with my Sacrifice, which is also yours, when you partake in it with a loveless heart? Is that not a betrayal? Go and reconcile yourself with your brothers! Then you should celebrate the Sacrifice!

The external fulfillment of the sixth commandment must proceed from an inner purity (Mt 5,27–32). It must be an honest and sincere self-conquest; it should not be a cowardly and melancholy repression, an acting-as-if, a weak and sickly fear of life, but it should be the attitude that was first brought into this world by Christ Himself. This attitude only makes sense in Christ and with Christ; it is only because of Him that it is not the ultimate in folly.

Again, according to Jesus' words (Mt 5,33–37), our truthfulness should be a clear proclamation that God has entered into conversation with us, and that He has raised to Himself the story of our human reality. It is said of clerics—frequently not without right—that they do not especially cultivate an honest, unvarnished openness. We should bear in mind that it is our duty to speak the words of eternal life, and that our falsity should really take our breath away. Christ said that those men are blessed who do not try to lie themselves out of every difficult situation by the use of all possible diplomatic skills. These are the men who possess in the Lord and in His truth the only wisdom and power that is worth anything.

Jesus demands that those who follow Him give up the right of revenge and learn to love their enemies with their whole heart (Mt 5,38–48). Otherwise, they will not be children of the Father in heaven, nor will they find that perfection that leads to God.

The first four verses of Matthew's sixth chapter deal with the giving of alms and with the true reward that only God can bestow—He who alone searches the heart of man. His reward is completely different from that of the world: It is the interior love of God; it is His glory that He alone gives; it is a living reward that must be believed, and that can only be received in a love that does not think of payment, but seeks God. Therefore, the "reward-ethic" of Christianity is in no way a kind of commercial policy in the moral order that reaches into the next world. It is something that a person who does not have deep faith, who is not loyal to the cross of Christ and does not derive from the cross his ability to forget himself and to abandon himself, cannot possibly possess.

The words of the Lord about the prayer of those who want to follow Him are also noted down in the Sermon on the Mount (Mt 6,5–15). Some of them sound almost like a disavowal of any form of solemn liturgy. The text does not actually mean this, but we should pay close attention to Jesus' criticism of a purely institutional cult. When a man's heart is not in it, and when the liturgy is not performed in a personal way (which does not mean "individualistically"), the Lord is not particularly interested in the liturgy even of His Church. The living power of our prayer comes to us from the heart of our Lord. The inner power of our prayer stems from Him and through Him has already reached into heaven. And when we pray in the Spirit of

Christ, then even if our prayer may appear to be very poor, empty and dull, it is still penetrated with the mystery of God.

"When you fast do not make contorted faces like those hypocrites . . ." (Mt 6,16–18). So we should keep our fasting to ourselves. Of course, Jesus does not want merely intellectual religiosity. He wants us to feel real hunger for the sake of the Kingdom of God. But precisely because the Lord wants us to give up material goods for the sake of God, He demands that it be done with a joyful expression. And the attitude of perfect openness to God cannot be made into some kind of a sensation. When we prefer the love of God to the comfort of our bodily life, when we, as it were, relativize our bodily needs and accept the fact of our indigence, then no Christian can lament over this. Hunger and thirst for God and the knowledge that man cannot live from the food of this world alone, but that God's goodness sustains him, are the basic diet of ordinary, everyday Christian living. This is true happiness.

Matthew 6,19–34 presents Jesus' teaching about the right way to go about gathering goods and about trust in the heavenly Father. Chapter seven relates different wise sayings. Heartless judgment of others is condemned in 7,1–5. Here Jesus demands that plain humility from us that requires us to present our case openly, seriously, and honestly without being dependent on the applause of others, and also without judging others when God has pointed out a different way to them. There are some more recommendations about prayer in Matthew 7,7–12. The final warnings (Mt 7,13–29) are penetrated with the spirit of the meditation on the Two Standards and the spirit of the other decision-meditations. We should reflect on Jesus' words about the small gate, the narrow way, about avoiding false teachers, the parable of the good and the bad tree, the refusal to utter empty "Lord-Lords," the story of the house built on rock. Let us think these things over and see how they apply to us.

The Sermon on the Mount tells each one of us what we need to know in order to make the right decision in this retreat. It presents us with the law and the spirit of Jesus Christ, with the courage of the eight beatitudes, with that plain humility that is based on God alone and is desirous of nothing else—and is prepared to lead a hidden life without sensations, with the troubling unrest that is rooted deep in our hearts which only God sees, and without whose presence the hours and paths of our life cannot bring forth what they should bring forth: that is, a believing, hoping, loving total surrender of the whole man to God Who will only be found as the Father of our Lord Jesus Christ. He will be found only through Jesus and in the spirit of His heart—that heart that loved all the way to the cross in order to make all things new.

21. The Three Classes of Men
(149–157)

As a further decision-meditation, St. Ignatius presents the parable of the three classes of men. By means of this consideration, the exercitant's attitude toward a right decision is supposed to be further developed. After the usual preparatory prayer, the exercitant should make the following preludes:

"FIRST PRELUDE. This is the history of the Three Classes of Men. Each of them acquired ten thousand ducats, but not entirely as they should have, for the love of God. They all wish to save their souls and find peace in God our Lord by ridding themselves of the burden arising from the attachment to the sum acquired, which impedes the attainment of this end.

"SECOND PRELUDE. This is a mental representation of the place. Here it will be to behold myself standing in the presence of God our Lord and of all His saints, that I may know and desire what is more pleasing to His Divine Goodness.

"THIRD PRELUDE. This is to ask for what I desire. Here it will be to beg for the grace to choose what is more for the glory of His Divine Majesty and the salvation of my soul."

Then Ignatius sketches the three different classes of men that we are supposed to consider:

"THE FIRST CLASS. They would like to rid themselves of the attachment they have to the sum acquired in order to find peace in God our Lord and assure their salvation, but the hour of death comes, and they have not made use of any means.

"THE SECOND CLASS. They want to rid themselves of the attachment, but they wish to do so in such a way that they retain what they have acquired, so that God is to come to what they desire, and they do not decide to give up the sum of money in order to go to God, though this would be the better way for them.

"THE THIRD CLASS. These want to rid themselves of the attachment, but they wish to do so in such a way that they desire neither to retain nor to relinquish the sum acquired. They seek only to will and not will as God our Lord inspires them, and as seems better for the service and praise of the Divine Majesty. Meanwhile, they will strive to conduct themselves as if every attachment to it had been broken. They will make efforts neither to want that, nor anything else, unless the service of God our Lord alone move them to do so. As a result, the desire to be better able to serve God our Lord will be the cause of their accepting anything or relinquishing it.

"I will make use of the same three colloquies employed in the preceding contemplation on the Two Standards.

"It should be noted that when we feel an attachment opposed to actual poverty or a repugnance to it, when we are not indifferent to poverty and riches, it will be very helpful in order to overcome the inordinate attachment, even though corrupt nature rebel against it, to beg our Lord in the colloquies to choose us to serve Him in actual poverty. We should insist that we desire it, beg for it, plead for it, provided, of course, that it be for the service and praise of the Divine Goodness."

In the meditation on the Foundation, the readiness for the "more" of the objectively better means, which is an essential attitude for making a retreat, found its concrete expression. If God demands that we make use of the means that is objectively better, then we must try to find this means. Therefore, through his indifference the exercitant is supposed to remove himself from the things he is familiar with, and he is supposed to try to see them as they really are. Given this attitude of indifference right at the beginning of the retreat, the presupposition is made that the will of God coincides with the objective order of things that is deducible from creation. Thus, he should arrive at the means that is "more" conducive to the end through an understanding of the objective inter-connection of things. This knowledge is guided by the unceasing battle against the prejudices and inclinations which are the result of original sin. For example, whoever would try to find out whether or not he should become a priest— by basing himself on his readiness to embrace the "more" (here this means: to embrace the objectively better means), and by taking his original indifference into consideration, must declare his willingness to enter the priesthood if he finds out that he has all the necessary requirements for this vocation.

If the exercitant has seen things as they are, then he has reflected on his own sinfulness and has discovered himself even more fundamentally subject to the complete disposition of God. For as a sinner before God, he is even much less than he was as a creature before God. When he fully experiences the ruin of his existence that is the result of his own guilt, and when, as it were, he tumbles into the abyss of his own guilt, then it is not the God Who is the builder of the world (which pertains more to the meditation on the Foundation!) that he encounters, but he encounters the Lord Who is merciful love itself. Man in his sinfulness must allow himself to be loved by this Lord without being able to find even a trace of a motive for it in himself. The incomprehensible element in this human existence is that it is able to receive from God the gift of coming before the Crucified who came in our weakness and necessity in order to try to win our love. We have already met the graceful King of our hearts— the King who loved us even to His death on the cross—in the meditations on the Kingdom of Christ and the Two Standards. We should surrender ourselves to this Lord unconditionally. At present, we do not know what God has in store for us, but we have offered ourselves to this Lord Who has shared our destiny and our painfully poor life and death—a death that is the final culmination of toil, poverty, and self-denial. We have offered to follow Him, insofar as it is pleasing to His Divine Majesty, in greater spiritual poverty, and even in actual poverty, if He should see fit to call us to it.

This attitude is presupposed in the meditation on the three classes of men, but then it is surpassed in a free and total surrender to the increasingly greater love of God—a surrender which, in a certain sense, even goes beyond the cross of Christ. This surrender does not take anything away from the cross. Rather, its true value lies in the ever greater, broader, and completely incomprehensible dimension of God's absolutely free love, and in the dimension of the unsearchable decree of his holy will that touches me and me alone. As a result of this very personal call from God, I should place myself in readiness for the greater and final "more." But with this step, the Foundation and the unconditional desire to follow Christ, which is the fruit of the meditation on the Kingdom of Christ, is actually surpassed. Of course, this choice of the love of God must be hidden in the apparent prosaism of my days and nights. Particularly in a retreat, this love must be brought to bear on all of the concrete questions that are related to my decision. I must love God right here in such a way that the determination of my own particular form of following Christ is completely in the hands of God. From His decision there is no appeal, and there is no other approach to Him but in Him. In the meditation on the three classes of men, St. Ignatius gives an example of the attitude required for such a choice.

Each of the classes of men presented here by St. Ignatius has acquired ten thousand ducats. In the place of money, we can easily substitute something else. We can, for example, imagine a number of priests who have each acquired an honored position in the Church. Each one wants the position, has the necessary talents for it, and can really accomplish great things for the Kingdom of God in it. As Ignatius does for his possessors of the ten thousand ducats, we also must presuppose that each of these priests has acquired his position honestly and exercises it in the way it should be exercised. There is no sin involved in the acquisition. Therefore, according to the principles of the moral law each one may retain his honored post. Everything seems to be in good order. What more can we ask?

It is possible for a cleric, even from very natural motives, to carry out his office with scrupulous honesty. From an ethical point of view, this is perfectly justifiable. Humanly speaking, this makes a lot of sense. And yet, each of the priests in our three classes can say to himself: I have not acquired my position from a complete and unreserved love of God; it is objectively possible for me to integrate it into this love, but I have not striven for it and acquired it as a part of my life as sketched out by God. To this extent, but only to this extent, each priest feels that his position is some kind of foreign body in his Christian existence.

Obviously, all of us find many things such as this in our own lives. Each of us must begin with the things of this world, and has already discovered many "positions" or many "ten thousand ducats" before it even occurred to us to ask how it is related to our love of God—a love that can only be an answer to the definite and unique love of God that goes out to each one in a different way. Since we do not begin our existence absolutely, and since we do not construct it, as it were, from nothing, since we do not build it up from the glowing coals of our love in such a way that everything else is a gradual and exclusive realization of our love of God, we cannot act otherwise. Nevertheless, a situation such as this which is perfectly legitimate from the point of view of moral theology, can seem to be a hindrance to a perfect incorporation of the love of God into the structure of our human reality. This is just the case with the priests in our meditation, as it is with the possessors of the ten thousand ducats in the parable of St. Ignatius. They do not know whether or not they can fulfill their office in their personal lives in such a way that it is a realization of their pure love and selfless dedication to God. Of course, it is obvious that this position is not opposed to their Christian existence in the same way that a sin would be, but neither can we say that something, which in itself can be integrated into the love of God, by that very fact can be integrated by a particular individual.

The priests of our parable do not want to save their souls by a minimum observance of the law. This would be legitimate, but it is not the problem of this meditation. They want to find God in the highest perfection and therefore "in all things." It is precisely for this reason that they are fearful of their salvation, even though they have not violated the objective norms of morality. In this fear for their salvation, they ask themselves about the order of everything in their lives. All may be in the best of order and in perfect conformity with the moral law—so much so that with a little effort they may produce much good. But can the individuals concerned be satisfied with this? The meditation on the Two Standards impressed upon us that everything not integrated into the love of God—even though it could be integrated—is a foreign body in the totality of our Christian existence, and is really a part of that wealth that seeks to absolutize itself and therefore become the starting point of true sin. The honored position of our priests is clearly a foreign body of this kind: It did not come to them from that love of God that is supposed to well forth from the depths of the human heart. Whatever takes place in the life of a man must always be integrated into this love, so that everything in his life can become the glorious carrying out and the blessed concretization of the one and only love of God. As long as there is anything in man's existence that is not absorbed by this love, he cannot find God in all things.

All of the clerics in the parable would like to attain the lofty goal of this love. They know that the weight of this impediment, of this foreign body that they are clinging to, must be put aside before they can reach it. Now they are faced with the question of how to accomplish this. Each one of them must free himself from the foreign body in his Christian existence before he can properly

191

hear the call of God directed to him: He must give up his attachment to the honored position he has acquired. This, too, must take place in the right way! The meditation on the three classes of men is supposed to lead to the avoidance of two false ways of solving this problem. One of the false solutions is simply to walk away from the position. The other would be the immediate decision to keep the acquired position and to reform it, that is, to try to inform it anew with the love of God. Actually, neither of these solutions gets at the real problem. Here it is neither a matter of a radical renunciation of the "thing" in question, nor of its incorporation into the dynamism of life that aims at God alone. For in both cases, a decision would have to be made. There is no question here of a concrete decision, but only of the proper religious *attitude* which should precede such a decision. This attitude is the absolutely open surrender of oneself to the sovereign will of God. He should decree what I choose. He should determine my relationship to everything that concretely hinders my total gift of myself to God. In this attitude, the carefully evaluating indifference of the Foundation is surpassed. The unappealable will of the ever greater God decides above and beyond all objective circumstances, yes, and even beyond the cross of Christ—and therefore, it even goes beyond the search for that which is more difficult. A genuine choice in this retreat should grow out of this abandonment to the will of God. The men in the three groups presented in the meditation know that very well. Nevertheless, they react differently.

Those in the first class would like to meet, out of a pure love of God, the immeasurable and irreducible will of God in all things—even in the honored position that is in question. But because they are afraid of the immeasurable love of God that can decree this or that, life or death, they just stay put, they do not go out of themselves, they do not surrender themselves to God's unconditioned love by which they would be able to receive from God either the acceptance or the rejection of the position. Therefore, in the last analysis they do not really love the ever greater God, but remain right where they are. And the strange thing is that they still honestly desire to save their souls. But from a fear of love, they do not employ any means to this end. Right up to the moment of their death, they remain steadfast in this situation, and so they leave the concrete questionability of human existence—that which has touched them personally—unanswered. They want to serve God, they want to belong to Him, they want to be saved, but only in their own way, and with reservations with regard to the love of God in the critical area of their own human existence.

The clerics in the second class also want to love God and to let Him guide them, but this desire is really a self-willed decision as to how they are going to realize their love of God. They say that they want to love God with their whole heart, but they want to do it in such a way that they keep their honored position and use it for the greater glory of God. They want to show how ready they are to sacrifice themselves, and to work for God in their beloved post. Even before they ask God how He wants them to serve Him, they have already decided what form their love will take. Thus, they do not really want to find Him in all things, but only in very definite things. They do not want to admit that there is a genuine possibility of loving God in the apparently senseless giving up of their position. They do not want to admit that folly and emptiness can be a true realization of the love of the cross. Persons of this class do not consider the giving up of something from the point of view of God and His love. In His eyes, renunciation and acceptance are the same thing, so that both of them are real possibilities for loving God. But it is up to God alone to dispose of these things. Those in this class are not one bit better than those in the first class. Both are equally far removed from the attitude of the third class.

The third class seeks to love God in the way that He wants to be loved. The men of this class do not prefer to keep or to give up those things that are to be integrated into their lives. Certainly, this form of the love of God is most difficult, and it

G   193 requires great effort to put it in practice. Even the love of the cross is both surpassed and humbled by this speechless, absolute openness toward God. Those in this group want Him to have the complete disposition of themselves. Because this is what the person of the third class wants, he first of all struggles against his own inner attachment to things in the spirit of the Kingdom of Christ and the Two Standards. Then he begs God actually to take these things away from him so that he can be ruled by God alone and His love. From this angle, the possibility of giving something up does not seem so terrifying. God alone is the source of all movement; now the Kingdom of God is really close, is contained either in giving up or in keeping, in life and in death. Now a man has really become a child who does not die of fright when God approaches either in the one garment or the other. In this class, the love of God for man and the love of man for God can meet each other in any form. God alone arranges the way in which that happens. This "way" is not a fate that man cannot avoid—it is God's response to man's love. If we have this disposition, then God can truly communicate His will to each and every one of us.

At the conclusion of this meditation, the retreatant should make the triple colloquies as he did in the meditation on the Two Standards: With Mary who said, "Be it done to me according to Your word!," with Jesus Who took up our life and death for our sake, and with the Father Who is the sourceless love from which the Incarnation of the Son proceeds—the love which is surpassed by no other, and which cannot be measured or established by any other.

The retreatant should let himself be led by the grace which the Mother of divine grace by the acceptance of her call from God mediated for him and will mediate for all eternity. He should open his heart to the free disposition of God because he has entered into a new dimension of reality which was made accessible to him by Jesus' death and resurrection. And finally, he should submit himself to the Father, Who gives us this love

194

for Himself in the way and in the form that He desires. When that happens, then the Kingdom of God has arrived for us, then we are men in whom the will of God is freely and perfectly realized. Christian and especially priestly existence should not be anything else.

22. The Three Degrees of Humility

(162–168)

Preliminary Consideration

St. Ignatius wants the retreatant to consider the three kinds of humility before making his decision. He should mull over these ideas for a whole day. "Before entering upon the Choice of a Way of Life, in order that we may be filled with love of the true doctrine of Christ our Lord, it will be very useful to consider attentively the following Three Kinds of Humility. These should be thought over from time to time during the whole day, and the three colloquies should also be added . . `.`" (no. 164). Actually, St. Ignatius is concerned here with the three degrees of the love of God, but he uses the word "love" only sparingly, and generally speaks of "humility"—the generous service of God. He feels that the essence of love does not consist of words, but of service and deeds.

It should be mentioned right in the beginning that the kinds of humility under consideration are of a positive nature. They cannot be distinguished clearly from one another. They are rather three sides of the one Christian approach to the service of God. Therefore, it is better to speak of three degrees of humility rather than three kinds or types.

St. Ignatius does not intend here to go beyond the readiness—

proposed in the meditation on the Two Standards—to share poverty and insults with Christ, and so to fight against the deceptive maneuvers of Satan that he employs against us by hiding behind things that are in themselves indifferent. Nor does St. Ignatius intend to go beyond the picture he drew for us in the meditation on the three classes of men—a picture of the love of the cross that is surpassed by a total surrender to the incalculable disposition of God's love. Here he no longer speaks explicitly of the lofty heights of the love of God that he described as characteristic of the third class. What he does here is simply to treat the decision-attitude, which has already been aroused, from another angle.

I. *The First Degree of Humility*

This first degree contains a modest, fundamentally humble, love of God. With a certain indifference, a person of this degree places himself as a creature squarely on a solid foundation of facts: He is fully committed to the will of God, which has given him an existence ordered to a supernatural end.

St. Ignatius connects the difference between the first and second degrees of humility with the distinction between mortal and venial sin. This is a repetition of the time-honored teaching, which was also proposed by St. Thomas Aquinas, that a man is absolutely deprived of the end of his existence by a mortal sin, and thus completely rejects the will of God. If he is guilty of a venial sin, he can still attain his end, but he is not really serious enough about the means. If someone is absolutely determined to avoid all mortal sin, but is determined to avoid mortal sin only, then this is equivalent to the resolve not to allow himself to be turned aside from the goal of his existence. But it is still an attitude subject to a certain amount of adaptation and improvisation. Such a person does not demand any more of himself than the attainment of his eternal goal. Such an attitude is no easy thing to achieve! St. Ignatius presupposes as a condition of this attitude that a person who has it would not even consider committing a mortal sin in order to save his life or to become the lord of all created things. Nevertheless, this kind of "humble" man does not order his life ruthlessly according to God's plan, nor does he open up all things in his life unconditionally to the will of God, so that he can see them as they truly are and use them as means to his goal. Despite his resolve never to commit a mortal sin, he is always in danger of compromising himself.

II. *The Second Degree of Humility*

"The second degree of humility is more perfect . . ." (no. 166). This degree of humility is identical with that distance from things which is attained in active indifference. The formula used here by St. Ignatius echoes the Foundation. In any event, a man of this degree is honestly striving for the *"Tantum-quantum"* of the Foundation, even if he is still not clearly trying to reach the *"magis."* He does not hesitate to choose a definite means when he sees that it is more suitable than others to attain the end established for him by God. To have attained this degree of humility in one's daily life is a great virtue. Who among us chooses the better means of serving God in the rush of everyday living, does not prefer riches to poverty or a long life to a short life? This shows that the second degree of humility is a continuation of the first. Ultimately, a person will only strive for the second degree of humility because he has set his sights on God alone, and has attained a state of active indifference with regard to all things. For the absolutizing of any created value produces a perversion of man's basic direction toward God. When a man identifies himself with a relative, contingent thing out of a false sense of anxiety, and in this way determines his attitude toward God, he has either already rejected God, or is at least ready to reject Him by committing a mortal sin. Therefore, if the desire for the first degree of humility is genuine and constant it must develop into the second degree.

III. *The Third Degree of Humility*

"The third degree of humility is the most perfect . . ." This degree
of humility consists simply in the will—which we have tried to
arouse in ourselves in the meditations on the Kingdom of Christ
and the Two Standards—to choose the cross from a love for
Christ and from the concrete experience of His life and death,
provided only that the honor of the Divine Majesty is not thereby
diminished. St. Ignatius realized in his own life the following of
the Crucified—but always with a discretion that was peculiar to
him. On some occasions in his following of the condemned Christ,
he accepted being held for a fool, and he bore the insults of the
world; on other occasions, he did not hesitate to bring another
into court in order to protect his own reputation, if he was
convinced that in the long run the honor and service of God
would also suffer if his own reputation were injured.

In the third degree of humility, a love for the cross of the
Lord is lived out that no longer seeks this-worldly reasons. It is
simply presupposed that whoever follows the Lord and Master,
the Crucified, Him Who is a scandal and foolishness to the
world, is on the right path. A person of the third degree desires
to walk no other path but that of an unconditional following of
Christ—always, of course, with that discretion which does not
neglect the greater honor of God. In order to grasp what is meant
here, we should consider Jesus' conduct before the High Priest.
When a servant struck Him, he protested and said: "If I have
spoken wrongly, bear witness to the wrong; but if I have spoken
rightly, why do you strike me?" (Jn 18,23). We should note
carefully: Through the added condition, namely, to choose the
poverty, insults, and foolishness of Christ "whenever the praise
and glory of the Divine Majesty would be equally served," a
following of Christ, which dispenses itself from the loftiness of
the love of the cross and therefore falls short of it, is not
proposed.

The third degree of humility contains an audacious love for

199

the crucified Lord—a love that does not seek a this-worldly foundation. For this reason, therefore, it is so subject to the unsearchable disposition of the love of God that it must, as it were, set itself at a distance from itself. The true lover of the crucified Christ has leaped out of self, and has left self completely; he no longer returns to self and reflects on himself—he remains standing under the cross of Christ. Therefore, it is no longer of great interest to him whether or not in his own actions, in these actions or those actions, God is objectively more honored and his own salvation made more secure. The Christian of the third degree of humility does not consider himself at all. As a follower of Christ, he is completely subject to the unconditioned disposition of God.

IV. *The Inner Unity of the Three Degrees of Humility*

We have already said that the first degree must grow into the active indifference of the second degree in order to assert itself, and that the second degree only exists to bring about the realization of man's progress toward his final end. The inner unity of humility also embraces the third degree. In this connection, we could also go into the theological question whether or not God has arranged things in this world in such a way that, when we have attained our final end, we have attained less than we really could have attained; or whether, when we have attained our final end, we have actually done everything that was concretely possible for us. In other words, does God not see to it with His grace (which does not mean that we have nothing to do with it!) that a man, who has attained the first degree of humility by the end of his life, has adequately realized the second degree because, at least in death, he has progressed from passive to active indifference?

We can gather from the words of St. Ignatius that the third degree is dependent on certain conditions, and therefore cannot be put into practice at all times and in all places. All of us cannot indulge in the folly of Christianity in the way that many saints of the past have done. We may not deliberately make a fool out of ourselves in the eyes of the world for the sake of Christ. No one can act in this way without being called to it. Conduct of this kind always demands the corresponding interior growth and disposition—the necessary external circumstances are not enough. Obviously, we should not look down on such extreme forms of the following of Christ as we find in the lives of certain people, for example in a Matt Talbot. But we should never forget that these things can only be done discreetly—no matter how odd they may seem.

Caution is required in this matter, and therefore heroic expressions of the desire to follow Christ must be formulated very discretely. In any event, they must be a concrete expression of our attachment to the Church. St. Ignatius says in number 170 of the book of the Exercises with regard to the retreat-decision: "It is necessary that all matters of which we wish to make a choice be either indifferent or good in themselves, and such that they are lawful within our Holy Mother, the hierarchical Church, and not bad or opposed to her." Perhaps we might consider in this regard what happened to St. Francis of Assisi with regard to his ideal of poverty. His passionate desire was to imitate Jesus' poverty down to the very last detail. The limitation of this ideal by the necessary Church authority became for St. Francis a life-long suffering that was both painful and tragic. A truly great love of the cross, therefore, must always be very skeptical of itself, because ultimately only from the observance of the commandments can we be sure that this love is really present. Thus, even in the third degree of humility we must always do what we are prepared to do in the first degree. The third degree is absolutely unattainable, if it is not carried along by the first and second degrees. "Every man who knows my commandments and obeys them is the man who really loves me . . ." (Jn 14,21).

Even though the third degree of humility is very holy, and even though it is very suitable for the priests of the New Testament who necessarily profess it through the sacramental offering of the Sacrifice of Christ, still it is anticipated and surpassed by the necessity of suffering and dying. At least in death, man is the poorest of all: empty, weak, and deprived of all the honors of this world. This is truly the end of the line. And if this is so, then it seems that the third degree of humility is a practicing anticipation of what God gives each man to do: to die in Christ absolutely poor and empty. But if a person wants to die as the first degree of humility demands that he should, then he must have approached death his whole life long by striving for the third degree of humility. The first degree can only be fully realized when the time comes for it to be exercised if there has been constant progress toward the third degree. Thus, the life of the Christian is necessarily a mixture of the three degrees of humility. But in the last analysis, only God decides which degree must be practiced and when.

23. The Priesthood

Note

After each of the programmatic decision-meditations, St. Ignatius puts the weight of the Exercises, as far as solving problems is concerned, right on the shoulders of the exercitant. In this way, he brings home to him that he should further consider certain points.

We want to close this section of the Exercises, corresponding to the "second week" of the thirty-day retreat, with a meditation on the priesthood of the New Testament. In the thirty-day retreat, there is plenty of time to consider the public life of our Lord. In the light of Jesus' public life, we who are priests, whose duty it is to continue His priestly mission, should discover how to shape our lives.

I. *The Priesthood and the Incarnation of the Word*

Just as human existence is radicated in Christ Jesus, so also is the priesthood of the New Testament. Its reality comes from Christ and is inseparable from him. The priesthood is not something accidentally tacked onto Jesus' life. Nor is it something that was only realized later on in His life. As the Incarnate Son of God, He is always a born priest. The moment the Word expresses Himself as a creature in order to be completely with us, and to announce what God thinks of human existence—from that moment Christ is essentially God's high priest, the true Mediator who actually binds God and the world together. This makes Him present to us as the openly revealed mystery of God and at the same time as a listening creature—as the one through Whom we all have access to the holiness of heaven and from Whom we all are truly born of God. Only the absolute nearness of God, given in the Incarnation, permits man's freedom to fulfill itself so completely that its worship of God always penetrates into the depths of God. By reason of His incarnational nature, Christ can give everything to God: true prayer that unites heaven and earth, a heart that captures God's love so that He can pour it out onto the whole world, a sacrifice that does not just mean emptiness and poverty, but a divine-human fullness. Thus, Christ is the eternal communication center who makes possible the holy conversation between God and men, between God and the whole world.

If our priesthood is essentially inseparable from the Incarnation of the Word, then it can only be the continuing realization of this medium between God and humanity. And if that is so, then we must conclude that it is the living sign of God's grace; it is the sign that His Kingdom has come and is safely planted in the world. For this reason, the world can manifest itself as God's own living room, as the physical tangibility of grace.

Of course, we must speak of the glorious power of our priesthood with great modesty and reservation. The priests of the New Testament are not magic wands of grace. Just as was the case for the Son of Man, the transcendent God does not gesticulate in them, hiding, as it were, under an earthly disguise that really has nothing in common with God. In their own human reality, they should bring to fulfillment the gift of God's grace and the unimaginable nearness of His mystery. In addition, priests must be aware of their own creaturehood. Thus, they must be ready to entrust themselves more and more to the mystery of the ever greater God, and so, exposed to the obscurity of God, allow their hearts to be absorbed by Him.

The unmixed, inseparable unity of the divine and the human that determines the reality of Jesus Christ is continued in our priesthood. His unity brings it about that our life is an ineffable mystery of being a human being—a mystery that only possesses itself by continually expressing God. Our inclusion in the priestly life of Jesus should be the boundless joy of our days and nights. But it should also be a terrifying experience that enflames our hearts to such an extent that there is no turning back, no escape. When God's call comes to us to continue Jesus' priestly life, nothing else has any real attraction for us. In that moment, the ineffable—the ineffable alone—has become the goal of our life in such a way that our life is dedicated to a pure and simple giving from then on. It is dedicated to a giving that is only itself if it is God's giving. If we really bring the grace of God with our words and with sacramental signs, and if we bring grace in such a way that we personally must be involved so that grace is not taken from us as candy from a vending machine, and if God lets us dispense grace as His *and* ours, it still remains unimpeachably true that He alone gives grace. He can also give his grace independently of us. No matter how exalted the priesthood of the New Testament may be, we can never force God to resign in our favor! Our authorization does not oblige Him to retreat into eternity and stay there.

II. *Cult and Kerygma in the Priesthood of the New Testament*

In the priesthood of the New Testament, liturgical functions and kerygmatic preaching are always inseparably united. A limitation of the priesthood to the liturgical service would not be in accord with Scripture. The priesthood of the New Law is not designated in Scripture from the liturgical function—the New Testament reserves this for Christ. The naming of priests and bishops is based on a missionary and directive function with regard to the community. Naturally, this is not meant to deny that the priests of the New Testament in a very true sense stand before God in the name of the community as official cult figures. Since our priesthood is the essential continuation of the high priestly office of the Incarnate Word of God, both elements—liturgical worship of God and speaking in His name—must form an inner unity. Our liturgical, strictly sacramental function can only have its validity from God's mystery that has been spoken to us; it is this mystery that ushers our cult into the depths of the divinity. And our prophetic kerygma is ultimately nothing but a repetition of the word of God that came into our world, bringing grace along with it. The teaching office of the New-Testament priesthood gets its inner power from the possession of the sacramental words. The living word, which gives a definite spatio-temporal reality to the transcendent grace of God, is spoken by the New-Testament minister of the divine worship primarily at the altar as a sacramental word. But since this "graced" word necessarily reaches out into the whole world, and since it only makes sense inasmuch as it is directed to all men, the priest of the New Testament must bring the word of grace to man by his preaching and teaching.

Despite their inseparability, liturgical worship and prophetic sending are two different functions of the priesthood of the New Testament. Depending on the concrete call of each individual, either the one or the other can be predominant. There are and should be priests who spend most of their time with the liturgy. Others are primarily involved in preaching or in doing acts of charity. A long time ago, St. Paul said that he did very little baptizing, since his mission was to preach the word. But no matter where the emphasis is placed, the liturgy and the sacraments should never be neglected, nor should the drive be abandoned to bring God to men and men to God. It takes a sending of this kind—in our own view, at least—for the priesthood of the New Testament to achieve the existential determination that distinguishes it from the other modes of Christian existence, that is, from the lay state or the life of a monk.

III. *Office and Life*

Corresponding to the nature of the New-Testament priesthood, the Western Church demands as a minimum that, in living a priestly life, the official and the personal mutually determine each other. Actually, many official powers as, for example, jurisdiction, the authoritative word, and sacramental power, are independent of the personal holiness and the pneumatic gifts of the office holder. This is true at least insofar as validity is concerned, and the matter in question does not represent the whole Church. Instances such as these can even be very frequent. But even so, the official and the personal cannot be totally separated in the Church! Fundamentally, the Church represents the historical tangibility of the victorious grace of God. She can never degenerate into a mere "salvation club" in an external, legal sense. Despite the fact that she is really a Church of sinners, she still always remains *the holy Church* to the very end. Through her existentially lived witness, she must announce that the grace of Jesus Christ cannot be destroyed, and that through Him the world has already achieved its blessed finality. This, of course, does not exclude the possibility that individuals can live in such a way as to lose the grace of Christ.

The Church as a whole could never say: I announce God's truth and I administer His sacraments, but the private lives of my office holders really have nothing to do with this. Were God to permit a separation of official acts from personal attitudes such as this, then the Church would no longer be the continuing Body of Christ in the power of the Holy Spirit, and thus the abiding epiphany of God in the world, but she would be instead a shocking lie and a horrible advent of the final defeat of God. For God did not enter into this world just to shake it up for a time and perhaps tear this or that "soul" from it—He made it into His own holy home by means of His own enfleshment. If the Church were to become a basic denial of the change of the world into the Kingdom of God, then she would be degrading herself into the

Synagogue. For the grace of God could actually be separated from the liturgy of the Synagogue, and as a matter of fact the Synagogue abolished itself because of this divergence. The holiness that belongs to the Church by reason of the grace that has been given to her must be the obligation of the lives of all her members, and especially of her priestly representatives. This means that each one of us must personally ratify his priestly state. *I* must bring my life into my priesthood to the best of my ability, and *I* must bring my priesthood completely into my personal life. In other words, I must be a holy priest. This is not a question of what is fitting. It is an obligation flowing from the essence of the New-Testament priesthood.

Like the Church as a whole, I must guarantee through my whole person the truth of my preaching and the validity of sacramental efficacy. Even if it is true, in spite of Donatism, that I possess priestly powers which remain effective in the face of personal sinfulness, still that only remains true because the holy Church is standing behind me, and I can only act in her name. Therefore, even my most non-holy official act will always appeal to the Church's holiness and be informed by it.

Our office gives us no guarantee that we will successfully integrate it with our priestly life. Therefore, we cannot take pride in ourselves before God because we have an official position. Rather, we should hold onto it with fear and trembling lest we be lost after preaching to others and bringing them the grace of God.

In this connection, we priests can consider further how personal holiness should interiorly permeate our priestly existence, and how the latter should shape the former. We can consider how the personal holiness of the priest must be different from the holiness of lay Christians, because his mission, his responsibility for the salvation of others, his familiarity with the word of God, and his performance of Christ's sacrifice put a special stamp on his holiness. We can also ask ourselves whether or not we have been infected by certain false forms of priestly existence. Under

208

these we would mention religious functionalism, clerical fanaticism, religious sterility, resignation, and clerical skepticism.

We should also consider in this meditation the relationship between the priesthood of the New Testament and celibacy. It is very important for us to apply what we have said so far to this specific sacrifice that the Western Church demands as a prerequisite from candidates to the priesthood. If what we said above about the relationship between the priesthood and its realization in personal holiness is true, then the celibacy of the priest of the New Testament, even if he has not made a vow of chastity, should not just be something that he must tolerate. Rather, it should be the heart and soul of his priesthood—a personal commitment that makes his priesthood alive and fruitful.

If the priest of the new law continues the mission of the Incarnate Word, if he is supposed to speak the words of eternal life and bring men the message of God's love, if he must preach this God as triune and as giving Himself to us—and preach it in such a way that, as the go-between and chosen one, he must live out in the world the generation and Incarnation of the Word plus the resultant generation of men to true supernatural childhood, then the sacrifice of his sexual love is no mere suitable or becoming way of life. No. This renunciation is fundamentally an efficacious sign of that which God Himself has implanted in us, and which surpasses all earthly life-communication: that is, His own life as the life of the new and eternal covenant!

We should consider what Jesus thought about the priesthood, how He trained the first priests of His new law, and what type of men He chose. Call to mind the words He uttered about the priesthood to His chosen ones and also to us. Finally, we should ask the Lord, who has called us to follow Him in the priesthood, to give us the grace to follow this call honorably, to love Him, to remain true to Him with all our hearts, to make every effort to accept the great gift of Himself worthily so that God's grace, which is always given to us—we who cannot be worthy of it and who are only made worthy by it, may not descend on priests who have become unworthy of their calling.

24. The Holy Eucharist

Note

St. Ignatius introduces the third part of the Exercises, the meditations on the passion, with the meditation on the Last Supper.

The sacrifice that Christ offers at the Last Supper is a perfectly valid cult-symbol of His approaching offering on the cross. In the Last Supper, the Lord offered a true sacrifice. This unbloody sacrifice is a visible expression of His offering of Himself to the Father; it is a cultic, liturgical, and perfectly valid expression of the same sacrificial attitude which was realized on the cross for the salvation of the world a few hours later in a bloody way.

I. *The Eucharist as a Participation in Christ*

In the Last Supper, the Lord gives the apostles His body and His blood as food and drink for life everlasting. He wanted this sign of His love—a sign that actually contains Him—to remain as the expression of unity with Him. Some time before, when He promised the Eucharist on the shore of the Lake of Galilee, He said: "Whoever eats my flesh and drinks my blood abides in me and I in him" (Jn 6,56). "To be in Christ Jesus" is the heart of Christian existence. It demands that everyone called by the Lord to participate in His sacrifice must accept in his own being this sacrifice and the life that it entails. Whoever receives the sacrament of Jesus' heart without preparing his own heart has missed

210

Jesus completely. Such a person has misunderstood the meaning of "*opus operatum*," and has degraded the Eucharist and the sacraments to mere magic. The sacraments have not been given to us to take the place of our own personal effort, or to make our effort easier! We can only approach the sacrament of the heart of Jesus Christ with an open heart. We can only receive the grace of the Eucharist insofar as we personally also realize the sacrifice contained in it.

The constant switch back and forth in John 6, where Jesus promises the Eucharist, between the acceptance of Christ in faith and the reception of Him in the tangibility of the sacrament as food and drink, also brings this point out. Therefore, preparation and thanksgiving, which are a personal association with the Christ who comes to us under the appearance of bread and wine, are also a part of the true reception of the sacrament—notwithstanding His presence to us that is fully independent of us. (Naturally, this should not be taken to mean that the preparation and thanksgiving for the Eucharist should take on one definite form. Our attitude toward the Eucharist can certainly be, depending on the circumstances, a tormenting silence of a persevering inner emptiness, an uneasiness toward God.)

In the Exercises, we do not encounter the demand for a participation in Christ's sacrifice for the first time in the meditation on the Eucharist. For our considerations on indifference, on the readiness to share the Lord's self-divestment, were directed toward bringing us to share in His most holy sacrifice. The Eucharist is the sacrament of the "greater offering" of the meditation on the Kingdom of Christ. The reception of the Eucharist corresponds to the attitude that is to be striven for in the meditation on the Two Standards—an attitude of putting away all feelings of reluctance to sacrifice for Christ, for it is with these feelings that the devil begins to tempt us. The Eucharist also helps us to develop interiorly in the third degree of humility.

Since everything in Jesus' previous life is ordered to His death on the cross as the high point and the culmination of His life, the Eucharist has a special meaning for us as the participation in His death. "Whenever you eat this bread and drink of this cup, you are proclaiming the death of the Lord until He comes again" (1 Cor 11,26). Is that not something really colossal? What is well known by men and likewise fiercely repressed, what is common and still very strange, what is mentioned only in hushed tones, what is truly a senseless catastrophe—this is the death of one man—and we make it into the central theme of the great liturgical feast that fills God's house with its grandeur. Through the remembrance of the death of a crucified criminal, we profess belief in joyful hope and victorious life. With all the pomp of the liturgy, we announce this death, the killing separation of flesh and blood, as the decisive event of world history which must be proclaimed and celebrated over and over again. We do not do this because we make little of death or because we try to pretend that basically everything is not so bad after all. Instead, we do it in order to understand that the destiny of our miserable human existence, which is to sink deeper into death as our life goes on—that this destiny is the merciful, eternal call of God's love. This is a love that redeems and fills our being because it is an absorption into the death of Christ.

In the Eucharistic celebration, therefore, we announce not only the death of Christ, but also our own death. Thus, we see that death is not just the last moment of life—it was not so for Christ and it cannot be so for us. Death is the final, fulfilling act that is always present in life and is born from life. Death is present when we make our first entrance into existence, and it reveals itself in its ultimate form in what we usually designate as "dying."

If we daily celebrate the death of our Lord in the Eucharist, then we should consider how Christ the Lord accepted death. First of all, the death that we must endure is something imposed on us without our consent. If Christ is really the Son of Man and our brother, then this also applies to Him—and it applies to Him in a special way because He did not deserve death. But the Lord obediently accepted this fate as the incomprehensible disposition of the Father. Obedient throughout his agony! The main thing to practice in this retreat is imitating Him in this. In spite of all restraint and reserve, and in spite of all our distractions, the meditation on the Eucharist should bring us to the point that we say to Christ: "I want to love you in your crucifixion; I want to practice right now the readiness that you will one day inexorably demand of me—how, I know not—so that I will not have to suffer my soul to be torn away from me in the despair of the Adamitic sinner; I want to give you my life with a final, silent, actively indifferent faith and love. This is the only way to endure your death." Still, all talk of willingness to love the cross would only be empty bombast, would only be the lifeless idol of a visionary, unless it came from the power of Jesus Christ Himself. Since the Eucharist immerses us in the death of the Lord, it is also a participation in His power on the cross. In order to be able to die our death in such a way that we can truly endure it as our salvation, or, in other words, in order to discover the death of Jesus Christ in our death, we receive the body that He offered for us and we drink the blood that flowed from His heart so that He might always be with us.

Even though it is the lot of every man to die, still each one dies his own death—a death that belongs only to him and cannot be changed for another. But the death of each man is also different according to the role he plays in the community of Christ's love. Men who are called by the Lord to the priesthood of the new law must die a priestly death. The liturgy for the ordination to the priesthood has these words to say to the newly ordained: "Imitate the One you handle!" Those are not just poetic words! As priests, we cannot really do anything else during the course of our whole lives but "go out with Him beyond the confines of the camp and share His disgrace" (Heb 13,13)—which was fulfilled in His death. What Paul says of his apostolic life is also applicable to us: "Even while alive we are constantly handed over to death for the sake of Christ" (2 Cor 4,11). As priests, we should continually celebrate the "memory of His suffering." We should celebrate it not only in the Mass where our lips and our pleading hearts become mute when we pronounce the most holy words of His sacrifice, but in addition to that we should celebrate it every day and every night of our lives and in every street on earth. In our flesh and blood, we must always and everywhere realize the presence of these death-dealing and at the same time life-giving words.

In this connection, we should remember that we must offer our silent, long-suffering everyday lives to our Lord present in the Holy Eucharist when we distribute it to others. If this sacrament is supposed to furnish the place in which every burden, all insignificance, all neglect of this life can be made good, then it must corporeally contain self-sacrificing, patient, and faithful love. Certainly, the sacrament of itself is an indication of this love, but this love only becomes something really precious when it also contains the selfless, faithful, dedicated life of the priest in addition to the sacramental species.

The Eucharist, certainly, means more to us than just a participation in the cross of the Lord! It would be false to consider it only as the sign of His bitter suffering, or to think of it as the continuation of His weakness. Ultimately, it is a sign of His powerful sacrifice. And the Eucharist is really the sacrament of Christ's glory. In accordance with the words of the liturgy, it is truly a "pledge of future glory" for us. Ignatius of Antioch calls it the "medicine of immortality." It is precisely through suffering, through being used up, that the priestly mission and power achieve their highest realization in this sacrament. Since Christ does not release us from His fate, let us hope that we will discover in our association with the sacrament of His heart what we will be and what we really are. Only from this association can we draw what we need, in order to become what God demands of us: priests who overcome the world in Christ, and win it over for God with their faith, hope, and love.

214

II. *The Eucharist and the Unity of the Church*

Our unity with Christ finds its historical tangibility in the unity of the Church. Therefore, the Eucharist should be spoken of as the sacrament of our ecclesiality, of our incorporation into the mission and fate of the Church. As often as we receive the Eucharist we affirm anew our attachment to the Church and her claim on us. Just as we identify ourselves with the crucified and glorified Lord, so also we are identified with His Mystical Body and its appearance in the Church. Our incorporation into the Church, which is the "elevated sign" of His Mystical Body, is increased by the sacramental reception of the body of Christ. The idea of the unity of the Mystical Body through the Eucharist is hardly known by the Eucharistic piety of our private devotions. We should try to make this truth of faith something living for ourselves and the people to whom we are sent. St. Paul writes in 1 Corinthians 10,17: "The very fact that we all share *one* bread makes us all *one* body."

When we receive the body and the blood of Jesus, it is really we who are received and incorporated. This is the Eucharistic teaching of the Didache and the apostolic Fathers! For whoever is received into Christ finds it even more difficult to remain alone than is normally possible for man. Augustine calls the Eucharist the "bond of love," and the Council of Trent clearly brings out that the Eucharist is the sacrament of the Church. This is not something vague and of little importance for the great community of the entire Church. It applies with concrete urgency to the men who are gathered together here and now in the name of Jesus Christ. Large Church organizations are illusions if they are not first fully realized in definite individuals.

As the sacrament of the heart of Christ, the Eucharist is the source of our love for our brothers and sisters, but it is also the judge of this love. The meaning of 1 Corinthians 11,29 will always remain true: By sins against the love of neighbor, we eat and drink judgment for ourselves in the Lord's Supper. If there

215

is and should be *one* Church in *one* body of the Lord, which is bound together with the bond of true love, then that must be especially true for those who approach the same altar.

For the priest, this sacrament of charity for men and of responsibility for their salvation contains a specific mission to them. In his priestly existence, he is perpetually bound to the men God has committed to his care. The Eucharist is the most fundamental sacramental expression of the service he is to render to his fellow men.

Through our priestly existence, we are sent out to others. The primary character of our life is simply that we are sent—just as the Word is sent by His Father. That which is most intimate in our lives is the fact that we are related to our brothers and sisters in the name of the Lord. Ours is a pressing vocation that does not proceed from our own inclinations or from our own life-situation. Our vocation far surpasses whatever is required of other Christians! The lay Christian must try to bring others to supernatural salvation when the circumstances of his daily life bring him in contact with them. We who are priests put our seal on the special nature of our calling, and on our closer connection to our brothers and sisters by means of the Eucharistic celebration. It is right here that we declare our special responsibility for their salvation, because Christ has ordained us to stand at His altar in front of the community and as its mediator. He wants us to be the spokesmen and the representatives of the community; He wants us to offer up the people of God to God when we utter the most holy words in His name and in the name of the Church: "This is My body!" and "This is the chalice of My blood . . ."

25. The Agony in the Garden
(200–204)

Note

St. Ignatius places the second meditation of the "third week" of the exercises under the title, "From the Last Supper to the Garden Inclusively."

The Gospel texts on which this meditation is based are: Matthew 26,36–46; Mark 14,32–42; and Luke 22,40–46.

For all the meditations on the passion of our Lord, we should consult the directions that Ignatius gives in numbers 193–199, 206, and 207 in the book of the Exercises.

I. *Jesus Goes to the Garden of Olives*

Jesus prayed often in this Garden. Judas knew where to find Him. Still, Jesus does not hesitate. He does not try to escape the impending fate. He is ready. "This is the reason why the Father loves Me— because I lay down My life . . . No one is taking it from Me, but I lay it down of My own free will. I have the power to lay it down and I have the power to take it up again . . ." (Jn 10,17–18). Nevertheless, His path toward Gethsemani is a path into scandal. "Tonight every one of you will lose his faith in Me," He says to his disciples (Mt 26,31). With His fate He places a terrible burden on them, and He knows that their faith and love will crumble under the weight of it. He goes because His Father

217

ordained it so. He accepted His Father's will completely, and therefore He lets his strength trickle out in weakness, His courage drown in fear, and His love sink into the darkness of Godforsakenness.

II. *The Agony and the Immediate Vision of God*

Even though it is theologically certain that Jesus always had the immediate vision of God, that still does not give us the right to water down the Gospel accounts of His agony, fear, weakness, and Godforsakenness.

The reconciliation of both the agony and the immediate vision of God may be very difficult, but in any event these facts cannot basically exclude one another. The effort to do justice to both of these data brings up anew the Christological mystery—and it furnishes some badly needed nuances of meaning. The attempt to reconcile these two by appealing to the tremendous depths of human existence in which many different things, even contrary things, can genuinely have their place *next to one another*, must certainly be rejected as insufficient. It is not as if the immediate vision of God as such must overflow into the other parts of the soul and confer blessedness so that there could be no room for a painful experience of Godforsakenness. But the immediate vision of God cannot be placed next to anything else in the soul. Metaphysically, it must correspond to the basic constitution of man's material-spiritual existence, that is, it is only conceivable as the unfolding of our luminous reality insofar as this is received as a gift from God that constitutes our human reality, and is only "present to itself" because it finds itself placed before God.

For a creature, the immediate vision of God cannot be anything else but the ultimate, unsurpassable self-communication of God in grace—a self-communication that really constitutes the existence of the creature. It cannot be just a part of our human reality, but it must constitute our whole reality. For our reality only exists because it has been called by God, and therefore has arrived at His interiority. In other words, the immediate vision of God must be considered the final, most intimate core of human existence, and the ultimate foundation of the other powers and acts of the soul. Nothing else is in its class, and nothing else can compete with it. But is the immediate vision of God necessarily a beatifying one for the Son of Man who is crushed to the ground in the Garden of Olives, weighed down with the sins of the world as a sacrificial lamb before the avenging, just God? May we not say—according to the teaching of Benedict XII and Pius XII—that the unimaginable nearness of the holy God is exactly the presupposition for the terrible weakness and the accursed abandonment of the Son of Man? If the immediate vision of God can only be formed according to the way in which God has chosen to give Himself to man, and if God only permits His Word to become man in such a way that He should carry out the kenosis and the agonizing catastrophe of the passion as true God and true man, then the immediate vision of God must be a human reality open to suffering; it must be, therefore, a vision of the hiddenness of God that casts Jesus into a Godless weakness and the bodily torment which is its result.

However that may be, we can honestly say this much: In Gethsemani, the night before his bitter death, the Son of Man submitted Himself with perfect love to the unsearchable ways of His Father, and descended to the lowest level of human existence —the fear of death. He knows that this terrifying thing will overtake and overpower Him, that from the courage, with which He accepts His fate, the opposite will proceed, that strength will turn into weakness, courage into powerlessness, burning love for the Father into Godforsakenness.

III. *Gethsemani and Tabor*

It makes a lot of sense that Jesus should take the three disciples, who accompanied Him on Mount Tabor, to witness the agony in the Garden. When He spoke with Moses and Elias on Mount

219

Tabor about the end of Jerusalem, these three disciples beheld Him, as it were, in an anticipated glorification as the fulfillment of the law and the prophecies of the Old Testament. In the Garden of Olives, they find out what this fulfillment really is. On Tabor, the representative of the law recognized Jesus as the Lord of the law. In Gethsemani, the law presses on to its historical culmination. Actually, we would expect the law to triumph and raise up the Just One—the only One Who kept it perfectly and of Whom God said that He was His beloved Son. Yet the high point of the law is—Jesus' fear of death, the loss of the Just One, and the defeat of God in His Son. It is something else again that this defeat is ultimately the victory which is a sign of the incomprehensible mercy and justice of God. But this remains hidden in the Garden and in the agony that is the beginning of his sufferings.

Apparently, even the ancient prophecies become absurd in Gethsemani. Can this man, who is here crawling on the ground in limitless weakness, horrible torment, and absolute abandonment, be the same one spoken of in the prophecies as the leader of the glorious Kingdom and the eternal covenant of God with men? This Son of Man flees from His Kingdom and His intimacy with God to his three disciples—and they do not even notice Him because their eyes are heavy with sleep.

IV. *The Agony*

We should try to form some picture of Jesus' agony from the expressions used in the Gospel accounts. Matthew (26,37) says of the grief that seized Jesus: "He began to be sad." Mark (14, 33) speaks of an ecstasy of shuddering and horror: "He began to tremble." According to both evangelists, Jesus is immersed in deadly anxiety, "And he began to be troubled." Luke (22,44) says that Jesus is, as it were, born in agony, "being in agony." Gathering up all His strength, He prepares Himself for the approaching catastrophe. Now He is baptized with the baptism of pain; now He is immersed in a sea of suffering that closes over Him. When He prophesied this baptism (Lk 12,50), He said: "How I am constrained until it is accomplished." At that time, He was not only driven, but also pressed on Himself into the unimaginable. Then He accepted with great courage what could not be avoided and what He still freely accepted. Now that He has attained what He so ardently desired, He is interiorly choked and overpowered by something He apparently cannot control.

We have all tried to come to grips with the problem of how the anxiety-laden prayer of Christ can be reconciled with His "immunity from concupiscence." In the meditation on the agony in the Garden, we should have more human feeling for the answer than is normally possible in the course of speculative thought. Now we should try to realize how the Incarnate Word opens His human heart to something overpowering, and how this enables Him to convert absolute suffering into His own total act. Thus, His suffering is not something accidental to Him— something distinct from His own being; it is not at all like scratching one's finger and then forgetting about it. No, this is not the case in Jesus' passion which begins in the Garden. Here He overcomes the unmanageable part of suffering by freely accepting it, and He integrates it into His total reality. Jesus *is*, as it were, His suffering—He is not just carrying it around like a cane. Perhaps that sounds a bit abstract. But try to penetrate the meaning of what was just said. Try to taste interiorly what is happening here: His sweat becomes drops of blood (Lk 22,44), and His suffering cries into the emptiness that all the power of His life is now nothing but suffering. Matthew says in this regard: "My soul is sorrowful even unto death" (26,38). He is exiled and threatened on all sides by death-dealing sorrow.

Only the Incarnate Son of God Who possesses perfect interior unity of soul—even though He assumed from the very beginning man's capacity for suffering and death, and therefore dies in the course of nature—can have a perfect knowledge of the approach of death. We have grown up, as it were, with death because of

221

our sinfulness and concupiscence, and have come to accept it as our just reward in spite of its horror and absurdity. But Jesus is different from us in this, and as the living Son of God He experiences death as completely senseless and as something that should not be. If the opposition to death in His being is supposed to be a real potency that must be actualized lest it negate itself to an empty incapacity—then it will manifest itself with regard to His approaching death as an experience of the utter incomprehensibility and absurdity of death: It will discover itself as a horror of sin.

We do not have to imagine Jesus' knowledge of sin in the agony, as if He had to get it from an open book. It is more important that we prayerfully immerse ourselves into His agony so that we get some idea of how the humanity of the Word, which can only be with us as boundless love for mankind and solidarity with it and as perfect freedom from an egotistic feeling of "Why bother about the others?", finds itself prostrate before God in solidarity with the sins of the whole world. And it is important for us to see that this realizaion is a collection of all these sins into one great burden that is not theoretically known, but immediately experienced. Let us try to put ourselves into a situation in which we can feel, as it were physically, this vileness, and where we are drenched with the presence of sin—not to recall past sins in order to count them, but rather to experience ourselves being dragged around in sin. The Son of Man, Who only possesses Himself by giving Himself in love to mankind, must have experienced the crushing weight of the sins of the world in some way similar to this.

From the very beginning, Jesus knew that His people would not listen to Him. He knew that He would end up on the cross. Nevertheless, He tried His utmost to find acceptance as the Messiah and to make His mission on earth a success. Therefore, He could let the futility of His mission to the people of Israel fall upon His soul—especially insofar as this futility was a sign of the fruitlessness of His salvation with regard to those who are

222

lost. Christ knew that many men would betray the grace of God, even after His sacrifice on the cross. He could not bring Himself to think with satisfaction that there would also be success, and that there would be those who would become saints by following Him in His grace. Each man is a whole world: In each one, Jesus either accomplishes His mission completely or He is a complete failure.

In the meditation on the agony in the Garden, the retreatant is supposed to make use of the "application of the senses" which was mentioned in the meditation on hell. Jesus' agony in the Garden is itself really a terrible "application" of His "senses," which are completely filled with lonesomeness and forsakenness, so much so that His words no longer reach the Father. His constant presence to God and His immediate vision of the Father intensify this experience immeasurably: We can only penetrate the depths of this experience if we are, so to speak, in a state of negative immediacy with God. The Godless man, whose forsakenness is not really a greater nearness to God, can feel that that which is not God is nice and pleasant. His Godforsakenness would lead him to say: "I am pleased that this God has finally gone elsewhere and left me alone!" But this is not what the Godlessness of hell is! For hell really to be hell it must contain a nearness to God—a nearness to God, though, that means damnation for the sinner. Consequently, Jesus' nearness to God is the real and ultimate reason why He experiences His entrance into the world—a sinful world standing before the damning judgment of God—as the Godforsakenness of the agony.

Listen to Jesus' prayer to the Father! Let us try to fill ourselves with its intensity. He who comes from heaven presses Himself into this sin-scarred earth, seeks protection in a hole where only death is master. He shouts His "Abba" to an impenetrable heaven, to God's infinite "No" to the world—a "No" that overshadows the horizon of His being. His "Abba" was a word that pierced the heart of the early Church, because she heard Him cry it forth. From an exegetical point of view, this cry in Gethsemani must have sounded very unceremonious, almost despairing and without respect; it was not a tender word of one united to His Father by perfect love. It is much more a cry of a creature Who almost oversteps the bounds of respect, and is so empty that His being retains only this dead cry. Through all of this, the Word is always the internal expression of the Father, but the incarnate form of this expression does not get a hearing.

Try to appreciate the content of His prayer. Jesus beseeches that the cup of His sacrifice might pass from Him. This is the same person Who "pressed on" toward Jerusalem (Mk 10,32), Who was "constrained until it is accomplished" (Lk 12,50)! Just a few days before, He had asked the two sons of Zebedee: "Can you drink the chalice that I will drink?" (Mt 20,22). And He had just said with determination and courage: ". . . I do as the Father has commanded me, so that the world may know that I love the Father. Rise, let us be going!" (Jn 14,31). At the Last Supper, He grasped this chalice—which now causes Him to shudder—and offered it to His disciples in anticipation of His sacrifice: This is the chalice of My blood, of the new and eternal testament, of the testament of reconciliation and salvation . . . ! His whole life long He desired "His hour." "His hour" is frequently mentioned throughout the Gospel of St. John. Now He cries out to God that this hour might pass from Him. Three times He prays. Always the same thing! Three times He apparently capitulates before the task for which He came and which is the decisive goal of His life. He stumbles helplessly into the sleepy silence of His disciples. He does not allow the angels to strengthen Him, and becomes so weak that He can hardly bring Himself to say "Yes" after His "No." The remarkable and even terrifying element in the agony in the Garden is that the Incarnate Son of God, Who could say: "He who sent Me is with Me; He has not left Me alone!" (Jn 8,29) and: "I and the Father are one!" (Jn 10,30), possesses this God, as it were, mediately only, and seems to be even more separated from Him in this possession. Even His cry of submission remains unanswered, in spite of the strength received from the angel. The Father does not budge; He leaves His Son crushed, covered with bloody sweat, powerless in fear and misery. The request for the passing of the chalice is drowned in silence. From out of the mute nothingness, into which the agony of His cry disappears, comes something wonderful. Even though nothing was changed, Jesus begins anew. The energy to go on flows from His empty, dead heart—on to the cross. It is as if a dead man has come to life. "Rise, let us be going!" (Mt 26,46).

To the question how this is possible, we can only say that the first and last truth of things is here revealed: a total submission to God that surpasses all else. We see here in the Son of Man that the creature about to die is just beginning to live with God, that when we are at the end God's power begins to be victorious and "is perfected in weakness" (2 Cor 12,9). His grace is victorious in our weakness, which we must fully experience right to the end because His grace does not take it away from us. In the recollection of Jesus' agony in the Garden, we can and should notice the remarkable make-up of God's grace. We should note that by His grace we are not "*simul justus et peccator*" in the Protestant sense, but that it does, as the power of God, really enter to take over our weakness. This is the power that constitutes the clarity of our hearts, so that we have it and still do not enjoy it, so that it operates in us and still does not glorify us.

We do not have to be braver than Jesus was in the Garden of Olives. Each one of us will have to empty the chalice of weakness, wretchedness, and cowardice in his own way—and this is measured out to each by God. Perhaps it will demand everything of us. But this and nothing else is the following of Christ. And God only has to give us the grace necessary to say: Not my will, but Yours be done! We have come under the law of this Jesus from Nazareth Who is crushed to the earth in the Garden of Olives and completely submits Himself: "Father . . . yet not as I will, but as You want it!" (Mt 26,39). He does not consider His surrender an act of His own power; He accepts it

H   225 as an incomprehensible miracle of grace—a miracle produced in Him by God alone. This is what we must become aware of with faith as a result of this meditation on the Lord's agony in the Garden. Only in this way, with the help of God Who descended to the depths of our agony, can we hope to shoulder the burden of our life and through it help so save ourselves and others.

We do not have to do very much. We do not have to do more than Jesus did in Gethsemani the night before His death. But if we are able to do that much—and we can only do it with the grace He merited for us in the Garden of Olives—then we are able to do everything. We should ask for this grace again and again.

26. From the Garden to the Cross

Note

Try to see our Lord's way of the cross with world history for its background. World history itself is really one big way of the cross leading either to ruin or salvation. The world's way of the cross and that of our Lord are open and transparent to one another: We can only understand the course of world history in the light of Christ's passion, and likewise we can only grasp the full meaning of Jesus' way of the cross by seeing that the crisis of world history is summed up in Him.

I. *Jesus Betrayed and Abandoned*

Jesus is betrayed by Judas and abandoned by His disciples—even by Peter, the rock of the Church, who wanted to go to death with Him and is now sifted by Satan.

The Godlessness of sin is clearly manifested in our abandoned and betrayed Lord. Here we see the love of God rejected. Sin is a fundamental perversion of loyalty, truthfulness, and love, at least insofar as these can be considered the attitudes corresponding to memory, intellect, and will. In itself, sin is a degradation of the creature's relationship to God, a darkening of one's own mind, and a hatred of the living God. The betrayed and abandoned Lord with His existence is a shocking proclamation that the ultimate, all-surpassing love of God remains without an answer. Of course, we must not forget what St. Paul says (Rom 11,29) in this regard: that the gifts of God are without repentance. God's faithfulness remains even in betrayal, and, in fact, achieves its end through betrayal.

II. *Jesus Before the Sanhedrin*

We should consider that this man, Who is dragged, spat upon, and struck in the face before the judgment seat of His people as a questionable figure and an accused criminal—that this man is God's living answer to all the world's questions, the questionless answer Who will question us when we finally stand before Him. The Sanhedrin had already condemned Him to death before hearing His sworn testimony that He is the Messiah, the Redeemer sent into the world by God, the fulfiller of the law and of history, the Son of the living God—they condemned Him even before they heard this, and interpreted His words as a blasphemy deserving death. They do not really take his avowal seriously. In fact, they misuse it as a pretext to secure the death penalty. There is no need for a Messiah such as this Jesus from Nazareth—there cannot even be such a Messiah! Thus, Jesus is condemned in the name of good order, national pride, the good of the country, truth, belief in Yahweh, theology and philosophy, beauty and symmetry—really in the name of everything on the face of the earth.

The mentality of the Sanhedrin has not yet died out—not even in the Church! There are many among us who think that they know God when they know the world. They, too, would condemn the Son of Man in the name of God's honor, which they cannot imagine to be anything else but agreement with the honor of the world. If a person stands unreservedly for the standpoint of the world, and affirms it unconditionally against the paradox, the incalculability and the unpredictability of the divine love hidden in this man Who holds His tongue, is kicked, buffeted, and spat upon—then he honestly must say: This Jesus has blasphemed. But this seemingly indisputable standpoint is false; it is sin itself! It presupposes a certain power over God, an ordering of things without consulting Him, a criticism of God in the name of one's own limited knowledge, and a confinement of His bottomless and always greater love to our limited measuring rods. Paradoxically, through His rejection and condemnation by the Sanhedrin, our Lord comes even closer to mankind: In this way, He becomes the Redeemer of the world.

III. *Jesus in Prison*

Christians of all ages have pondered the metaphysical and salvation-historical depths of Jesus' hours spent in prison.

Because of sin and our subjection to death, Jesus really entered into the prison of our finiteness, loneliness, and inescapability—into the prison of our hopeless self-deception. Because He has descended into the prison of my human reality, the gates are now thrown open—and I will not accept it as true, I will not sum up the courage to go out, I think that I will never escape. I feel that my situation is hopeless, and yet Jesus is still standing by me. Sooner or later, the same thing will happen to me that happened to Peter in the prison in Jerusalem when the angel of the Lord shook him and said: Get up, gird yourself, put on your sandals and go! (Acts 12,7–8) . . . and the bronze doors of my imprisonment are open.

IV. *Jesus Rejected by the Jews and Pagans*

The Sanhedrin's death sentence on Jesus must be ratified and carried out by Pilate. In the courtyard of the Roman Guard, the scene is played in which the Jews and Pilate, who represents the pagan world, condemn Jesus.

The Jews reject Him as a scandal to them even in the name of God. We could almost say that a supernatural demonism is

229

exercising its power in the hatred of this people against the true Kingdom of God. But even here, Israel remains the people of God—a people so closely bound to God that its very existence is a divinely willed sign of salvation. This people can never separate itself from God in such a way that it would cease to belong to the God of grace. As St. Paul penetratingly says in the eleventh chapter of this Letter to the Romans, this people remains forever bound up with God's plan of salvation. But it is precisely this closeness to God that makes the monstrosity of this people's actions against Jesus intelligible—actions which are a visible symbol of the sins of the whole world. A person can only perform such an evil act when he is in close contact with the God of love.

The conduct of the Jewish people in Jesus' trial is nothing else but the terrifying realization of the attitude of the second class of men that we spoke about earlier. As we said before, the men of this group want God to come where they are. They do not consider following God. They determine how God is supposed to conduct Himself. And this attitude—we should tell ourselves this again and again—is also present in the Church and in her clergy. It can also appear in us! Even if the Church as a whole—in this it differs from the Synagogue—is so seized by God's love that she cannot escape His grace, still the individual Christian, the individual priest, and entire social groups in the Church, can do the same thing the Jewish people did when they rejected Jesus before Pilate and thus demanded another Messiah more pleasing to them.

On the other hand, Pilate and along with him the pagans with their worldly wisdom cannot stand the foolishness of this Jesus. Listen to the governor's apparently tolerant but really cold rejection of Jesus. Consider his apparent level-headedness and his morbid skepticism! Note the wisdom presented by Pilate which does not want to dirty itself with the affairs of this world, and which is so indignant about the fanatical dispute surrounding Jesus that, very logically, it is prepared to let an innocent man be killed so that there might be peace and quiet. Are we really strangers to the unconcern that abandons others in need, to the coldness contained in the question: "What is truth?", to the spiritless rejection of the mystery of love? Frequently, this false and basically superficial worldly wisdom seems very clever! In fact, things can go so far that it even seems necessary to us for the development and preservation of Church interests. In God's eyes, what ultimately counts is not an intellect that is pleasingly skeptical and coolly calculating. What He wants is a simplicity and a total dedication that come out for Him alone, and we must not try to avoid His love by opting for something apparently better.

V. *The Scourging and Crowning with Thorns*

Then Pilate "released to them Barabbas, but Jesus he scourged and delivered to them to be crucified" (Mt 27,26).

We cannot consider man's body something that is only accidental to him, or something that is only temporarily given to furnish him with a dumb instrument so that he can come in contact with spatio-temporal things. Rather, our human reality is *essentially* a unity of body and spirit. We only possess our intelligence and our freedom insofar as we are in this world united to a body. The existence of our spiritual soul is rooted in matter! The sadistic attack made by a callous soldier in the Roman prison on the body of Jesus is a direct violation of His whole Person. The scandal of death, which must be carried out in the body and which is now tangibly moving in on the Lord, is not imposed on Him by a cruel, spiritless nature—it is inflicted by human malice and depravity. The miserable sight of the afflicted Son of Man— a sight produced by men themselves—encourages them in their contempt of Him.

Basically, every sinner who persists in his sin (which is a form of self-deception) winds up by making his deeds their own justification. For if we can act like that, then obviously it must be right because, so the argument goes, facts are always right! Surely, God is on the side of the stronger battalion! In the Church, this kind of argumentation, which we could call Hegelian, is operative wherever people unreservedly think that the Church must shine in order to prove the truth of her claim, that there must be visible success in the apostolate in order to be a good apostle, and that those who have little or no success must be stupid or naïve (this charge is sometimes, of course, not without foundation). But before we argue in this way, we should consider the mystery of evil and the mystery of God's love—a love coming down from above to counteract evil: Both of these mysteries are revealed in the passion of the Lord. We can only hope to achieve some understanding of God's love if we find God more truly present in the sight of the afflicted, thorn-crowned Son of Man than in the sight of other men. The body of Christ, which is being disfigured in the Roman prison by the scourging, the mocking, the crowning of thorns, and the bodily exposure, is the body in which God wants to give Himself to us. And the essence of sin is the violation of God in the body of the world.

The attack on Christ's body is continued in the abuses inflicted on His Church. And she receives her most scandalous disfigurations from her own members! We also are capable of this! Through our tepidity, through our hardness and coldness, through our selfishness, and through the vices with which we misuse our priesthood!

See the picture of the "*Ecce Homo!*"—Behold the Man! We should ask the Lord to give us some understanding of His passion. We should ask Him to impress upon us the picture of His suffering, so that we may at least begin to get some idea of how each man and the whole history of the world with its sinfulness carry the marks of His love and grace. This is the man we are following. Of Him, Pilate cried out in his helplessness: "Look at this poor excuse for a man!" By following Him, we achieve a true humanism that has value in God's eyes—a humanism that has no illusions about what man is, but rather is able to perceive the face of God in this disfigured man. And therefore, it knows for a certainty that the most ideal plans for producing the "noble man" are infinitely surpassed in this abused Son of Man. This Son of Man Whom all of us crowned with thorns, struck and mocked, Whom we dared to judge, Whom we permitted to be destroyed —He will look at us for all eternity. He will be the Glorified One, of course, but still He will aways remain the One who carried His passion into glory. And this face that will behold us for all eternity is the face of God Himself.

27. Our Lord's Death on the Cross

Note

We will next meditate on our Lord's death on the cross, taken from the "third week" of the Spiritual Exercises. To accomplish this, all we really have to do is to repeat what the entire Exercises say about Christ crucified. The whole meditation can be summed up in the already-quoted words of St. Paul: ". . . the word of the cross is folly to those who are perishing, but to us who are being saved it is the power of God" (1 Cor 1,18). We can take this thought or the one that closely follows it in the same letter: ". . . but we preach Christ crucified, a stumbling block to Jews and folly to Gentiles, but to those who are called, both Jews and Greeks, Christ the power of God and the wisdom of God" (1 Cor 1,23–24), as the leitmotiv of our meditation. According to St. Paul, the true philo-sophy is the love of God's wisdom which is offered to the world in Christ crucified. The cross of the Lord is and remains the fork in the road of world history. "He is set for the fall and rising of many . . . and for a sign that is spoken against" (Lk 2,34b).

I. *To the Jews a Stumbling Block, to the Gentiles Foolishness*

When St. Paul says that the crucified Lord is a stumbling block to the Jews, he is thinking primarily of his own contemporaries who opposed Jesus with fanatical hatred. But St. Paul also enunciated a certain human way of thinking here that extends beyond the Jews and appears in all ages: Those who try to direct God according to their own little categories, those who only see God in the images of the triumphant Lord that they themselves have constructed, those who are not prepared to include in their picture of God an end on the cross—they are just like the Jews who rejected Jesus. Their idea of God may be correct for the most part. But they falsify it by the addition of this one characteristic, inasmuch as they are not willing to surrender themselves to a God Who, not only in Himself but also with regard to us, is infinitely greater than anything we can think of Him—even after He has revealed Himself to us. A person with the attitude characterized by St. Paul as "Jewish" defends "his" God against anything that could shake him loose from this theological concept. Anything different from what "his" God is supposed to be, is so scandalous that he must fight against it with all the fury of religion, with all the fury of the theological image of God which he constructed—with honest, hard work!—a long time ago, so that he can destroy it as a God-opposed, blasphemous scandal.

The monstrosity of persecuting God for the sake of God can also occur in our lives. Naturally, as heirs of the New Testament we are in the holy Church in which God is really present, and which He is drawing to Himself with a steady hand. But still, we are always open to the temptation of adopting the Jews' Christ-opposed attitude, and in the name of God and of His Christ of opposing everything that the Lord wants to be as the result of His sovereign freedom and unsearchable love.

The attitude criticized by St. Paul as "Greek" evaporates into a happy or tragic existence restricted to this world. For men of this persuasion, God is really only a glimmer of the perfection and absoluteness of this world. Whether or not they consider their state blessed or catastrophic is beside the point. In any event, they will not allow themselves to be drawn out of their confinement in this world. They entrench themselves either in a tragic finiteness or in an apparently happy worldliness. For them, a crucified God, Who really is God and still dies on the cross, is an abstruse phantasy, a "foolishness" (1 Cor 1,18) that is by-passed without comment, since it would be a shame to waste time on it.

We can find an attraction for this attitude in ourselves! We must constantly strive and pray for faith in the crucified Lord. Only those who have been "called" (1 Cor 1,24) by His incomprehensible grace can grasp its reality. Of course, we must follow the promptings of grace, and muster up the courage to break away from ourselves and to place our complete trust in the ineffable God. And whoever gives himself in this way completely to God will discover that the crucified Christ is the power of God. Actually, it is precisely the weakness of God in the world and even in the Church that is *the* appearance of God's power. The Lord's cross is the "wisdom" of God, and the true "love of wisdom" (philo-sophy) is ultimately nothing else but loyalty to the foolish love of God in Christ Jesus. When we have once grasped the incomprehensibility of God's power hidden in weakness and the mystery of his foolish wisdom, then everything else will be given to us.

II. *The Cross in Jesus' Earthly Life*

On the cross, the Son of Man attains the high point of His mission. For the sake of this "hour," He came into the world. The glorification which He asks of the Father in His priestly prayer— "Father, the hour has come; glorify Your Son that the Son may glorify You . . ." (Jn 17,1–2)—is nothing else but God's will that the Incarnate Word descend into death's incomprehensibility with all the love of His heart. His glorification begins when He is nailed to the cross and hung between the highest and the lowest, abandoned and rejected by heaven and earth alike. Now He is the lamb of God who takes the sins of the world upon Himself, the perfectly obedient One who came into the world to serve so that He might hand over His life as a ransom for many. On the cross, the saying of His that He "must" suffer is realized (Lk 24,26). This is the remarkable and incomprehensible "*dei*" of the original Greek text of Scripture by means of which the seemingly insoluble connection between God's sovereign direction and man's freedom, between God's love and man's guilt, is proclaimed to all. In its own way, it also announces that contingent world history has taken on a certain aspect of absoluteness. That Jesus die on the cross "had to be," and everything else, His life and work, all of His words—and even the totality of world history, can only be properly interpreted from that starting point.

Of course, this high point of Jesus' mission is also the supreme catastrophe of His life. This is so true that even His mission seems to disappear into deathly silence! The crucified Lord is betrayed and abandoned by His friends, rejected by His people, repudiated by the Church of the Old Testament. When He dies a painful death, He is even abandoned by God Himself. He who did not know sin has become sin in this abandonment (2 Cor 5,21), so that His life is given over completely to death.

The catastrophe of Jesus' life, however, is also the deepest and most personal act of His life: For, by His obedience, He is able to absorb that which is absolutely foreign to Him and that which is threatening to destroy Him, so much so that, being changed into Him, it becomes something absolutely near and something breaking forth in power. Obedience has many different functions in our lives. For example, it is necessary for the existence and growth of any kind of common life; it is necessary for learning, since only the person who believes another actually and not just theoretically—and directs his life accordingly—is able to transcend himself to such an extent that he is not locked within himself, and thus deprived of any real knowledge of himself.

Jesus' obedience, His own desire to be "obedient" (Phil 2,8), His submission to the will of the Father, cannot be described even approximately with worldly categories. There is a certain mystical sense about them that is proper to Jesus. This certain something is present in our obedience when we follow Christ. When Jesus could have destroyed His vulgar, ignorant enemies, and when He could have had ten legions of angels at His disposal—if God's will had not been otherwise, then we encounter in His obedience the silent "Yes" to His end, to an excruciating death in abandonment, to that which is not known by another, which is not taken away by another and in which a person has already attained the acceptance of the Father. If we can enter into this attitude even partially, then we will begin to understand that the saints, who could obey without getting angry or bitter, who were dumb enough to obey when commanded, could, as it were, tumble into the most holy life of God with this silent obedience of theirs—an obedience brought into this world by the Incarnate Son of God.

Jesus' greatest act on the cross is not only His "Yes" to abandonment and suffering, but it is also His "Yes" to the incomprehensibility of God. Jesus' death is His own free act of falling into the consuming judgment of God. But Jesus can only accomplish this as a perfect act of His unconditioned love of God. For the ordination of the sovereign freedom of God, when it is seen to proceed from His absolute holiness, justice, and goodness, can only be accepted and born by another lover who lets himself go in love. In this way, He accomplishes the incomprehensible—something that must be present in every love if it is really going to be love. Since love is the only act rooted in man's essence by which he can let go of himself in order to get away from himself and so really find himself for the first time, love alone is somehow a "given" that is itself inexplicable and incomprehensible. Only love can adequately express what is really characteristic of man. Thus, he can only attain his own true reality by giving himself in love.

Of course, a man should protect himself. He should take care of himself and worry about the salvation of his soul. There is and must be a legitimate self-love! But in the last analysis, we can only love ourselves by loving God and not ourselves, by loving His ways and not our ways, by loving the One who is not a metaphysical abstraction of infinite perfections, but the living God who ordains the cross and death and all those things that "ought not" to be. For the person who does not love but just wants to know, who therefore necessarily only agrees with the god of his own making—for this person, a God who is the sum total of everything incomprehensible must be a frightful scandal. The endurance of God's incomprehensibility reached its peak for Jesus on the cross. It becomes so much a part of Him that His very life is poured out in the death-dealing cry, "My God, My God, why have You abandoned Me?" (Mt 27,46). Jesus experiences death not as a biological fact, but as the absolute darkness of hell. We could almost say that He Himself becomes this darkness, which, of course, does not justify the contention that Jesus underwent the pains of hell. For this darkness of His debilitated life is not the ultimate fact of His existence. The ultimate fact is the great love which prompted Him, in the midst of His own darkness, to say to another who was crucified with Him: ". . . this day you will be with Me in paradise!" (Lk 23,43), and to utter with confidence: "Father, into your hands I commend My spirit!" (Lk 23,46). These words do away with hell! In fact, we could say that the only reason Jesus is not in hell is because He brought the incomprehensible, absolute power of His love into hell with Him. It is a terrible thing to fall into the hands of the living God. On the cross, Jesus handed Himself over to this God in perfect obedience and love—and there was no endless terror. There was only the blessedness of entering into the still greater love of the God of grace.

Jesus' sacrifice on the cross is not an unsurpassable moral event because—in the sense of a superficial "satisfaction theory" —it can be attributed to the Word and so achieve a certain infinite "value" or "worth." Rather, this sacrifice is the personal act of the Word Himself! And this does not make it less creaturely and free, but it makes it even more genuinely so. For the closer a creature comes to God, the more autonomous it is, the more free it is, the more it "is" simply. Therefore, the Incarnate Word is really able to experience all the dimensions of human existence as His very own: the dignity of a mission,

239

the abyss of ruin, the consummation of obedience, and the deep love of the heart—a heart that can say "Father" to this God who still stands before Him as the consuming fire of judgment, a heart that can surrender its poor life into His hands.

III. *The Meaning of the Cross in Salvation History*

The cross of the Lord is the revelation of what sin really is. The true world is the one that appears right here: the world in which the cross of the Incarnate God is raised on high. The cross of Christ mercilessly reveals what the world hides from itself: that she, as it were, devours the Son of God in the insane blindness of her sin—a sin whose Godless hate is truly set on fire upon contact with the love of God. How could she have even a ray of hope when she kills this man, when she destroys Him and blots Him out right at the point where He came into His own? Even though it is true that a person cannot sin without knowing what he is doing, and without being guilty for his sin in the eyes of the God of love and merciful understanding, still it is no less true —no matter how paradoxical it may seem—that sin and the malice of sin appear to be harmless, that sin tries to manufacture a good conscience; it is no less true that sin can act as if everything is not really so bad after all, so that finally its presence in the world is hardly noticed.

Although most of us are rather dull, ordinary clods rendered harmless by our tepidity, it still remains true that the sins we commit really and truly "crucify the Son of God on our own account . . ." (Heb 6,6). We are deceived if we think that we could not actually do that, or that, at most, it could only "happen" to us in such a way that we would not be responsible for it. What our own experience leads us to feel about ourselves is basically the consequence of many sins—of our first parents, of the whole world, or our own. The truth about ourselves is what the cross of Christ says to us about our baseness and its hellish possibilities. Therefore, we should turn our gaze to the crucified Jesus and

240

tell ourselves in the midst of our sinfulness: He loved me and offered Himself up for me. "In this the love of God was made manifest among us, that God sent his only Son into the world, so that we might live through him. In this is love, not that we loved God but that he loved us and sent his Son to be the expiation for our sins" (1 Jn 4,9–10). We should meditate on that; we should also consider these words of St. Paul: "But God shows His love for us in that while we were yet sinners Christ died for us" (Rom 5,8).

Also, from a theological point of view, it is not easy to understand why we are loved by God precisely through Christ's death, why He transformed this death into the revelation, yes, into the only revelation of His love, with the final result that we only receive His love through His death. All we can do in our meditation is simply to accept this fact with love. "He loved them to the end!" says St. John (Jn 13,1). That goes for us, too! The Word loved us to the end! With his own life, He shared our end and our death. Because He was a lover and remains a lover for all eternity, the world is saved. The salvation of the world grows out of the strangely incomprehensible, even paradoxical, unity between the death-dealing revelation of sin which inflicts a terrible paroxysm on God Himself who came into the world in order to destroy death by His own death, and between the ineffable outpouring of His love which did not hesitate to sustain sin and death. Out of death and love! "Where sin increased, grace abounded all the more!" (Rom 5,20), and, "God has consigned all men to disobedience, that He may have mercy upon all!" (Rom 11,32).

All of us try to block God's door to the world in such a way that it can never be opened again, and we try to lock ourselves in the prison of our own finiteness so that we can never get out again—even if we wanted to. But if we turn around in our prison so that we can see what a pitiable state we are in, then we encounter Christ Who has entered into our loneliness and embraces us there with the outstretched arms of the Crucified. Because He

241

is present where we have incarcerated ourselves, we are no longer able to close the prison of our finiteness. We can still be lost, but then we lose our life in the midst of salvation. And so long as we are walking in this "present time," in the "now," we really do not have to do anything but allow ourselves to be embraced by the Crucified. We could almost say that it is much more difficult to be lost than to be saved, for the One who wants to save us is God Himself, who showed His supreme love for us by dying on the cross. It can be important for us to tell ourselves this frequently, for we are always tempted to stay in sin because we do not dare to believe in the magnificent love of God, and because we do not want to believe that God will forgive us our sins.

When we consider the Crucified in this way, we should also look at His pierced heart—that heart which is open "so that there might be a refuge of salvation for all penitents!" If properly understood, the devotion to the Sacred Heart of Jesus belongs to the very essence of Christianity. Therefore, it is always present wherever true Christianity is present, even if it might not be recognized explicitly as such. The only reason we are saved is because the heart of the Incarnate Word was pierced through and streams of living water flowed from it. The pierced heart of Jesus Christ is the center of the world in which all the powers and currents of world history are, as it were, bound together into one. The ultimate meaning of the frightful multiplicity of all the things God has created and His most comprehensive statement about them is—the heart, in which His love was pierced through.

IV. *The Cross in Our Life*

Man needs a simple, realistic courage in order to put up with a life of suffering and failure. Non-Christians are able to do this—and we should not feel sorrier for ourselves than they do for themselves! But the pagans' hardened attitude can sometimes result in the danger of a pseudo-ethical or pseudo-religious paroxysm of sacrifice which is not willed by God and which is basically not a real loving surrender to God's will. Rather, it is nothing but an escape of despairing individuals into greater ruin, because they are bewitched by a compulsive feeling that everything will end anyway in the very near future.

Human living, however, offers an abundance of suffering and futility which cannot be mastered by sober courage alone, and which ultimately must lead to boundless despair without the crucified Lord. This despair may be camouflaged with cynicism or resignation, but in reality its emptiness produces only death. In response to this hopelessness of human existence, we Christians are called on to continue the sacrifice of the Lord in our lives, which alone has saving power, as the act of our faith, hope, and love. The person of the new covenant should take upon himself something of "what is lacking in Christ's afflictions" (Col 1,24). Can we say of ourselves that we carry the mark of Christ's death on us as the sign of our election?

Finally, we should think over once again what we said earlier about asceticism as a training in readiness for the passion of Christ. With our eyes raised to the cross, we should ask ourselves: Where in my life am I trying to avoid the cross? Naturally, I do not call that which I am trying to escape and that which I bitterly protest against in the depths of my being—I do not call that the cross of Christ. But that is exactly the place where I should accept it. If I do, it will bless me with the fullness of its grace.

28. The Resurrection and Ascension of the Lord
(218–229)

Note

Now we will enter into the so-called "fourth week" of the Exercises. In this week, we should "ask for the grace to be glad and rejoice intensely because of the great joy and the glory of Christ our Lord" (no. 221). In this week, we should particularly relish the fruit of our redemption—life from the Holy Spirit as the beginning and the finality of our new and redeemed life.

In this present contemplation, we are going to take up the Resurrection and Ascension of our Lord. First of all, we will consider the Resurrection in the life of Jesus Himself, then we will consider its meaning for salvation history. This will lead us to contemplate the glorified Lord who is sitting at the right hand of the Father; it will also cause us to reflect on the effects of His Resurrection and Ascension in us. The point of this contemplation is to bring us to see the meaning of the fourth week of the Exercises. And the goal of the fourth week is to impress on the retreatant that he can only achieve the glory of the Resurrection through the cross.

I. *The Resurrection in the Life of Jesus*

We can only get a complete picture of Christian existence, such as it is given by God and such as we should make it, if we take

244

a good look at the whole life of Christ. Even though we should not forget the *crucified* Lord, still we cannot really understand Him if we do not at the same time believe in Him as the *resurrected* Lord Who, by means of His death, entered into the eternal life of His Father. The purpose of His life is perfectly accomplished in His Resurrection. In it, He overcame both death and the world. The love of the Father is now brilliantly present to Him—that love to which He clung amidst the power of the world's sinfulness, before the judgment seat of the thrice-holy God, and in the darkness of His Godforsakenness. This love seizes the totality of His concrete human existence—including His body. The whole Christ with His whole destiny and with everything He experienced and suffered on earth with His human nature, has now entered into the glory of the Father. The *glorification of His body* is not something accidental—a second thought, but it is given to Him because He has attained the great end and purpose of His history. This is so true that everything that He was in the course of His history has entered into the glory of the Father.

Jesus has not lost a thing. He has not only saved His physical being intact, but everything has remained present, as it were, in its hidden, sublime essence. Because the events of His life truly happened before, now there is nothing but eternal happiness. In His descent into the world, he was, just like us, a man of history, of everyday occurrences, of interference from others, of self-fulfillment through the deeds of His temporal existence. As long as we are on this earth, we only have, as it were, a small piece of our life in our hand for a moment, and then we lay it down behind us—in fact, it seems to slip from our grasp almost unnoticed. But with Jesus, the situation is very different: He possesses His life completely. Certainly, the fact that we are getting older does not mean that we are getting poorer! What is really questionable is the future which we do not yet have. The past is not lost—it is our final possession. But for us, this finality is, so to speak, hidden; it has fallen into an abyss so that it cannot be reached by our conscious experience. (What will we be like when the same thing happens to us that happened to the resurrected Lord,

245

when our whole past is brought back to us and must be experienced as a unified reality?) He has not left His cross, His abandonment, His death completely behind Himself in such a way that one could say: At last, it's over with! Let's forget it as fast as we can! When He meets us now as the resurrected Lord, He is Who He is because of His past. What He experienced during His life now shows, as it were, it absolute and final face. He took His whole life and everything in it with Him into glory. He is the resurrected Victor over death and the world. And He is that in the glorification of His body!

II. *The Ascension of Christ and Its Meaning for Salvation*

Christ is also the Lord Who ascended into heaven! His Resurrection and Ascension are the fruits of salvation—a salvation bringing the destiny of the world to its appointed end. In this regard, St. Paul says that "the end of the ages" has come upon us (1 Cor 10,11). If God accepts the world, if He carries out His descent into it in such a way that He experiences the abandonment of death as the appearance of sin and Godlessness in order to include it in His glorification, if He takes a piece of this world, which always remains just that, into His glory with Him, then the world is indeed irrevocably accepted, and no one can ever wrench it from the hand of the resurrected and ascended Lord. Then the world has ascended to heaven in His Person. In this way, the world entered into its final phase. We might even say that thus the heart of this despairing world has been changed into something good. Ultimately, the world has already been set right, for He, the living center of history and even of nature, became flesh and is even now glorified. Thus, everything that happens in the world now is either an effect of His victory or a last-ditch battle of those worldly powers that were conquered by His cross.

It will always be difficult for us to look at the world and the world's history in this way. But this only means that we have

246

not yet come to the inner realization that the final victory is really already present in our hearts—hearts into which Christ has poured His spirit of victory over the world.

The resurrected, ascended Lord is the end of the ages! He is the heart of the world! He is standing before the throne of the Father as the Son of Man. The words of Psalm 110 apply to Him: "Sit at my right hand!" Here He is the High Priest celebrating the eternal liturgy of creation (Heb 8–10), for He has truly ascended to heaven, taking with Himself what is ours. In such wise is He standing before the Father! As One belonging to us, He has thus actually become our blessedness, a piece of God's inner life. Naturally, this "piece" remains a creature, but for all that it still belongs irrevocably to God. If our knowledge of metaphysics helps us to see how God is absolute in the full sense of the word, outside of time and history, beyond becoming and progress (to borrow an expression from the mysticism of the Middle Ages), then this does not mean that He interferes with His creation from time to time. Rather, its true significance is that He holds eternally within Himself the results of creation's history as His own reality, and lets it participate in His own life for all eternity. This is nothing else but the glorification of the world and of man, which can only happen through grace. Of course, this glorification can only be believed in grace, for only under the influence of grace can a person muster up the boundless optimism to be convinced that God has already begun to be "all in all" (1 Cor 15,28).

That is what must be continued in our own "private" saving history. We are the ones who "live together with Christ," who makes us "sit with him in the heavenly places" (Eph 2,6), because we "were buried together with him . . . and in him also rose again" (Col 2,12). In other words, just as His cross and the totality of His life have become a part of our life, so also is His Resurrection a factor in our present existence. We would have a mistaken notion of our imitation of Christ if we thought it would bring us into one stage of His life after another. We have already risen with Christ! Because He has risen and because we possess His Spirit, we already have the "pledge" of our future glory (Eph 1,14) in that Spirit about Whom St. Paul writes to the Philippians that He will make our body like to the body of His glory (Phil 3,10). Basically, this resemblance is already present in us, but it still must be made manifest!

The Resurrection of Christ is not only a saving event that tells us now what we will one day become, but is not actually ours at this moment. Rather, it is *the* reality that determines, right now, all history and therefore the personal situation of each one of us—both externally and internally. Externally, because we live in the aeon of Christ and are thus at the end of the ages! Internally, because we already possess His glorifying Spirit! This must be the source of Christians' confidence in ultimate victory! And such confidence cannot be based on the cleverness of Church politics. It is also very far removed from the expectation that we will always be successful in this world. There is no this-worldly advantage for the Church's persecuted and for her martyrs to tell them in the midst of their sufferings that the Church will be even more glorious after they are gone. This is not the kind of victory-confidence that has been given to us! We can only understand it as an inner conviction proceeding from these words of Christ: Have confidence, I have overcome the world! What we consider to be our field of existence, what we feel to be the "powers" influencing our destiny—these things are more appearance than anything else. Actually, our whole situation is much different from that. Of course, Jesus also says: You will be afflicted in the world. We would surely be surprised if it were not so. But then He immediately added that He has already overcome the world, and that therefore we should have trust. If the world in which we live has already been overcome by Christ, then we are not justified in saying: "Sure, He has done all right, but we are still in the same old predicament." That is not so! Of course, we are with Him in the new order only because we believe. Naturally, the situation is not such that we first have the experience: Aha, everything is going just fine!—so that we are then led to believe. Instead, somehow or other this faith and this experience mutually determine each other. Only the believer can have this experience—and because he has it, he believes.

We read in Hebrews (3,6) that Christ stands as the Son over his own house: "We are that house, if we hold fast our confidence and the hope in which we glory unto the end." Now we can really approach the throne of grace with confidence. In the power of Jesus' blood, we also have access to the Most Holy. We should not throw this confidence away. We should tell ourselves again and again: The love and mercy of God are final. The love of the Lord will never again be overcome! In the eighth chapter of his Letter to the Romans, St. Paul lists the worldly powers he had experienced: life and death, the world, angels and principalities, good and evil, things present and things to come, height and depth, all creation—and then he says that nothing can separate us from the love of God that has appeared in Christ Jesus our Lord. We should gradually come to a realization of the superiority of those who have risen with Christ to life. Not in the sense that we become bold in a worldly sense; nor in the sense that we would imagine ourselves to be freed from all further sadness and affliction. But in the sense that, in spite of everything, we are somehow mysteriously surrounded by something greater, by the victory of Christ—and from that we get our courage. Truly, through Christ we are already beyond time and the power of time, beyond past history, beyond sin and the weight of the flesh, beyond death.

Of course, this victory-confidence of ours is almost identical with the weakness of the cross, because the victory was obtained on the cross. Therefore, we are still walking in fear and trembling. But still in a fear that is self-composed. We must consider the cross the test of our faith, and at the same time realize that God is stronger in us than is our own fear of the cross. We should have this viewpoint in mind when we consider the future of the Church and our own future: Nothing can separate us from the love of God in Christ Jesus our Lord! In accordance with the mind of St. Paul we should add to that: . . . the resurrected and elevated Lord! This view is also a grace—one that must be prayed for and one that makes us blessed. But it also demands the complete gift of our hearts: We must, as it were, break away from ourselves with a realization supported by faith that everything that happens in this world, no matter how painful and cross-filled, is really already penetrated with the victory of Christ—the same Christ Who rose from the dead and ascended into heaven.

29. The Spirit as the Fruit of the Redemption

Note

The retreatant should occupy himself in the "fourth week" of the Exercises with the meaning of the glorification of the Son of Man for the salvation of the world. Along this same line, we will now propose a few ideas with regard to Pentecost and the outpouring of the Spirit. As the Lord who rose from the dead and ascended on high, Christ can send out the Spirit. The fact that He has done just that and is still doing it is a sign that He has truly entered into the most holy sanctuary of God. If we want to get some idea from the life of Jesus just how our lives are going to turn out, then we cannot ignore the impact of Pentecost and the outpouring of the Spirit as the fruit of the redemption.

I. *The Spirit in the Trinity*

We should try first of all to consider the Holy Spirit as the third Person of the one Godhead. And we should not forget that we have real relations to each of the three divine Persons. Our knowledge of them is not something that is unimportant to us. The God Who gives Himself to us in grace, in Whose life we participate by grace, and Whom we will one day see face to face, is a Trinitarian God Whose nature subsists in three Persons. Of course, the "how" of this subsisting is absolutely incomprehensible for us. If our theology is cold and abstract, then it can easily happen that the possession of this absolute mystery seems unfruitful in our lives. But the fact still remains that God is triune in His inner life, and that we are involved through grace in His interiority. If we accept the words of Scripture as we find them, then we do not get involved in "appropriations" in the sense that statements applicable to God in general are distributed haphazardly to the three Persons. No. The relations of the Father, the Son, and the Spirit to us—relations which are expressed in Scripture—are fundamentally the immanent Trinity Itself. Therefore, we do not have to occupy ourselves so much with psychological speculation on the Trinity (in the vein of St. Augustine), which, though it may be very sublime, leads to a dead end. Such speculation may be very profound and beautiful and magnificent; it even deserves our respect, since it is the result of a thousand years of theologizing about the Trinity. But the first thing we must do is listen simply to what Scripture tells us about the Spirit. *That* accepted, believed, lived, embraced, and loved in the depths of one's being . . . that is the Holy Spirit! There He encounters us as He is and not as a mere abstract appropriation. In any event, our true, supernatural life consists in the communication of the divine Spirit, and everything a person can say about the essence, glory, and end of the Christian can be summed up by saying that he has received the Spirit of the Father and in this way has been filled with the divine life. That explains everything else!

II. *The Source of the Spirit*

A further consideration would be that the elevated Lord is the source or fountainhead of this Spirit. We can add to that: "The Lord with His pierced heart." St. John says: ". . . for as yet the Spirit had not been given, because Jesus was not yet glorified" (7,39). But Jesus was glorified because as the corporeal love of

252

God He was raised on the cross and pierced through by the guilt of the world. He became the source of the Spirit for us because He sacrificed Himself and poured out His blood for us. According to 1 John 5,6ff., there is no Spirit except in the blood of the Redeemer. The living water that flows out of the heart of the Messiah (Jn 7,38) comes from the pierced side of Christ immersed in futility and weakness.

If we have the feeling sometimes that God has left us without buoyancy and enthusiasm, without an interior glow, and even without the Spirit, then we should ask ourselves whether or not we are refusing to accept the cross, penance, failure, weakness, and the emptying out of our own hearts. Could it not be that this is the reason why we have so little experience of the powerful movements of the Spirit in our own lives and in the life of the Church? "Give your blood and you will possess the Spirit!" is an adage of the early monks. That is still true today. Without being touched in the heart, there is no Spirit, for the source of this Spirit is the elevated Lord Who gained His triumph on the cross in the midst of weakness and Godforsakenness. The fountains of everlasting life, according to St. John, spring forth from the depths of the earth. Because He came in water and blood, we are saved! For those of us who are close to Him, blood and the water of the living Spirit are very closely related.

III. *The Testimony of Scripture*

We should try to get inside of the reality of the "graced" man— a reality which is given through the communication of the Spirit from the Father and the Son—by quietly going over what Scripture has to say about the Spirit of God and of Jesus Christ.

In this connection, we should think of the names given to the Spirit in the New Testament. He is the "Holy Spirit," the "Spirit of the thrice-holy God," the "Spirit of the Father and of the Son," the "Spirit who was poured into us," the "Paraclete," the "Comforter" and "Advocate," the "Spirit of freedom," the "seal

253

of our redemption" by which we are truly stamped as those accepted by God and belonging to Him, the "first fruit of the redemption," the "pledge" in which the beginning of eternal glory is already given to us, as it were, by pre-payment, the "strengthening and comforting anointing." He "enlightens" and "inspires"; He it is "Who lives in our bodies as in a temple," "sanctifies us into a dwelling place of God," "makes of us the sanctuary of His Church." He is the "Spirit of the new creation through Whom the Lord makes all things new," "out of Whom a person must be born again" in order to really be the person he is supposed to be for all eternity. His goal is life and freedom. He is the divine opposite of what the New Testament calls *sarx*, that is, the flesh which is weak and perishable, attached to sin, sullenly closed to God, and a stranger to the Spirit. That flesh is marked out for death, but nevertheless it fancies itself to be life. In contrast, the Spirit is the arouser of the glorified body, the "Spirit of adoption giving us testimony that we are the children of God." St. Paul says of this Spirit (1 Cor 2,10ff.) that "He searches the depths of God," and as such imparts to us the true basis of our knowledge of God.

We should never forget that our theology is not just the product of human cleverness striving for its own deification with the use of certain metaphysical and historical data. Its real source is Christ's gift to us of everything He received from the Father. Ultimately, we can theologize because the Spirit is given to us as the Searcher of the depths of God, and as the living anointing of wisdom. The theological system we have so carefully worked out is a faint shadow touching only the surface of that luminous nature of ours which struggles along in concepts. It is only a reflection of what is present in the center of our human existence —much more clearly and really, in actual self-reflection, yes, and in a true possession of the known. Even when we are speaking about the mystery of the life of the triune God, we are not speaking in mere concepts, but from experience, because, prior to all theology, the Spirit, Who searches the deep things of God, has already become our Spirit.

The Spirit of God breathes where He will; He does not ask our permission; He meets us on His own terms and distributes His charisms as He pleases. Therefore, we must always be awake and ready; we must be pliable so that He can use us in new enterprises. We cannot lay down the law to the Spirit of God! He is only present with His gifts where He knows that they are joined with the multiplicity of charisms in the one Church. All the gifts of this Church stem from one source—God. What Paul says in the twelfth chapter of his First Epistle to the Corinthians is still true today! This should give us the strength to overcome every form of clerical jealousy, mutual suspicion, power-grabbing, and the refusal to let others—who have their own gifts of the Spirit—go their own way. That is what the Spirit wants from us! He is not as narrow-minded as we sometimes are with our recipes! He can lead to Himself in different ways, and He wants to direct the Church through a multiplicity of functions, offices, and gifts. The Church is not supposed to be a military academy in which everything is uniform, but she is supposed to be the Body of Christ in which He, the one Spirit, exerts His power in all the members. Each one of these members proves that he really is a member of this Body by letting the other members be.

If we read the seventh chapter of the First Epistle to the Corinthians carefully, we will note that the Spirit is also the Spirit of virginity. After St. Paul has defended his teaching in this matter, he closes with the words: "And I think that I have the Spirit of God." —Even in this regard! This connection also shows up in other passages where St. Paul characterizes the Spirit as a Spirit of prayer; and again where he relates the Spirit to the practice of continence in marriage.

In the New Testament, the Holy Spirit is also called the principle of the Christian community—the principle of "*koinonia*." In second Corinthians (13,13), He is spoken of as the giver of this community in which the redeemed are open to the Father and the Son. God's intercourse with the creature and the creature's with God, and even the intercourse of creatures between themselves—which is only possible and truly free under the influence of charity, where everything belongs to one and still every other can truly be himself, without being reduced to nothing because he has been deprived by the others and without himself being compelled to deprive others in order to assert himself—this intercourse really *is* the Holy Spirit.

According to Jesus' words contained in John 20,23, the Spirit is the principle of the forgiveness of sins: The Lord equipped His disciples with the Spirit so that they could forgive sins. Moreover, the Spirit is introduced as the principle of prayer: He it is Who goes in for us with ineffable signs, because we have been sanctified by Him. He prays in us so that our prayer acquires an almost infinite range and a divine depth. The New Testament keeps telling us again and again to pray in the Holy Spirit. We should remind ourselves occasionally of the dignity and depth of our prayer.

According to second Timothy (1,7), the Holy Spirit is communicated to priests through the laying on of the hands of the apostles as the Spirit of power, love, and self-control. The Spirit is also characterized in the writings of the New Testament according to His fruits. In this connection, we should read the fifth chapter of the Letter to the Galatians. In sharp contrast to human self-seeking, St. Paul enumerates as the fruits of the Spirit: love, joy, peace, patience, kindness, goodness, faithfulness, gentleness, continence.

IV. *The Spirit and the Church*

In this meditation, we should also delve into the relationship of the Spirit to the Church! On Pentecost, the Church made her appearance possessing the Spirit. She was not only juridically organized and constituted, she was not only a "perfect society," but she was also the Church of the final, victorious, justifying, and sanctifying Spirit. And this Spirit will never leave her because, to use the words of St. Irenaeus, He has found his final abode in the Church. Before the coming of Christ, we could only say that "He spoke through the prophets," that here and there He descended on certain men and intruded into human history, but up to that time He had not yet achieved a sign-presence, a bodiliness, which is eternally and inseparably bound up with Him but without any mixing together of natures. He was still on the way. But now He is here! Before this time, He was the One who was coming, and now He is so present that St. John speaks of a "non-presence" of the Spirit before the glorification of Jesus (John 7,39).

Of course, we must understand that in the right way. Before Jesus Christ, there was grace, justification, and Spirit, but they really proceeded from Him and had Him as their goal. But still, there is more than a difference of degree between the presence of the Spirit in the world now and formerly. The differentiating element is the Incarnation of God, which is the final assumption of the world into His spiritual life. Because there was a Pentecost in this sense, there is now a Church. This Church is the unity and difference of the letter and the Spirit, of the sacraments and their grace, of office and sanctity. Those things are different, but still they are inextricably bound up together as the result of the Incarnation. We have to reach this viewpoint before we can have the proper attitude toward the Church. We will meditate on this point later on, but right now we should think over how it is that only in the Church can we find the Spirit of God who sanctifies us, saves us, leads us to the truth, comforts us, liberates us, glorifies us. We should also consider how, according to the intention of the "*asynchytos*" (Greek="Without any mixing together of natures") contained in the teaching of the Council of Chalcedon, the Church, as a juridically constituted organization, and the Spirit, are not simply to be identified with one another.

V. *The Spirit and Official Positions*

The relationship between Spirit and office is crucial in our priestly lives. It is always helpful to remember that the bestowal of an office in the Church is a sanctifying sacrament. Through this simple fact, which has become almost routine for our conscious life, our entire priestly life and our asceticism are shaped in a special, decisive way. This same fact says that our mission and call to the hierarchical priesthood, in spite of all anti-Donatism and in spite of the legitimate distinction between the powers of office and subjective holiness, are still inseparably connected with holiness. This is so because the Spirit of holiness, Who proceeds from the Father and the Son, Who is given to us and produces in us love, faithfulness to God and men, courage and willingness to bear the cross—this Spirit it is Who confers our office on us in His coming. If we accept His office and at the same time reject Him as the Spirit of holiness, if we reject the love given us by the Father and poured out by the Son, then we insult Him and act against His inner nature. By such conduct we do wrong to our office, for, even when we are vested with God's power and retain it in the midst of maliciousness and Godlessness, the actual exercise and success of this power depend decisively on our personal holiness. Of course, we can thank God that it also depends on the holiness of the universal Church—a product of God's grace and power.

But what good would these powers be to us if people refuse to make use of them? For we can only administer the sacraments if there are people around who want and accept them. All saving power of office is to no avail and remains, as it were, in the minister, if there is no one to take advantage of it. The Church's objective truth-charism and her last-recourse infallibility are also to no avail if men do not listen to the truth. In the final analysis, they will only listen to the truth and make use of the sacraments if, in the power of the Holy Spirit, we give witness in our own lives to the credibility and holiness of Christ and His message. Thus Spirit and official position belong together!

VI. *The Experience of the Spirit*

Finally, we should ask ourselves about our experience of the Spirit. If we read the New Testament impartially, we do not get the impression that we experience the existential-supernatural elevation of our acts only from hearing the Gospel, but from within ourselves have no knowledge of it at all. St. Paul says: "The Spirit himself bears witness with our spirit that we are children of God . . ." (Rom 8,15). Right there where He bears this witness, He is unction and power, peace and joy, patience and love. For our life in the Spirit it is not necessary to be able to penetrate reflectively into our souls in order to show that the Spirit is there. But in accordance with the meaning of Scripture, we should realize that He is at work in us, that everything we experience in our intellectual-spiritual life has a breadth, depth, and infinity which is really a gift of the Spirit of Christ! We should not have a smaller estimation of ourselves and our spiritual life than revelation permits us to have! It does not do any good to be too modest in an area where God Himself thought more of us than we do of ourselves.

Perhaps our present taste of the Spirit is very weak. But of itself it presses on to further development. Whoever carries the cross of the Lord, whoever can hold his tongue when he is attacked, whoever does something that is only seen by God who searches the heart, whoever prays on his own and not just to fulfill a legal obligation, whoever summons up the courage and the patience to meet death in trust without exaggerated fear, whoever can calmly disregard the world and its squabbles—that person truly experiences an inner expansion and immeasurability of the heart. If we could plumb the depths of this transcendent experience, not just speculatively but also existentially, then we would already be so far that we could never stop; we would have penetrated into the depths of God—all the way to the point where we would stand before Him face to face. In this sense, there really is something like an experience of the Spirit, even though in the course of a self-examination we could never say for certain that we are filled with God's spirit and grace. But when we abandon self without seeking self, when we are true to the cross of Christ, at that moment something unheard of takes place in us—the Spirit of love from the Father and the Son takes us as it were with Himself, pulls us away from ourselves in order to lead us with His divine freedom beyond everything created, and in order to make us participators in the divine life.

If we live in the Spirit and do not persist in a false sense under the law, then each thing that we do as Christians and priests must be performed not only as a matter of obligation, not just because otherwise the Lord would punish us; rather, each action should proceed from within in such a way that it proclaims the happiness, freedom, and inner law of the heart. Of course, we are still journeying between the old and the new. We are still on the way; we have not yet become what St. Paul describes as a human reality free from the law. But that is what we are supposed to become! We are still on the path between Adam and Christ; we are still living, as it were, a forced existence under the prick of the law, under the pedagogue whose job it is to lead us to the Lord. For this reason, the humility to place oneself under norms that are imposed from without also belongs to the whole picture, so that we can share the life of the free, powerful, and unimpeded Spirit Who breathes where He will.

As time goes by, we should become more and more aware of the fact that we are already on this path. To be sure, this path is built on the poverty and shame of Christ, His renunciation, the living of the beatitudes and the practice of the following of Christ. But the more we allow the Spirit to take hold of us, the more we will note that this difficult life of following Christ is really a life filled with the Spirit, the fruit of the redemption. We will note that it is a life directed not just toward a happiness that is completely in the future as the result of some vague promise, but rather that it already possesses what it hopes for. We will note that it is a life that is free even in the area where it seems to be buried under the restraint of law, death, concupiscence, and all the wretchedness of this world. We are supposed to be the kind of redeemed men who are able to draw out of this knowledge of the Spirit the free magnanimity to become what God wants us to become: Christians who take themselves and others to God in the Holy Spirit.

30. Mary and the Church

Note

St. Ignatius did not treat this theme expressly, but it fits very well into the total structure of the Spiritual Exercises. For mention of Mary is made again and again in them: She is mentioned in the Triple Colloquy where St. Ignatius presents his magnanimous offer before the whole heavenly court, in the meditations on the Annunciation and the birth of Jesus. The Triple Colloquy shows us that Mary held a special place in the saint's piety. There is no doubt that the Church also has a decisive role in the Exercises. She is presented to us as the final dwelling place of the Spirit. The Rules for Thinking with the Church (nos. 353–370) are witnesses of the importance St. Ignatius attached to the theme of the Church.

In the course of the "fourth week" of the Exercises, we consider Mary from a very definite point of view. During this entire retreat, we have not really been pondering theology, but saving history: from sin to the Resurrection and Ascension of the Lord. But the result of saving history is redemption. Now we can ask ourselves: Is the idea of a redeemed, new, sinless person, who has been incorporated into the inner life of God, only an abstract ideal? Or does it truly find its realization in us? To this we must answer that it is in no sense an unattainable goal, but has been realized in a definite case. If we ask ourselves once again what our love of God is supposed to be like, then we do not have to be satisfied with an abstract answer. In the Kingdom of the living

God, the ideals are not merely general postulates, but concrete persons—just as God Himself is. For we find the actualized ideal of the absolutely redeemed, sinless, holy, perfect person in the blessed Virgin and Mother of our Lord Jesus Christ.

I. *Mary, the Perfectly Redeemed*

The ideal picture we have before us must naturally be determined by Christ. For this reason, it cannot be He, so it must be realized by some other person through a perfect following of Him. Now the ideal of perfect openness to Christ is found concretely realized in Mary. She is the one who is perfectly redeemed. And, of course, she is perfectly redeemed in a very definite way belonging to her alone! But this way is at the same time the ideal case, the perfect fulfillment of what is and must be the law and goal of our lives through the inner structure of our existence in grace. There are many ways in which we could consider this idea which attained its historical, concrete form in Mary, and has become tangible in our flesh and blood. Here we are not going to discuss which principle of Mariology is the fundamental one. But we can, nonetheless, easily arrive at the fact of Mary's perfect redemption from what the faith says about her again and again: that she is the blessed Mother of our Redeemer.

As the perfectly redeemed, Mary is the absolute unity—not identity!—of spirit, body and soul. In her, everything is summed up in the act of her personal surrender to God. In her, we find the perfect integration spoken about in the meditation on the Three Classes of Men. The act of God's love is completely successful in Mary. Election by grace and openness to grace are one in her. We could even say that here God is received by the creature in the most basic way possible. Therefore, Mary is so much the Mother of God that she both conceived the incarnate grace of God corporeally in her womb, and—because in her conception and personal act, spirit and body, belong together in inseparable unity—is the one whose faith is praised in Scripture, because she responded to God with her *"Fiat"* at that crucial

263

point in salvation history where the efficacy of His grace asserted itself in a decisive way for all history. Mary stands at this point! She speaks her "Yes" and conceives God; she speaks her "Yes" in faith and in the concreteness of her earthly life. She conceives the Word, to borrow a phrase from the Fathers, simultaneously in faith, heart, and womb.

Mary's perfect redemption indicates that in her the beginning and the end, both of which were established by God, are in perfect harmony. Thus, she was immaculately conceived and finally assumed into heaven body and soul, that is, she went into heaven with her total human reality. Deed and destiny, which are always painfully separated in us, achieved a blessed integration in her. In us, either the deed is not done, or else destiny encounters someone who is not ready for it, so that it cannot be incorporated into his personal self-fulfillment and ultimately passes him by. But in Mary, everything is present in her "*Fiat*." Even in becoming the mother of the Word, she can accept the absolute disposition of God in her regard in an act of free love and free obedience.

If we find the unity of the given and the accepted in Mary, the perfectly redeemed, then that has a very special meaning for us priests. Of course, we should not make Mary into a priestess or anything like that! Nevertheless, we should not forget that she does not have a haphazard function in salvation history; rather, her function is decisive for all of mankind.

All of us, says St. Paul, are built on the foundation of the apostles and prophets (Eph 2,20), and we share in the faith of our father Abraham (Rom 4,16). Each one of us, in his own historical situation, is essentially dependent on the life history of others. If that is true of the deeds that remain, as it were, anonymous, then it is especially true of those that belong to the public, official history of the people of God and as such have entered into the reflection of the Church. Thus, Mary's destiny is not just her own affair: She is not the Mother of God for herself alone—in a purely biological sense or with a love that only

264

concerns her. Her motherhood introduces the salvation of all! This means, then, that Mary belongs in a special way to the official representation of the Church, even if her position is not one that could be perpetuated. That is just the point: Her function is essentially unique! And she exercised her unique function in the Church in perfect correspondence with her personal, interior life. There is no separation in her between her office and her subjectivity. Despite the Church's vigorous anti-Donatism, she was so clear on this point that she always took it for granted that the Mother of the Lord is also the holy Mother. In other words, the Church proceeds in this matter from the theological axiom that, in such a case as this, office and person could not be separated. Of course, this is not to say that Mary was not free, but that she was pre-ordained for this perfect correspondence between official function and personal holiness by reason of the efficacious grace of God which alone makes a person free. Today, Mary with her unity of office and personal holiness is urgently calling to us: You also should be what I am! Our celibate, single-minded service of God, Christ, the Church, and men is really just a part of the coincidence of official position and personal realization which we have in common with Mary.

As the perfectly redeemed, Mary in her human reality also stands for the unity of individual self-fulfillment and service of others, or, we might say, the unity of personal holiness and the apostolate. In her, these mutually determine one another. She is holy because she conceives the Word as the lamb of God for the salvation of the world, because under the cross she joins her motherhood to the sacrifice of her Child, and because her life is nothing but a complete self-oblation in the service of her Son for the good of souls. Her individuality is, as it were, submerged in her mission; it disappears in the apostolate, but it is precisely in this way that she becomes the unique person that she is supposed to be.

In this matter also, we can learn something from Mary. A

.*

humanistic cult of personality—such as was the mode in the nineteenth century—which is really a form of egotism, does not lead positively to Christ, and is certainly very "un-Marian." This Virgin who led her miserable, poor, simple life in a remote corner of Palestine, through her selfless, self-consuming service as the handmaid of the Lord achieved a uniqueness all her own —she became, as it were, the absolutely human individuality. Nothing remained empty, nothing remained undone in her human reality. And the reason for this is that she was not concerned about herself, but thought only of the others, of her Son, of her duty. "Behold the handmaid of the Lord . . ." who is totally absorbed in the Lord Whom she serves. It is exactly in this way that she became the Queen of heaven and earth!

It is, therefore, easy to understand that in Mary, the perfectly redeemed, grace and freedom have attained an absolute, blessed unity. All the gifts and privileges of the Blessed Virgin and Mother of our Lord should be looked at from this point of view. The same is true of her virginity, which is one of the first fruits of the New Testament. As the first representative of this virginity, Mary's special mission in the world was to represent the Church of the end-time—a Church completely turned over to Christ. And that is what priests and religious are supposed to do by their celibacy.

II. *Mary and the Church*

The foregoing brings us to the consideration of Mary's relationship to the Church. If the pure, immaculate, and virginal Church is the community of those who are following Christ, and thereby are realizing now in their own lives what Mary accomplished long ago, then this means that Mary is the prototype of the Church. A Catholic, or better, "incarnational" religiosity cannot consist in some exalted act of freedom which is directed toward the transcendent God alone, and which, as it were, annihilates everything else. God descended into this world and communicated

266

to it His own life. But this means, then, that the creature with its plurality, peculiarity, and beauty, which is distinct from God, has become religiously meaningful. Incarnational Christianity does not permit its glimpse of God to reduce everything else to nothingness. If we want to accompany God in His descent, then we must learn how to find God in the magnificent figures of His salvation history. Therefore, in a very special sense, we must learn how to find Him in Mary! In this matter, we should have no part of the anxiety of an un-Christian religiosity—un-Christian because it is not incarnational. This religiosity fears that God and perhaps even Christ Himself will escape its grasp if it has anything at all to do with others within the framework of religion.

If it were true that only God could be, then we should destroy ourselves so that honor could be given to God alone. But that is not the way things are! God is honored because we are here, because we praise Him in the great deeds of His love—deeds by which He establishes that which is different from Himself. If this is true as a general rule, if the basic religious act in Christianity can be directed to a multiplicity of realities, then it is true with regard to all the saints and in a special and unique way with regard to our relationship to Mary. We must come to realize that all things point beyond themselves to the infinity of God's love. At the same time, we must realize that we are greatly tempted to try to get to God directly and by-pass His creatures. We usually ignore this tendency in ourselves, instead of overcoming it in the straight-forward Catholic piety which recognizes Mary and loves her, and does not reject her praise as something out of place.

III. *The Church and Us*

Finally, we should ponder over the Church as the people of God, the Body of Christ, and the primordial sacrament of grace. Do not forget: The Church is not just a teacher of abstract truths; she is also the fullness of grace because she possesses the infinite life of God. Consider that the Church is the unity of love, that she is also the promise of that which is still to come, a witness for Christ before the world, the community of redeemed sinners.

After we have looked at the Church in this way, we—priests especially—should ask ourselves about the condition of our love for the Church; we should ask ourselves what form our love must take if we are going to be priests and representatives of the Church. What sort of a figure must we cut if the Church, as she really is, is going to confront men in our words and actions, in our faithfulness, selflessness, propriety, and reliability? Can perfect truth, unity in love, patience, awareness of being a redeemed sinner, consciousness of being surrounded by the love of God in Jesus Christ—can all of that be seen in me? Is my life a witness to at least something of this? And in a way that shows that I am even prepared to do more?

Most likely, love for the Church develops just like any other love. In the process, we are attracted by the goodness and beauty of another, then we draw the other to ourselves, and then the crises and the pain of love begin to appear. We discover that the beloved is not all that he appeared to be, that he does not meet all of my requests but demands that I adapt myself to him and abandon my attempt to make him into what I want him to be. Through tension, suffering, and disappointment perhaps he gradually brings me to the point where I actually do attain genuine love, where I am selfless, abandon myself and give myself to him completely. Our love for the Church should be something like that! Perhaps like youngsters we have falsely idealized the Church—a Church that is pilgrimaging at a distance from the Lord and is immersed in the history of this world. And perhaps that false idealism has made us forget just what it is that makes the bride of Christ spotless and without a wrinkle. If so, then we have been disappointed. But this disappointment should lead to the fullness of love. We should acquire a love that believes, hopes, is loyal; a love that endures, prays, perseveres, and does not seek self, but truly seeks the Church and God in her—the God Who is always greater than our expectations and Who put the Spirit in the Church as the mysterious source of her life.

We should ask ourselves if we love the Church in this way. Do we love her teaching and her institutions, her representatives, the bishops and the pope, the prelates, her Canon Law, her customs and traditions, yes, and even what is old-fashioned, threadbare, and clumsy in her? Do we love her as one person loves another by simply being with the beloved, even though the lover sees the faults of the beloved? Only when we learn to accept the Church as she is will our love for her reach full maturity. We should ask ourselves whether or not we pray and make sacrifices for the Church. Do we have confidence in her? Do we truly live with her and think with her as St. Ignatius recommends in his Rules, which, of course, are colored with the spirit of his age? We should think about what the Church expects of us priests and future priests: faith, hope, love, service, confidence, patience, courage, humility. She expects us to begin with ourselves if we want to criticize her. She expects us to see that each one of us in his own way compromises the Church in the eyes of the world. Compromise is not the monopoly of those at whom we are so ready to be scandalized.

31. The Contemplation on Love
(230–237)

In this contemplation, the only thing we can do is make some preliminary remarks.

In the text of the Exercises, a certain parallelism is noticeable between the Contemplation on Love and the Foundation. Christ is hardly mentioned in either one. Both seem to be dry philosophical considerations. Apparently, principles of a metaphysics of love and philosophical reflections on the God of love are all that is offered. But that is only apparently so! Things are proposed here in a formal way which by reason of their pregnancy get right to the heart of the matter. Ultimately, these things are possible only in Christianity, and they are available to us only through revelation and the cross of the Lord. Both the Foundation and the Contemplation on Love are outside of the body of the Exercises. Nevertheless, both of them are present in all the meditations, and contain the whole Spiritual Exercises on their own right. For if we take the *"Tantum-quantum,"* detachment, and the "more" of the Foundation in a concrete way, then the Contemplation on Love and the Foundation reveal themselves as the "more" of the love that was proposed to us in the meditation on the Three Classes of Men, where we saw that perfect peace is achieved only through being moved by the love of God.

If we examine the connection of the Contemplation on Love with the other meditations and contemplations, we will note that

St. Ignatius speaks of love in his first preliminary remarks (especially no. 15), where he demands of the retreatant that he strive for immediate communion with the Creator. Therefore, the goal of the present contemplation is really the same as the goal of the entire retreat: that God Himself in the sublimity of His love should say something to us that surpasses philosophical and theological speculation. In other words, the Contemplation on Love is really the result of the decision, which is the heart of the Exercises, arrived at in the course of the retreat. It is a movement proceeding from the love of God that surpasses legal and speculative activities, yes, and it even surpasses the cross of the Lord.

As in the meditations on the Kingdom of Christ and the Three Classes of Men, the love spoken of here is the love of surrender to God and Christ. If we did not offer ourselves for the following of Christ in those meditations, then perhaps we can get something out of this meditation by speculating on it philosophically, but we will not be able to realize it interiorly the way that St. Ignatius wants us to. Moreover, the love mentioned here is the humble love of the sin-meditations of the first week; it is the same love that came to realize in the hell-meditation that of itself it is not able to avoid sin, that of itself it might even forget its weakness, and that, therefore, it must develop a wholesome fear lest it be lost.

Even though this love of the Contemplation seems to be based on creatures, nevertheless it is really the love communicated to me by Jesus and His grace. To be sure, St. Ignatius speaks of God's kindnesses and favors in nature, so that it might seem that there is nothing specifically Christian about this love. But truly to find God in the hard, cruel, divided, and threatening world, despite and even because of the world's oppressive contradictions to search out a reconciliation in love—a person can only do that if he does not shun the cross of the Savior, and if he believes in God's love, even though he himself must hang on a cross in this world. Finding God in all things and experiencing the transparence of things toward God is accomplished only by the person who meets this God at that point where He descended into utter darkness and abandonment: on the cross of Jesus Christ! In this way alone will the sinner's eye become bright, will detachment become possible for him, will he be able to find God also in those things that come to him as crosses, and not just where he wants to find God.

It is interesting to note that St. Ignatius' first and fourth points in this meditation really refer to the love which is a realization of God's descent into the world. But a love that enters into the world with God in order, apparently, to be lost in it, only becomes possible for us when we have accepted the truth of the meditation on the Kingdom of Christ and the truth of the "third week," that is, this love can only be attained in Christ and the Church. Therefore, this love is also a service! "I ask for what I desire. Here it will be to ask for in intimate knowledge of the many blessings received, that filled with gratitude for all, I may in all things love and serve the Divine Majesty" (no. 233). Since this love is a realization of God's descent in which He served His creatures, it does not terminate in the ecstatic *élan* of an abstract metaphysical eros of God, but in a service which is added to God's work in the world.

This love is also the movement of the image of the Trinity in us. Is it not oddly magnificent that, when a person gives himself completely to God in the "*Suscipe*," the first thing he gives to God is his freedom—something modern existential theology considers to be the most basic in man, and after that his memory, his intellect, and his will? Whoever commits himself to God the way he is supposed to with the help of grace and by using the three powers of the soul, enters into the Trinitarian life of God Himself. If this love is carried by the Spirit of God and His grace, then it will bring us into communion with the Father and the Son and the Holy Spirit. But at the same time, this love also produces deeds.

In number 230, Ignatius says: "Before presenting this exercise

272

it will be good to call attention to two points: The first is that love ought to manifest itself in deeds rather than in words!" Throughout the Exercises, the retreatant is called on to act. Recall the frequent recurrence of the phrases, "What I must do," and, "Whoever desires to follow me must be ready to labor with me," and so forth. These sentiments are presented again in this contemplation. Therefore, love surges beyond itself, is not self-satisfied, lets God be greater than itself, can become adoration, praise, and a faithful servant, is able to come closer to God while the distance from Him increases. This love prompts the retreatant to ask of God: "What do You want me to do?" This love does not feel that greater reverence for God will diminish its own happiness. Nor is it naïve trust that, as it were, taps God on the shoulder and brashly intrudes into His privacy. It knows very well that the closer a person comes to God, the more he experiences His surpassing glory and His great distance.

The Contemplation on Love seems to be tightly woven into the fabric of the complete Exercises, especially when it leads to the discovery of God in all things through the detachment so much insisted on by St. Ignatius, and through that distance from things that is won only on the cross of the Lord. As we saw in the meditation on the Three Classes of Men, the things of this world are so transparent toward God that they really only attain their true worth and purpose by revealing Him. They are not set off from Him or opposed to Him. The love of the "finding God in all things" is certainly aware of a tender, chaste immediacy of the God it seeks and clings to in the Holy Spirit. Nevertheless, or better, therefore, St. Ignatius does not ignore the world. For it can always be a means to God. Not, of course, in the sense that we can greedily grasp everything in it and say: "Aha, now I have found God!" Nor in the sense that we need not follow the Crucified in His abandonment and death. But for St. Ignatius there is no such thing as "one way" that is *a priori* better than any other way—God can be found in each thing and in every thing.

We can descend with God into the world to die there with Him. We can find Him in using things and in leaving them, for all things are supposed to be transparent toward God and saved in Him through the cross which leads to glory, and through the detachment which is truly a realization in the Christian of Christ's death. In addition to that, the love intended by Ignatius goes through the Church out into the world. Think back for a moment on the meditation on the Kingdom of Christ. Even though Ignatius is more interested there in the pure desire to follow Christ than he is an apostolic enthusiasm, still the crucified Lord is portrayed as the One who calls us to self-renunciation so that we might thereby conquer the Kingdom. Therefore, the love we have concerned ourselves about during the whole retreat contains the unconditioned desire to begin with God to save the world, and to take it with us to God even if we must die in the process. This attitude is also expressed in the Ignatian formula: "To find devotion in all things!" Because of this attitude, St. Ignatius was able to walk away from the tears of mystical experience and study Latin instead; he wept while assisting at the liturgy, but he was able to leave it because the sovereign will of God called him elsewhere. He was able to suppress his gift of tears because the doctors told him it would ruin his eyesight. A St. Francis would have told the doctors: "Well good, so I lose my eyesight!"

St. Ignatius is looking for a person who is really dead to self and thus has acquired the capacity, like an angel both to look into the face of God and to be ready to be sent to serve, or—according to Ruysbroeck—like a mirror both to be open to God and to be ready to serve others. Another formula for the attitude of "finding God in all things" is the frequently quoted and more frequently misunderstood "contemplation in action." The retreatant should find God in all things. But that presupposes a perfect conformity with the will of God that takes precedence over everything else, even over the present forms of religious expression.

If we carefully examine each of the points of the Contemplation on Love, we will notice that each one throws light on the others. The love of God is presented to us from a constantly changing point of view, and our love should answer each of its aspects. We might express these different points of view as: God gives, God inhabits, God works, God descends.

God gives. "The first point is to recall to mind the blessing of creation and redemption, and the special favors I have received. I will ponder with great affection how much God our Lord has done for me, and how much He has given me of what He possesses, and finally, how much, as far as He can, the same Lord desires to give Himself to me according to His divine decrees. Then I will reflect upon myself, and consider, according to all reason and justice, what I ought to offer the Divine Majesty, that is, all I possess and myself with it. Thus, as one would do who is moved by great feeling, I will make this offering of myself . . ." (no. 234). Then St. Ignatius has the retreatant say the *"Suscipe,"* which contains no mention of our love. But there should not be a high-sounding name for this love, since it should only be uttered in the stillness of the heart where it can simply be reduced to a fact. And it can be reduced to a fact in man's perfect surrender of himself to God along with the fountain of his freedom —that image of the Trinity in him. Thus, God can freely dispose of man according to His own good pleasure, and man needs only to wait for that which surpasses everything else: God's love and grace.

God inhabits. In the second point, St. Ignatius says: "Reflect how God dwells in creatures: in the elements giving them existence, in the plants giving them life, in the animals conferring upon them sensation, in man bestowing understanding. So He dwells in me and gives me being, life, sensation, intelligence, and makes a temple of me, besides having created me in the likeness and image of the Divine majesty. Then I will reflect upon myself again in the manner stated in the first point, or in some other way that may seem better" (no. 235).

God works. "Consider how God works and labors for me in

all creatures upon the face of the earth, that is, He conducts Himself as one Who labors. Thus, in the elements, the plants, the fruits, the cattle, etc., He gives being, conserves them, confers life and sensation, etc. Then I will reflect upon myself" (no. 236).

God descends. "Consider all blessings and gifts as descending from above. Thus, my limited power comes from the supreme and infinite power above, and so, too, my justice, goodness, mercy, etc., descend from above as the rays of light descend from the sun, and as the waters flow from their fountains, etc. Then I will reflect upon myself, as has been said" (no. 237).

The common element in all of this is the "finding God in all things" so that I and the redeemed world might be transparent toward God and God toward the world. Is that anything different from the basic truth of Christianity which says that God not only places creation outside of Himself, but also retains it in Himself by the unsurpassable mystery of His grace? In order not to just formulate that in theological propositions, but really to experience Him in all things, in order to see that the world is open to Him and to feel His nearness in it, in order not to feel that we are shut off from God and to be able to integrate everything in the love of God—for all of that, the ultimate commitment of the creature is necessary. This pure commitment should find God in all things. Of course, it will find Him in a world whose prison of finiteness and sin must first be broken open. But this has already been done on the cross of Christ, and it constantly recurs in the following of the Crucified.

Thus, everything should be attributed to God in a song of praise. Whoever can do that, whoever can say the "*Suscipe*" with his whole heart and soul and mean every word of it, whoever is capable of that because he is free from sin and has broken away from himself in the following of Christ, he has arrived at that point where St. Ignatius wants him to be at the end of the Spiritual Exercises. He is the kind of person St. Ignatius can send back into the world of daily life so that he can find the living

God of love there in his work, in his destiny, in his gifts and sufferings, in life and death, in using and leaving the things of this earth. If he truly attains such love, he will possess God, not in opposition to the world, but as the only One who gives value and dignity to the world.

"If I speak with the eloquence of men and of angels, but have no love, I become no more than blaring brass or crashing cymbal. If I have the gift of foretelling the future and hold in my mind not only all human knowledge but the very secrets of God, and if I also have that absolute faith which can move mountains, but have no love, I amount to nothing at all. If I dispose of all that I possess, yes, even if I give my own body to be burned, but have no love, I achieve precisely nothing.

"This love of which I speak is slow to lose patience—it looks for a way of being constructive. It is not possessive; it is neither anxious to impress nor does it cherish inflated ideas of its own importance.

"Love has good manners and does not pursue selfish advantage. It is not touchy. It does not keep account of evil or gloat over the wickedness of other people. On the contrary, it is glad with all good men when truth prevails.

"Love knows no limit to its endurance, no end to its trust, no fading of its hope; it can outlast anything. It is, in fact, the one thing that still stands when all else has fallen.

"When I was a little child I talked and felt and thought like a little child. Now that I am a man my childish speech and feeling and thought have no further significance for me.

"At present we are men looking at puzzling reflections in a mirror. The time will come when we shall see reality whole and face to face! At present, all I know is a little fraction of the truth, but the time will come when I shall know it as fully as God now knows me! In this life, we have three great lasting qualities—faith, hope, and love. But the greatest of them is love" (1 Cor 13).

32. The Grace of Perseverance

Note

In the thirteenth chapter of Session VI, the Council of Trent said: "The same is to be said of the gift of perseverance, about which it is written, 'He who has persevered to the end will be saved.' This gift can be had only from Him Who has the power to determine that he who does stand shall stand with perseverance, and Who can lift up him who falls. Let no one feel assured of this gift with an absolute certitude, although all ought to have most secure hope in the help of God. For unless men are unfaithful to His grace, God will bring the good work to perfection, just as He began it, working both the will and the performance. Yet, let them who think they stand take heed lest they fall, and let them work out their salvation with fear and trembling in labors, in sleepless nights, in almsgiving, in prayers and offerings, in fastings, and in chastity. Knowing that they are reborn unto the hope of glory and not yet unto glory itself, they should be in dread about the battle they must wage with the flesh, the world, and the devil. For in this battle they cannot be the victors unless, with God's grace, they obey the Apostle who says: 'We are debtors, not to the flesh, that we should live according to the flesh. For if you live according to the flesh you will die; but if by the Spirit you put to death the deeds of the flesh, you will live.'"

It would be out of place here to comment at length on these words of the Council. But at the same time, we should realize that apprehension about the hidden future, of which the problem of perseverance is a part, is an essential moment in the reality of a finite spirit in matter. We do not live out our present life just in anticipation and projection of the future. For the future is necessarily hidden from us because of the free character of our creaturehood—free because under the disposition of God—and it must be accepted in its hiddenness. The future would not be hidden from us if we paid no attention to it whatever. It is really only hidden if we consciously venture into the unknown and consider it as in some way belonging to us. If this is our attitude not only with regard to this or that particular event of our lives, but also with regard to our whole future, which is obscure even though it really grows out of our freedom, and which, though not completely in our power, still has a determining effect on us, then we are asking a theological question about ourselves which is the question of perseverance. To raise the theological question of perseverance is the same thing as to ask whether or not a person will finally be what he now is or at least hopes to be.

I. *The Essence and Origin of Christian Perseverance*

The teaching of the Council of Trent quoted above gives us some information on this topic: "This gift can be had only from Him Who has the power to determine that he who does stand shall stand with perseverance, and Who can lift up him who falls."

The strange thing that immediately presents itself when it comes to questioning the essence and origin of perseverance is that, on the one hand, our future will certainly be worked out by our freedom, and that, on the other hand, we are completely in the hand of God. Only when a person has experienced, believed, feared, and loved God in the absolute surrender of his whole being—and therefore also of his whole future, can he begin to realize the full meaning of God's power and freedom. We can only live in close contact with God when we believe in Him as the only true love, and when we accept our future from Him as a gift which, as the result of our own freedom, still really belongs to God.

It takes a consideration such as this to bring us to see how completely different God is. We could not, as it were, share our freedom with anyone else but God. If we were to share it with anyone or anything, then the inexorable conclusion would be: Either I or the other will determine my destiny. But this does not apply to God! And therefore, a person is perfectly right when he sees that the question about the future is really a question about the acts of his freedom, because he has come to realize that he cannot answer this question by himself, and nevertheless must go on to encounter the incomprehensible vagueness of the future as something really belonging to him. God is the One who gives, and His gifts are so unique that when we accept them they become our own free acts.

From a theological point of view, perseverance is efficacious grace. This is something that no theology of revelation can ignore. Protestant theology cannot ignore it, even though the Protestants frequently do not understand how it is that we beg of God something that we ourselves must do. In other words, they do not see how we can truly realize our freedom by abandoning ourselves to God in love and freedom. Actually, we effect our perseverance by seriously and constantly trying to do just that, by praying, by serving God, by using and leaving the things of this world with genuine detachment, by always being ready for the direction of God that surpasses all else. To be sure, this situation means that there is a deep and urgent restlessness in our being. Having seen this, St. Augustine asked how he could be serene before God. Then he answered himself by asking whether or not he would be more serene if he had his destiny in his own hand, or whether he should not be more confident if he knew that he was in the hand of God. To accept this situation in faith and love is salvation, and those who are perishing are not being lost because they are in the hand of God and being led by His grace, but because they have not accepted His grace and believed in it. The person who knows that he is under God's power and humbly surrenders himself to Him with hope and trust—loves God. As long as he does this, he is surrounded by the grace of God. Every sin is fundamentally a drawing back from God and His direction because the sinner has more confidence in himself than he does in God. And it is mistrust of God that brings about damnation.

Therefore, our first conclusion with regard to perseverance is: Our heart can be composed and serene only in God's grace, and it can only attain serenity if it is restless in the love of God. We are not seized by a suspicious fear when we are with someone we truly love. Perfect love drives out fear. But we can also say: Perfect love effects a holy fear of God that renders us happy, calm, and confident.

II. *Signs of Divine Election*

If we were to ask ourselves whether or not there are signs of belonging to God's "elect," we would have to say that there are no signs, such as legal documents, that can be adduced as proof of certain perseverance in grace. If there are any signs of election, then they can only be those effected by our own actions, which are signs that God is working in us. Such signs are, for example, constancy in prayer, steady progress in doing good, God-fearing concern for salvation, selfless love, and so forth. We might also mention those special experiences a person has that lead him on gently and irresistibly so that, amazed, he asks himself occasionally how he escaped this or that disaster; or he might ask himself how he was able to accomplish certain things for which there was really no indication in his physical or psychological make-up.

Francis Thompson has compared the choosing love of God, which surrounds a man and pursues him down every path so that he cannot escape, with keen hounds which encircle the stag and close in on it for the kill. In this sense, therefore, there definitely are signs of election. However, they are not there to be enjoyed, but to be done. The runner may hope to reach the goal, and the one who is striving may hope that God will accomplish in him the eternal work of His mercy.

III. *The Sacred Heart Devotion and Devotion to Mary as Means of Acquiring Perseverance*

The question whether or not there are any means that can be employed—speaking anthropomorphically—to obtain and secure the grace of perseverance, can be reduced to the question treated above about the signs of divine election. The real answer is that such a means can be had only in doing. We could also approach this question by examining the various elements that make up our spiritual life, to see whether or not they are more suited or less suited to merit the grace of perseverance. Such an examination will certainly bring to light the fact that those forms of the religious life are useful which, by their very nature, are least apt to become institutionalized, which will normally either not be practiced at all or else will be genuinely performed, and which will not tolerate that weird, superficial no-man's-land where legal pretenses are kept up, but where the heart and spirit are not involved.

It is not difficult to point to many elements in an organized program for the spiritual life whose practice tends toward a disassociation from the personal core. For example, it is very easy to change the regular early rising into a mere habit, so that one ultimately comes to the conclusion: That which crawls out of bed in the wee hours of the morning is not a spiritually alive person, but a mere shadow who satisfies his conscience by faithfully sitting out the time for prayer. Reciting the Breviary can also easily become the performance of a merely institutional, legal "obligation."

On the other hand, it can be said of other forms of the spiritual life: If I use them at all, then I have a relatively good chance of performing them properly; if I use them at all, then I notice not only, as it were, that I have some success in them, but also that I am coming closer to God in them. On the basis of this consideration, among the many traditional devotions two can easily be singled out as important for the acquisition of the grace of final perseverance. They are the devotion to the Mother of God and the Sacred Heart devotion. These devotions must be truly interior and personal if they are to be practiced at all. This is all the more true in an age when the attraction of both devotions has suffered in the eyes of the clergy and the laity. Therefore, if Christian tradition assures us that devotion to Mary and to the Sacred Heart are practically signs of final perseverance, then that is rather easy to understand. It could be that this argument smacks a bit of theological rationalism. Perhaps we should add: The Church, which possesses the Spirit of God, knows through her supernatural instinct that God has attached very special graces to both of these devotions.

If I ask myself with all seriousness and in a truly Christian way whether or not I will remain faithful to the grace of God my whole life long right up to my death, then I must come to realize that the ultimate guarantee of this is the grace of God Himself. Everything depends on Him alone, the faithful One, Whose love is unchangeable. Moreover, if I ask how I can know for sure whether or not I still possess the living love which is necessary for final perseverance, and which surpasses every sort of perfunctory affirmation of definitions, the Church, her glory, my office, my duties, the commandments, and so forth, then I can reduce this question to concrete terms by examining myself to see if I truly love the Mother of God.

I can also ask myself: Does the mention of the Sacred Heart of Jesus seem repulsive and tasteless to me, as words of true love are felt by those who do not love, or is it something for which I have understanding, something I am seeking from the depths of my heart, and something about which I say to myself quietly at least once in a while: "Heart of Jesus, Son of the eternal Father, have mercy on me; Heart of Jesus, kingly center of all

283

hearts, have mercy on me"? Am I trying to understand something of this center of the world, of this pierced Heart that poured out its love into the deadly darkness of the world? If I can honestly answer myself: Yes, I am really trying to love the Lord—and that is evident in my religious life; if I can say the same thing about Mary, then I can be sure that the love of God is still alive in me, still throbbing, that it has not vanished under the pressure of daily living, that it has not been choked by formality and habit. Then I am still on the way, and it is clear that my faithful God has not abandoned me. And then he will lead me on from grace to grace until it has become final.

IV. *Retreat Resolutions*

If in the course of this retreat we have resolved to make certain changes in our spiritual life, then at the end of the retreat we cannot easily avoid the question of how successful we will be in carrying out our new resolutions.

The first thing to say is this: Begin immediately. If we put off the realization of our resolutions to some future date, then they hardly have a chance for survival. By now, we should know exactly what our resolutions are, and should begin to practice them at once. Our resolutions should truly saturate our daily life. They should not be like a trinket in our pocket, occasionally noticed, but really of little importance. We should have made some sensible, concrete resolutions that can be tangibly carried out and controlled. We should go over our spiritual program regularly with our spiritual advisor or with our confessor—and we should take the initiative in this matter.

We can do all of that right now! We cannot possess the eternal future now, but we can begin now—perhaps by being faithful to a small grace of God. Each one of us receives much more grace than he is able to assimilate. Perhaps the distance between these two is very small. Perhaps this abundance of grace enables us to call on God for help in our perplexity, to say to Him: Please give me what I am not able to accomplish! We can always do at least that much! But that must really be done—it must be a personal act. There we find the miracle, as it were, of breaking out of possibility and going to deeds. And if someone says: "But that's exactly what I can't bring myself to do!"—then he should be told: "Begin right now at least to cry out to God, and don't give up!" Then we will suddenly notice that we also can break into the world of deeds. That is precisely the experience St. Augustine had. In his despair, he paced back and forth in front of God's closed door, and he did not give up. He persisted in beating on that door and crying out until, all at once, he was able to accomplish what he had for years thought to be impossible.

To take the end of the retreat and the beginning of daily life seriously in this sense may be a very small step toward an infinitely distant goal. We do not want to dramatize, but nevertheless it is true that perhaps it is the most decisive step of all. In any event, we should have trust in God, we should lovingly do right now what we can, we should begin with our program as soon as possible, and recognize in our love for the Mother of God and the Heart of Christ an assurance that we are still open for the love of God. If we can do that, then love can drive out fear, and we can go forward to meet God with an open heart, thankfully and joyously, calmly and also without a detailed knowledge of our future. Then it will be clear that "He who began the good work in you is faithful, and will bring His work to completion."

Glossary

Anticipation: *Vorgriff*.

Being turned toward: *Verwiesenheit*.

Co-realize: *mitvollziehen*.

Elevation: *Aufhebung*.

Essence: *Grundbestand*.

Existential: *seinshafter*.

Existential: *existential* (= previous to and independent of personal choice); *existentiell* (= resulting from personal choice)—see the context.

Fulfillment: *Vollzug*.

Fulfillment of human existence: *Daseinsvollzug*.

Fundamental event: *Urereignis*.

Getting away from: *Distanzierung*.

Historical: *historisch* (= the historic event that merely happens); *geschichtlich* (= the historic event that is personally significant or challenging)—see the context.

Historical character: *Geschichtlichkeit*.

Human existence (or reality): *Dasein*.

Human situation: *Daseinsverfassung*.

Incomprehensibility: *Unbegreiflichkeit*.

Indefinibility: *Undefinierbarkeit*.

Internal luminosity: *Gelichtetsein*.

Non-relativity: *Unbezüglichkeit*.

Non-salvation: *Unheil*.

Obscurity: *Verhülltheit*.

Onceness: *Einmaligkeit*.

Ordination: *Verfügung*.

Other-existence: *Anderssein*.

Performance: *Vollzug*.

Pre-decision: *Vorentscheidung*.

Pre-given: *vorgegeben*.

Priestly existence: *Priesterdasein*.

Realization: *Vollzug*.

Realize: *vollziehen, mitvollziehen*.

Reference: *Verwiesenheit*.

Remembrance (or recollection): *Anamnese*.

Self-divestment: *Selbstentäusserung*.

Self-possession: *Fürsichsein*.

Self-presumption: *Selbstüberhebung*.

Self-reflecting or personal: *bei-sich-seiendes*.

Spirit: *Geist*.

Surrounding world: *Umwelt*.

Tangibility, tangible: *Greifbarkeit, greifbar*.

Thematic, explicit: *thematisch*.

Transformation: *Aufhebung*.